ISLAMIC LAW IN EUROPE?

Cultural Diversity and Law

Series Editor:
Prakash Shah, School of Law, Queen Mary, University of London, UK

Around the world, most states are faced with difficult issues arising out of cultural diversity in their territories. Within the legal field, such issues span across matters of private law through to public and constitutional law. At international level too there is now considerable jurisprudence regarding ethnic, religious and cultural diversity. In addition, there are several layers of legal control – from communal and religious regulation to state and international regulation. This multiplicity of norm setting has been variously termed legal pluralism, inter-legality or inter-normativity and provides a fascinating lens for academic analysis that links up to cultural diversity in new and interesting ways. The umbrella of cultural diversity encompasses various population groups throughout the world ranging from national, ethnic, religious or indigenous groupings. This series particularly welcomes work that is of comparative interest, concerning various state jurisdictions as well as different population groups.

Also in the series

Law and Religion in the 21st Century
Relations between States and Religious Communities
Edited by Silvio Ferrari and Rinaldo Cristofori
ISBN 978-1-4094-1143-7

Muslim Marriage in Western Courts
Lost in Transplantation
Pascale Fournier
ISBN 978-1-4094-0441-5

Shari'a As Discourse
Legal Traditions and the Encounter with Europe
Jørgen S. Nielsen and Lisbet Christoffersen
ISBN 978-0-7546-7955-4

Legal Practice and Cultural Diversity
Edited by Ralph Grillo, Roger Ballard, Alessandro Ferrari, André J. Hoekema, Marcel Maussen and Prakash Shah
ISBN 978-0-7546-7547-1

Islamic Law in Europe?
Legal Pluralism and its Limits in European Family Laws

ANDREA BÜCHLER
University of Zurich, Switzerland

Routledge
Taylor & Francis Group
LONDON AND NEW YORK

First published 2011 by Ashgate Publishing

Published 2016 by Routledge
2 Park Square, Milton Park, Abingdon, Oxfordshire OX14 4RN
711 Third Avenue, New York, NY 10017, USA

First issued in paperback 2016

Routledge is an imprint of the Taylor & Francis Group, an informa business

British Library Cataloguing in Publication Data
Büchler, Andrea.
Islamic law in Europe? : legal pluralism and its limits in
European family laws. – (Cultural diversity and law)
1. Legal polycentricity – Europe. 2. Conflict of laws –
Domestic relations – Europe. 3. Domestic relations (Islamic
law) – Europe. 4. Religion and law – Europe.
I. Title II. Series
340.9'15-dc22

Library of Congress Cataloging-in-Publication Data
Büchler, Andrea.
Islamic law in Europe? : legal pluralism and its limits in European family laws /
by Andrea Büchler.
p. cm.
Includes bibliographical references and index.
ISBN 978-1-4094-2849-7 (hardback : alk. paper)
1. Domestic relations—Europe. 2. Domestic relations—Europe—Cases.
3. Legal polycentricity—Europe. I. Title.
KJC1105.B83 2011
346.401'5—dc23

2011017889

ISBN 13: 978-1-138-27890-5 (pbk)
ISBN 13: 978-1-4094-2849-7 (hbk)

Contents

Preface

Family-law codes in Europe have been subject to a succession of reforms over many years. 'Modernisation' has been the leitmotif of all the changes which have been made. It is these modernising initiatives which, in numerous countries in Europe, have resulted in family-law codes which are capable, at least partially, of embracing a whole range of family living arrangements – single-parent families, step-families, unmarried couples, same-sex couples. Migration from countries with a predominantly Muslim population has presented an additional challenge to Europe's family-law codes. Are these modernised codes also able to accommodate alien concepts and understandings of what constitutes a family and of the purpose of family law? Where do these family-law codes reach the limit of what they can achieve, and how are those limits justified? Is Europe about to see its family reality reverting to more traditional models, which will, at the very least, irritate certain fundamental concepts of the relationship between the sexes, of autonomy and of inter-generational ties? To rephrase the question somewhat: where, and how, are alien concepts of family law gaining entry into European countries' legal systems? Is it desirable for there to be a plurality of family-law codes comprising different provisions for different cultural and religious groups? Given the human right to cultural and religious identity, may such plurality indeed even be a necessity? What are the alternatives?

I first examined these issues – which are now attracting much attention from European social scientists, lawyers and politicians – in a paper I presented at a conference of the German Society of International Law in Halle in 2007.[1] During the 2008/2009 academic year, the Institute for Advanced Study in Berlin then provided me with an ideal environment in which to develop my initial ideas in greater detail and to expose them to debate. This text is the result of that process. Many fellows and friends have joined in the discussion of the issues examined here. I am deeply grateful to them all.

I should also like to thank Nicholas MacCabe for taking care of the English manuscript.

Andrea Büchler
Zurich, November 2010

1 A. Büchler, Kulturelle Vielfalt und Familienrecht. Die Bedeutung kultureller Identität für die Ausgestaltung europäischer Familienrechtsordnungen – am Beispiel islamischer Rechtsverständnisse, in G. Nolte, H. Keller, A. von Bogdandy, H.P. Mansel, A. Büchler, C. Walter, *Pluralistische Gesellschaften und Internationales Recht. Berichte der Deutschen Gesellschaft für Völkerrecht*, Heidelberg: C.F. Müller, 2008, 215–252.

Introduction

'Rencontrer un homme, c'est être tenu en éveil par une énigme.'*

Emmanuel Levinas

These words were written by the French philosopher Emmanuel Levinas.[1] In writing that sentence, Levinas combined memories of his physical and spiritual encounters with his teacher Edmund Husserl which are of almost tender fondness. Yet, concealed within those same words is the very essence of the unique depth and seriousness of his fascination with the other, for it is man himself who is that infinitely unique other. Encountering man means becoming aware of his existence. It is that encounter which gives birth to language and which kindles feelings of responsibility.[2] For Levinas it is that confusing manifestation of alterity which constitutes the puzzle, the enigma, the dialectic transcendence.[3] That is what keeps us alert, indeed it is a prerequisite for our very awareness of our own existence.

That is why this irritatingly pristine statement is of such unimagined significance for the present day, and for its somewhat restless dealings with all that is other.

Ethnic, religious and cultural diversity is increasingly evident in Western Europe. In a number of European countries there are fears that foreign or, more specifically, Islamic family law is becoming entrenched. All parties to this discussion see themselves as under threat. Migrant populations are afraid of losing their cultural identity, while their adopted countries' established populations see a risk to social cohesion and a threat to modernity. Cultural diversity and equality, autonomy and inclusion. These are the faultlines, and the tensions which are building up along them are becoming increasingly noticeable, especially as the volume of migration from countries with a predominantly Muslim population has increased. Family law brings these underlying tensions into sharp focus, probably because it is widely perceived and understood to be both closely intertwined with culture and a key source of identity. Furthermore, Europe's current modernity is the product of a long and hard struggle, especially where family law is concerned.

---

* Levinas 1967, 125.

1 Emmanuel Levinas, a Jewish philosopher, was born in Lithuania in 1906 and died in France in 1995. He was awarded a doctorate in Paris in 1930 for his dissertation on the philosophy of Husserl, gaining his *venia legendi* in 1961 for his work on totality and infinity. He was awarded a chair at Nanterre in 1967 and at the Sorbonne in 1973.

2 Cf. Levinas 1991, *passim*.

3 Cf. Levinas 1967, 208: 'Cette façon pour l'Autre de quérir ma reconnaissance tout en conservant son *incognito*, en dédaignant le recours au clin d'œil d'entente ou de complicité, cette façon de se manifester, nous l'appelons – en remontant à l'étymologie de ce terme grec et par opposition à l'apparoir indiscret et victorieux du *phénomène* – énigme.'

There is no doubt that the last few decades have seen European nations' family-law codes subjected to fundamental changes. As family living arrangements have become increasingly pluralised, strict family-law models have needed special justification. The state is in retreat. There is talk of family law becoming de-institutionalised and contractualised, particularly as couples are now largely free to define their living arrangements themselves, with individual agreements taking the place of universal institutions. This widespread trend in Western family law, which modernisation has brought in its wake, has recently been accompanied by a second development which, while its traditional inspiration may initially make it appear contradictory to the first, nevertheless also represents a challenge to the loosening of family-law codes. As migrants from countries of origin with a Muslim population have established themselves in Europe, there have been calls for cultural and religious plurality to be reflected in European laws, and for these also to pay heed to Islamic legal concepts, processes and values. The proponents of these claims base their argument on the fact that cultural and religious identity is now recognised as a fundamental human right, upheld by a whole series of international treaties.

Differing concepts of family law have, at one time or another, inflamed the entire debate on such critical issues as human rights, equality, progress, secularisation, revelation, universality, identity and imperialism. Europe's legal systems have reacted to the new challenges posed by migration from countries of origin with a Muslim population in many different ways. Often, their response has taken the form of an *apologia*. Rarely has it been informed by theory. Traditional solutions of the kind offered by private international law rules are too clear-cut to accommodate the complexities involved. New answers have yet to establish themselves. The theoretical and practical challenges involved are forcing us to re-evaluate the concepts of European countries' family laws in a culturally diverse, pluralistic society.

Cultural and religious identity and family law are interrelated in a number of ways and raise various complex issues. I shall endeavour to describe areas in which conflicts may arise (chapter 1), with a view to mapping out the field of tension between cultural diversity, equality, autonomy and inclusion, to indicating possible paths towards addressing these conflicts in an affirmative and productive manner and towards reconciling the protection of cultural identity and autonomy with the advancement of social and legal inclusion. My thoughts primarily take the form of broad outlines and are perhaps overly biased towards theory. They are ideas about something which is necessarily subject to political contingencies and the unpredictable ways in which societies evolve. I shall examine international and European private law, defining my own critical, and admittedly somewhat apodictic, position within that framework (chapter 2). The following sections will include a description of, and some and comments on, the various degrees of consideration accorded to cultural identity within substantive family law (chapter 3) and some remarks on models of legal pluralism (chapter 4). I conclude with an evaluation of various approaches which are process-based rather than institution-centred (chapter 5), before presenting my main theses (chapter 6).

Despite all the efforts made to achieve harmonisation, Europe's various individual jurisdictions remain characterised by numerous specific differences in the very broad area covered by family law. This book does not present a systematic analysis of Europe's various family-law codes. Rather, by reference to examples from legislation and court decisions, it discusses various approaches to questions relating to cultural and religious identity and to diversity in family-law matters. Examples will be drawn from considerations of the paths adopted by Germany as a culture-based nation, Switzerland as a nation based on political will, France as a secular republic, England with its colonial past and Spain with its historical Islamic imprint. These countries represent the nuances between various concepts of the role of the state and how those concepts have influenced their approach to religious freedom and the tension between religious pluralism and social cohesion.

Chapter 1
Cultural and Religious Diversity in the Context of Family Law

Some Reflections on the Semantics of Cultural Identities

Abstractions and Binary Codes

The semantics of cultural diversity incorporate the concept of otherness in a number of ways. Differentiation is a prerequisite for inclusion, however. What is this cultural identity which has the ability to distinguish between the self and all that is 'other'?

On the one hand, cultural identity is an expressive, non-purposeful, non-rational emanation of the personal. On the other hand, it is a construct, invoked to articulate and recreate itself assertively and continuously in the social and institutional context. We often experience a more or less overtly stated binary logic, based on purported attributes of 'us' and 'them'. These attributes exert substantial influence throughout society, giving rise to concepts of social groups which are entrenched in the collective memory such as 'Islam' or 'the Muslims'. Cultural perceptions and ascriptions operating like a binary code play a considerable part in encouraging depersonalised abstractions. In certain socio-cultural configurations, this can lead to processes of forced identification or delimitation, or to the attribution and appropriation of identities which are absolute.[1] Turks, Pakistanis, North Africans and Malaysians are all reduced to their common religious affiliations and simply declared to belong to a single collective. Muslims in Europe, however, are not one homogeneous, clearly defined and delimited group. They are a set of different individuals, each with different religious practices and attachments.

The Renaissance and Pluralisation of Religion

How, though, are the religion and the religious identity of Muslim men and women actually evolving in European societies? Let it first be noted that this very question is a relatively recent one. The first generation of Muslim immigrants which arrived in Europe in the aftermath of the Second World War were perceived largely in terms of their economic role as migrant workers, and their residence in Europe was wrongly assumed to be temporary. As additional family members joined those

1 On this 'compulsive explicitness' (in German 'Zwang zur Eindeutigkeit') and its attendant dangers, see Schiffauer 2008, 88 and 93.

who had already established themselves in Europe, and the myth of a subsequent return to their homelands was abandoned, Muslim men and women began to establish organisational structures of their own and make their voices heard. For the first time, questions were raised as to how their religious affiliation should be treated, and religious templates also began to be applied to social issues as well. Chronologically speaking, this new Islamic presence in Europe can now be said to be about thirty years old.[2]

Religion is indeed experiencing something of a renaissance in the discourse of cultural diversity and is becoming an ever more important form of self-identification. Diaspora communities increasingly emphasise links to the religious identities they have brought with them, as exemplified by their use of emblems such as the headscarf.[3] Indeed, emigration often raises people's consciousness of their religious affiliations, as a symbolic means of reinforcing their own identity. Or, as van der Veer puts it: 'paradoxically, migration to the lands of unbelievers strengthens the religious commitment of the migrants'.[4] The particular circumstances of migration make the issue of identity more pressing and increase the need for identifiable points of reference by which individuals can gauge themselves.[5] Religion offers people both a meaningful framework and a network of contacts on which they can depend during times of crisis.

Conversely, over the last ten years or so, the focus of debate on religions has shifted from their potentially pacifying aspects to the perspective of threat and conflict. Islam has been most notably affected by this shift, and is often perceived, as it were, as the symbol of cataclysm, the quintessence of everything which threatens modernity, not least because of the religious determinism of its discourse on family law.[6] Shortly after the terrorist attacks of 11 September 2001, Habermas spoke of a 'post-secular society'.[7] Of course, it is certainly also true that the classic paradigm of secularisation[8] itself has met with increasing criticism – a paradigm exemplified partly by the idea that religious observance was practised more intensely in former times and that religion's very significance and purpose have

2 Tiesler 2007, 25.

3 On the phenomenon of re-ethnicisation, cf. Reuter 2002, 407; about the increasing visibility of Islam in the European public space, cf. Cherribi 2003, 195.

4 van der Veer 1994, 119.

5 Lauser, Weissköppel 2008, 7 and 9, which contains numerous references to research on migration.

6 For Germany, cf. Bielefeldt 2010, 173–174.

7 Habermas 2001, *passim*, in particular 12.

8 Admittedly, the term 'secularisation' has itself been the subject of intense debate. In essence, the process of secularisation is characterised by differentiation between religious institutions and the state and between knowledge and belief, though the significance and function of religion in a society has also been addressed.

been diminished, and partly by Weber's thesis[9] that modernisation will necessarily bring about changes in religion.[10]

Whether we are now witnessing the return of religion, or merely its transformation, there seems to be little doubt that religion is assuming a more public profile and that it is demanding recognition, that religious references have proliferated, and European societies have become far more pluralised, both ethnically and religiously. There can be no doubt that European societies now have multifarious religious strands running through them. Religion can provide an anchor for the individual confronting societal, technical and economic complexities which he or she can neither control nor fathom. To those uprooted by modernising and postmodernising trends, religion offers a basis for addressing existential questions – what is feasible, what is permitted, what is available? – as well as the prospect both of answering them with a degree of certainty and definition, and of dealing with new contingencies as they arise.[11] There can be no doubt that Europe must be prepared for religious communities to endure in a secularised environment.[12] Europe must thus attempt to reincorporate religion into its civil and social structures, making religion part of the modern secular society it understands and proclaims itself to be.[13]

The Focus on Difference and the Shifts Caused by Globalisation

Culture is indisputably imbued with specific historical and social meaning. Culture lends significance to individual existence, tying the individual to society with a tacit sense of belonging. But culture, as Clifford puts it, is 'not an object to be described, neither is it a unified corpus of symbols and meanings that can be definitively interpreted. Culture is contested, temporal, and emergent. Representation and explanation – both by insiders and outsiders – is implicated in this emergence.'[14]

9 Cf. Weber 1968, 577: 'The needs of economic life make themselves manifest either through a reinterpretation of the sacred commandments or through their casuistic by-passing. Occasionally we also come upon a simple, practical elimination of religious injunctions in the course of the ecclesiastical dispensation of penance and grace.'

10 For detailed criticism of the secularisation paradigm, see Zachuber 2007, 17.

11 Cf. Gräb 2007, 81, also Mahlmann 2006, 75 and 77.

12 Cf. Habermas 2001, 13.

13 For a detailed discussion of the necessity for these efforts and of the theory of religion as a resource for social integration, see Sellmann 2007, *passim*.

14 Clifford 1986, 19. A discussion of the concept of culture is not intended here, nor would it be feasible. In this context, culture is understood as 'ein komplexes Ganzes, welches Wissen und seine Anwendung, Glaubensvorstellungen, Kunst, Moral, Gesetze und Bräuche sowie all jene Fähigkeiten und Eigenschaften einschliesst, die sich Menschen als Mitglieder einer bestimmten Gesellschaft aneignen und wodurch sie sich von anderen Gruppierungen unterscheiden', as in Kälin 2000, 21.

The concepts of culture current in European countries today appear to focus on difference, and the relevance of diversity is increasing inexorably. This may simply be interpreted as a recognition that it is culture which lends purpose to life. Yet this emphasis on differences in culture and identity arises not only because diversity is perceived as a desirable end in itself, it is also sometimes expressive of the – erroneous – idea that there are a variety of entities, distinct from each other, self-contained, with precedence over the subjective, possessed of logics of their own and with the power to induce uniformity within themselves.[15]

Some legal discourse appears to suggest that this notion of culture is congruent with national identity, which, in turn, would imply that cultures are firmly delineated within national boundaries. This is, of course, something of an oversimplification. Culture is not ontologically evident nor is it an anthropological constant. Globalisation[16] has been a key factor in reshaping identity-determining areas beyond nation-states.[17] Transnational areas – for example the spaces linking migrant communities with their country of origin – allow contradictory and cosmopolitan identities to evolve which are not only multi-pillared, but are also universal, hybrid, multi-lingual and ubiquitous. On a sub-national level, this phenomenon is accompanied by the formation of identity patterns whose intent is defensive, and which regularly have recourse to primordial categories such as ethnic origin and religious affiliation. In contrast to their cosmopolitan counterparts, such identity configurations are local, authentic, homogeneous and coherent. Globalisation has produced two contrasting and parallel outcomes. It has not only made society more pluralistic, it has also made social groups more ethnic.

Cultural identity unfolds through discourse, narration and action. It is the result of social interaction. Culture is thus the product of numerous, complex cultural perceptions, attributions and definitions, all of which are shaped by individual concepts of that which is other and thus by individual attitudes towards otherness. Migration has played a significant part in producing today's transnational social spaces. It has unbound nations, creating societies whose individual and collective cultural foundations are pluricentric, and whose loyalties are ambivalent. If migrants to a new country have recourse to religious and cultural symbols and signs of their own,[18] even if they present these as ascribed manifestations of their own selves, these symbols and signs will not have the same significance in the emotional identity of their offspring, born in the country to which their parents

---

15 On the genesis of the concept of culture, cf. Wicker 1998, 26.

16 A discussion of the ramifications surrounding the concept of globalisation is not intended here. It is important, however, to point at Teubner's observation that the globalisation being witnessed today 'nicht die von der internationalen Politik allmählich gestaltete Weltgesellschaft [ist], sondern ein höchst widersprüchlicher, durch und durch fragmentierter Vorgang der Globalisierung, der von einzelnen Teilsystemen der Gesellschaft in unterschiedlicher Geschwindigkeit vorangetrieben wird'. Cf. Teubner 1996, 258.

17 Wicker 1998, 31.

18 Cf. Belhoul 2005, 159.

emigrated. Caught between the Scylla of a home where parents have vivid and emotional memories of the cultural environment from which they originate and want to hand these down to their children, and the Charybdis of a demanding, often distrustful social majority,[19] this second generation finds its identity split, if not indeed broken, if it is unable to derive productive benefit from its various cultural roots. Members of this second generation are often adept at navigating their cross-cultural environments, well aware of the differing expectations and modes of behaviour which apply within and outside their own ethnic community, able to avail themselves of both sets of values and even skilled in playing off both sides against each other.[20] Transnational ties are often maintained, with families remaining in contact with the region from which they originated, with 'back home', not least with a view to future marriages. Indeed, members of European diasporic minority communities often marry spouses from their countries of origin, and also celebrate the marriage in that country, thus making such marriages both transnational and trans-jurisdictional.[21] It is then the members of the younger, second generation who have multiple senses of belonging and are exposed to conflicting ethnic, national, cultural and legal points of reference. Their identity is shaped by the interplay between synchronic and diachronic perspectives.[22]

It is certainly true that the integration process, which may span several generations, can gradually blur the differences between a country's native population and its migrant groups, so that ethnic, religious and cultural affiliation

---

19 Speelman 1995, 71.

20 For an arresting description of a specific case, cf. Ballard 2006, 35. The case involved the successful carrying out of an arranged marriage between a 17-year-old Pakistani woman who had been living in England since the age of six and her cousin, who until then had been living in Pakistan. Two years elapsed before the couple were reunited, during which time the young woman availed herself of her new freedom as a married woman and entered into relationships which were not tolerated by her community. When her husband finally arrived in England, she rejected him. She made plans to run away. She decided that she could best extricate herself from her predicament by presenting herself to a whole set of institutions as a young Asian woman in serious domestic distress, being put through a forced marriage to a violent husband by authoritarian parents who would kill her if they discovered that she was planning to run away. Nobody made a serious effort to establish the story's veracity. The case ended tragically. The woman died in a fire that she almost certainly started herself. A case was brought against her husband but then dismissed due to lack of evidence. On the self-identification of second-generation migrants, see also Schiffauer 2008, *passim*, in particular 91.

21 See the review of research and the discussion of the motivations for transnational marriages in Beck-Gernsheim 2007, 275.

22 See the detailed investigation in Ehringfeld 1997, 38, in particular 60. The term 'transdifference' has also been used to describe the elements of contradiction, inconclusiveness, undecidability and uncertainty which the order of this binary logic suppresses, thus implicitly questioning the validity of binary differential constructs without resolving the differences inscribed. Cf. Lösch 2005.

becomes less important over time. That is not to say that the integration process is simply linear. Indeed, many factors, such as the establishment of relatively stable diaspora structures, or practices such as disrespect, discrimination and marginalisation, can halt it, slow it down or even reverse it.

The family is one of the most private environments, yet it is here that there is intense public discussion about the roles of the sexes, personal autonomy and personal responsibility. As a social construct, a conceptual entity and a moral order, there is hardly any other area of life which is confronted so forcefully by legal and societal expectations as the family. It is thus not surprising that family-law dogma of one kind or another is often at the root of private confrontation and public dispute about the opportunities and threats presented by cultural diversity in Europe.

Family Law in the Islamic Context

Classical Islamic law comprises a system of rules whose development had been more or less completed by the end of the ninth century. It represents a particular interpretation of the religious sources on which it is based. It is not codified, but is set out in a number of substantial private works promulgated by renowned Islamic jurists and scholars who saw it as their task not to develop a new set of laws, but rather to lend formal substance to a set of laws which were already given and which would endure forever. Islamic law is thus not a national law, but rather a source and a point of reference for a legal order. Hence one has to distinguish the legal codifications of individual countries, such as Egypt, Syria, Iran or Sudan, from classical Islamic law. The relationship between these national legal orders and the *sharia* varies, as does the Islamic imprint of the laws of these individual states. Islamic law and Islamic legal concepts and perceptions thus refer to transnational phenomena which are linked to the past.

According to classical doctrine, Islamic law is essentially based on four sources, which are ranked as follows: the Qur'an and the *sunna* (the way, the sayings and the manners of the prophet) – the two primary sources of Islamic law –, the *ijma'* (the consensus of legal scholars) and the *qiyas* (interpretation through analogy) – the two secondary sources.[23] The Qur'an is the supreme source of law and is considered an imperative. It consists of 114 *suras* and more than 6,000 verses. Of this total of over 6,000 verses, however, only relatively few – the figure is variously given as anything from 50 to 800 – deal with questions of law.[24] Numerous methods and principles, the *usul al-fiqh*,[25] serve to derive legal rules

23 Cf. Kamali 2003, 16, 228; Vikør 2005, 3.

24 Cf. Kamali 2003, 25; Saeed 2006, 16. The legal section deals with the issues of marriage, divorce, alimony, child custody, paternity, inheritance law, law on the sale of goods, rent, murder, space, military law and the laws of evidence. They constitute the basis of what is called Islamic law.

25 See Kamali 2003, 117.

from the religious sources and to guide the exercise of *ijtihad*,[26] the independent and personal reasoning and interpretation of those sources. The result is a highly elaborate and well-defined, yet at the same time flexible and adaptable, system of jurisprudence, the *fiqh*. The various schools of legal thought also have their own individual methods for interpreting source texts and take differing views on specific legal matters.[27]

The core of *sharia* law is family law. Family law is at the heart of Islamic law, because, within the *sharia*, it is the branch of the law with the greatest density of regulation emanating from the highest-ranking sources. The reason for its relevance up to the present day is that it is the part of *sharia* law which was successfully protected against encroachment by European codes during the late Ottoman Empire and the colonial era, and has also remained untouched by the various degrees of secularisation which have occurred in Arab and Islamic countries. While the nineteenth century saw large swathes of Islamic law being eradicated and replaced by codifications on the continental European model, most countries with a predominantly Islamic population have maintained *sharia* based family law to this day.[28]

Thus, for many Muslim men and women, family law has become a symbol of collective identity, and adherence to it an absolute and inviolable core of belonging to the Muslim religious community.[29] While, in Islamic countries themselves, family law is an instrument of patriarchal, conservative power and policy, it is also an indispensable source of protection and order for family units both large and small. The way in which religious pronouncements have been codified varies significantly from country to country. Comparative analysis of family-law provisions based on Islamic principles reveals not only the diversity and dynamism of Islamic legal tradition, but also the flexibility and interpretative openness of Islamic legal rules. Given the sheer size of the territory under Islamic influence, the number of individual historical, social, economic and political factors which have shaped the various legal systems is vast, and the range of provisions is correspondingly wide.[30]

In Europe, however, Islamic family law as a whole is clearly perceived as a threat. Modern states, when promulgating their laws, have developed an almost automatic aversion to arguments based on religious considerations. Yet it must also be remembered that Europe's current modernity has itself not come without a struggle. Nowhere is this more evident that in the field of family law. Divorce

---

26 See Kamali 2003, 469.

27 There are four main schools of legal thought in Sunni Islam: the Hanafi school, the Maliki school, the Shafi'i school and the Hanbali school. The names of the schools refer to the names of the leading legal scholars Abu Hanifa, Malik ibn Anas, Muhammad ibn Idris al-Shafi'i and Ahmad ibn Hanbal. Cf. Hallaq 2005, 150; Vikør 2005, 89.

28 Cf. Coulson 1964, 149.

29 Cf. Poulter 1990, 147.

30 Cf. An-Na'im 2002, 16, *passim*; Welchman 2007, *passim*; Nasir 2009, 34.

was first legalised in Spain in 1982, and until 1988, the Swiss Civil Code stated that the husband was the head of the family, that it was the wife's duty to run the household and that – in the event of divorce – she was entitled to only one third of any increase in the couple's joint wealth. The attainments therefore remain fragile. Authoritarian structures within specific communities are perceived as thwarting hard-won principles of equality which have often yet to be fully put into effect. It is certainly true that confrontation with other forms of law tends to initiate a process of self-affirmation. In reviewing theses issues, we should, however, also not forget recent European family-law history.

Is there a Right to Cultural Identity in the Context of Family Law?

Cultural and Religious Identity in International Law

From its beginnings, Islam has been just as interested in law as in theology, the more so as law is central to its message. Moreover, Islamic family law has a direct bearing on Muslim men and women living in Europe, especially since family life and religious conviction are closely linked. The question of whether there is a right to cultural identity in a family-law context is one which Europe is predisposed to take seriously, since there are essential human rights aspects to cultural and religious identity, and these aspects have a sound normative foundation, both in the constitutions of European countries and in international law, which is no longer disputed to any significant extent. Facets of cultural and religious identity are protected by a whole series of international provisions, most notably article 8, paragraph 1 of the European Convention on Human Rights, article 29, paragraph 1, section c and article 30 of the Convention on the Rights of the Child.[31]

Nevertheless, unlike the right to religious freedom, cultural identity is not the sole content of a specific human right.[32] Furthermore, it is certainly true that human rights apply universally, and their primacy cannot therefore be qualified by invoking culture and culturally based practices. Human rights set implicit limits to what can be tolerated in the name of cultural diversity. It follows that it is not necessarily the explicit aim of human rights to promote cultural diversity. Nevertheless, the interpretation of a certain concept or term such as that of 'the family' may include cultural considerations. Cultural identity is an element of human dignity and, as a matter of principle, it should be used to interpret, develop and implement human rights. What is more important is that human rights in their emancipative objectives are directed at diversity of life paths, modes of living and

31 Further indications are contained in articles 7, 8 and 21, subsection b of the UN Convention on the Rights of the Child.

32 Donders 2002, 337, takes the view that cultural identity should not be developed as a separate human right, considering the concept of cultural identity to be too broad and vague.

world views by recognising and protecting the equal right to self-determination of all individuals. Rights of freedom guarantee individuals' scope to practise and experience and to unfold a whole range of different life cultures, and it is these freedoms which provide life choices with their cultural dimension.[33] Article 8, paragraph 1 of the European Convention on Human Rights protects the individual's freedom to conduct his or her life and relationships with others as he or she sees fit and also protects the individual's social identity.[34] In this way human rights make the development of cultural diversity by way of the collective exercise of individual freedom possible, so that it is not the individual's religious or cultural convictions which are recognised as human rights in themselves, but rather the individual's freedom to have such convictions in the first place, the freedom to develop them, but also the freedom to abandon them.

Protection of our cultural identity encompasses the protection of our belonging to a community, to an environment in which we can define ourselves in relation to others, and from which we can derive self-worth. This means that those rights of the individual enshrined in human rights law which make the establishment of communities possible are at odds both with authoritative collectivism and involuntary social exclusion.

Furthermore, the recognition of cultural identity is also important in guaranteeing equal access to justice, since equality of opportunity and treatment in this context requires an appreciation of uniqueness, and of the cultural dimensions of each specific case, with all its cultural implications. Moreover, the recognition of difference must be at the root of the Enlightenment idea that human dignity is inviolable and that human rights are universal, since the uniqueness of the human individual which human rights seek to protect, as Taylor rightly points out, would be inconceivable without the existence of different others.[35]

The right to freedom of thought, conscience and religion is expressly promulgated in article 9 of the European Convention on Human Rights,[36] and this freedom relates to convictions and modes of behaviour which are of crucial importance in determining personal identity and are closely linked with human dignity.[37] In a landmark judgment, the European Court of Human Rights ruled that:

> As enshrined in Article 9 …, freedom of thought, conscience and religion is one of the foundations of a 'democratic society' within the meaning of the

33 For a fundamental discussion, see Bielefeldt 2007, 49.

34 Cf. Harris, Boyle, Bates, Buckley 2009, 363.

35 Cf. Taylor 1992, *passim.*

36 Cf. also article 18 of the International Covenant on Civil and Political Rights of 16 December 1966; article 22 of the Charter of Fundamental Rights of the European Union (7 December 2000).

37 For the German legal concept of dignity in relation to article 9 of the European Convention on Human Rights, see Grabenwarter 2009, 252.

> Convention. It is, in its religious dimension, one of the most vital elements that go to make up the identity of believers and their conception of life, but it is also a precious asset for atheists, agnostics, sceptics and the unconcerned. The pluralism indissociable from a democratic society, which has been dearly won over the centuries, depends on it.[38]

Article 9 is connected to article 14 of the European Convention on Human Rights, which explicitly forbids discrimination, including discrimination on grounds of religion. Exercise of religious freedom is subject to restrictions, but these restrictions must have a basis in law, must pursue legitimate objectives and must be proportionate. Circumstances under which interventions restricting the exercise of religious freedom are justified include, in particular, cases where the rights and freedoms of others must be protected – against the exertion of abusive influence, for example. Article 9 of the European Convention on Human Rights also requires the state to uphold the freedom to change religion or belief.[39]

Freedom of religion is primarily a matter of individual conscience, but it also implies freedom to manifest one's religion alone or in community with others and in public or in private. Article 9 of the European Convention on Human Rights lists a number of forms which manifestation of a religion or belief may take, namely worship, teaching, practice and observance. Muslims sometimes argue that, as members of the Islamic community, they are duty-bound to follow the precepts of *sharia* in organising their family lives rather than to do so according to established European law. They view the right to adhere to *sharia* as an essential part of their religious freedom. The European Court of Human Rights, however, decided in the *Refah Partisi (The Welfare Party) and Others v. Turkey* case[40] that religions are confined to the sphere of private religious practice. Henceforth, according to the court, the call for application of religious private law rules is not part of the claims protected by the religious freedom disposition of the Convention and such a policy goes beyond the freedom of individuals to observe the precepts of their religion. The court stressed that freedom of religion is primarily a matter of individual

38 *Kokkinakis v. Greece*, ECHR, Judgment of 25 May 1993, (Application no. 14307/88), note 31.

39 Cf. Harris, Boyle, Bates, Buckley 2009, 429, and references.

40 In 1998, the Turkish Constitutional Court dissolved the Refah Party as a 'center of activities contrary to the principle of secularism' and banned six of its leaders from political-party activities for five years. The party, and the politicians affected, appealed to the European Court of Human Rights; *Refah Partisi (The Welfare Party) and Others v. Turkey*, ECHR, Judgment of 31 July 2001, (Applications nos. 41340/98, 41342/98, 41343/98 and 41344/98); at the request of the applicants, the case was referred to the Grand Chamber of the Court, which confirmed the previous judgment; *Refah Partisi (The Welfare Party) and Others v. Turkey*, ECHR Grand Chamber, Judgment of 13 February 2003, (Applications nos. 41340/98, 41342/98, 41343/98 and 41344/98).

conscience and quite different from the field of private law, which is concerned with the organisation and functioning of society as a whole.[41]

However, this cannot obscure the fact that religious belief, legal principles and family relationships are closely intertwined in Islamic doctrine. Even if freedom of religion cannot justify a parallel system of religious family law, religious convictions in family matters do have a cultural dimension and are thus part of the right to self-determination. It should also be noted that Islamic doctrine recognises the distinction between the transcendental, governing the relationship between man and God (*'ibadat*), and matters which are between individual humans (*mu'amalat*). This differentiation makes it possible for reformers to justify ongoing development of the law in the second area.[42]

Traditionally, human rights have been conceived of as rights of the individual, that is, rights of individual people, even though they often have a collective dimension or are exercised collectively, as in the case of freedom of religion. Whether the right of self-determination can be interpreted as extending to encompass a right of protection and autonomy for culturally, ethnically or religiously defined groups which goes beyond the individual freedoms guaranteed by human rights law is the subject of controversy,[43] and it is a question which may well be answered differently in different national contexts. Many international agreements protecting ethnic minorities have not only an individual rights content but also a collective rights content, article 27 of the International Covenant on Civil and Political Rights[44] or article 5 of the Framework Convention for the Protection of National Minorities, enacted by the Council of Europe in 1995,[45] being prominent examples.[46] Nevertheless, these Conventions are also primarily

---

41 *Refah Partisi (The Welfare Party) and Others v. Turkey*, ECHR Grand Chamber, Judgment of 13 February 2003, (Applications nos. 41340/98, 41342/98, 41343/98 and 41344/98), notes 127 and 128.

42 Cf. references in An-Na'im 1992, 26 and 32.

43 See the extensive discussion in Donders 2002, 53, 93.

44 Although this provision protects collective groups, only individuals may invoke it. On article 27 of the International Covenant on Civil and Political Rights, see Jayawickrama 2002, 843; and the extensive review in Donders 2002, 166.

45 Article 5: '1) The Parties undertake to promote the conditions necessary for persons belonging to national minorities to maintain and develop their culture, and to preserve the essential elements of their identity, namely their religion, language, traditions and cultural heritage. 2) Without prejudice to measures taken in pursuance of their general integration policy, the Parties shall refrain from policies or practices aimed at assimilation of persons belonging to national minorities against their will and shall protect these persons from any action aimed at such assimilation.' For a detailed discussion of the Framework Convention for the Protection of National Minorities, see Donders 2002, 252.

46 The Universal Declaration on Cultural Diversity adopted by the General Conference of UNESCO on 2 November 2001 deserves mention here (particularly article 4); see the detailed discussion in Donders 2002, 134.

aimed at ensuring that persons belonging to minorities can maintain and develop their culture and preserve their identity.

Conflicts between Law, Culture and Religion

There are essential human rights aspects to cultural identity. It follows that if the Islamic concept of law is religiously determined and if religion is viewed as an integral part of cultural identity, conflicts between law and culture, and between freedom and equality, can potentially arise and must be addressed.[47] Nevertheless, the law should be viewed as part of the cultural fabric of society, since every law and normative system is a product of the social, cultural and political contexts from which it has evolved. Furthermore, because they are integral to cultural identity, legal customs will be all the more respected the greater the religious legitimacy they enjoy, especially as in this case they will be perceived as less subject to human influence. If law and culture become dissociated from each other, if the individual, with his or her particular self-image, perceives the law to which he or she is subject as somehow alien, or becomes estranged from that law, the individual will either attempt to withdraw from society and its law or will feel increasingly detached from it. So, for the law to be respected by the community, it must reflect and consider the values of those it governs and must therefore also recognise a variety of cultural opinions. The law thus has a role in defining the boundaries of societal belonging.

Should the pluralised society which migration has brought in its wake also result in legal pluralisation? How can homogeneity in family law be reconciled with cultural identity? What relevance do Islamic legal norms, expectations and practices have in the context of family law in Europe? Is there an obligation to accommodate or even incorporate Islamic family-law norms into national European legal systems? What are the limits of legal or normative pluralism? Do European family-law codes have the openness to incorporate cultural diversity, or is there an implicit assumption of homogeneity which impedes an adequate response to ethnic and religious plurality in family practices? These are some of the major questions confronting the family-law codes of European countries.

Convergences: Pluralisation of Family Forms and Harmonisation of Family Law

Pluralisation of Family Forms and Family Values

Developments are very rarely linear or uniform, and they are never the result of one single cause. However, an examination of how family forms have developed in European countries since the end of the nineteenth century shows that they have

47 Cf., generally, Grimm 2001, 118, in particular 122.

been subject to a profound transformation, and that there have been unmistakable shifts in one and the same direction, even though this transformation undoubtedly exhibits some differences in its specific characteristics from one European country to another,[48] especially as far as acceptance of change is concerned.[49] The socio-demographic metrics which document this transformation are well known: rising numbers of divorces, declining birth rates, an increasing number of couples co-habiting outside marriage and the rapid increase in single-parent and patchwork families. This list could be extended to include medically assisted forms of reproduction, which make it possible for a man and a woman to produce offspring without physical contact. Current forms of family life are characterised by a contradictory mixture of traditional longings and new expectations, in which a multiplicity of forms of life, love and relationships has been constructed from pieces borrowed here and there and is hoped for by some, endured by others and vigorously opposed by many.[50] Family forms have been subject to rapid change for decades and have become pluralised. Cultural pessimists are keen to see in these trends the incipient disintegration of the family. I do not share this apocalyptic view. The trends we observe today can be traced back to modernity. Indeed, processes of individualisation always result both in a desire for some element of a life of one's own, coupled with a yearning for belonging, propinquity and community. The idea of partnership has not become less plausible. The only concept which has become less compelling is the exemplary icon of the life-long, biological and social unit of father, mother and child, legitimated by marriage, which, despite being inscribed in collective memory and despite the undoubtedly profound influence it exerts on society, is a relatively recent phenomenon in historical terms. The family remains a symbol of hope, though traditional certainties about its constitution have vanished.

The same applies to family values. While the Christian idea of marriage as an institution is integral to collective memory,[51] ontological examination shows that its key constitutive elements – enduring for a lifetime, monogamous and between members of opposite sexes – have little normative effect.[52] The idea that there is a coherent, shared body of common Western family values is a fiction. It is a fiction which confuses what ought to be with what is, and one which disguises existing heterogeneity, the coexistence of a transient superficial text – in the form of a dynamic diversity of values – and a persistent subtext – in the form of an unspecified residue of metaphysical structures of meaning.

---

48 Cf. Kaufmann 2002, 419 and 423.

49 Cf. Fux 2002, 363

50 Beck-Gernsheim 2000, 10.

51 This applies particularly to the civil law countries The protection afforded to marriage as an institution is far less explicit in the common law countries; cf. Meulders-Klein 2004, 477.

52 Cf. Bainham 1995, 237: 'It seems likely that if we were to concentrate on the practice rather than the theory of matrimonial obligations, at least as strong a case could be made for identifying a community norm of marital infidelity as one of marital fidelity.'

It is certainly true that migration from countries with a Muslim population has resulted in a re-traditionalisation of family forms and family values, which is reflected in social statistics in as far as the signs of continuing erosion of the traditional family unit are still evident, but are to some extent offset by contrary trends. This re-traditionalisation, which is at least to some extent attributable to migration, has meant that the entire spectrum of family forms and family values has become even more pluralised. To take two highly stereotypical examples, it runs the gamut from the 40-year old female neuroscientist from Germany, now on her fourth long-term relationship, with two children from two different men, currently maintaining a same-sex partnership and experiencing the desire to have a third child, all the way to the woman who has recently emigrated from Anatolia, and has a powerful need for care, support and the upholding of Islamic conventions of marriage and community. Of course, these opposites can be reversed, as exemplified by the hypothetical case of the farmer's wife living in a traditional rural community in the Swiss mountains and the single Iranian female professor of biochemistry working in the Swiss pharmaceutical industry. These examples illustrate that the pluralisation of family forms in Europe is not a phenomenon which can be explained solely by the erosion of traditional family life brought about by individualisation, but that it should be thought of as an ambivalent process, characterised by opposing trends, which is in no way linear and is creating tensions across numerous planes. The range of family structures in Europe today exhibits the contemporaneity of the uncontemporary, so that traditional, newer and alien forms of family life exist side by side.

Harmonisation of Family Law

The convergent development of European family-law codes and the search for a shared legal framework do not in any way contradict this contention.[53] Admittedly, family law is reputed to be the branch of law upon which traditions, religions and cultural values have impinged the most. In Krause's words:

> In contrast to laws involving commerce, however, family law has resisted secularization and amalgamation. At its cultural foundations, humanity remains

53 A multitude of publications address the perspective of a harmonised system of family law at the European level, as does the Commission on European Family Law established in 2001. Such discussions are highly productive, as they not only compel us to reflect on our own positions but also prompt consideration of what family law can and should achieve and how individual countries position themselves in the European context. Converging developments in this area can thus be consciously considered, critically examined and scientifically assessed. Cf. Antokolskaia 2004, 29; Pintens 2006, 137; Schwenzer 2003, 318; Boele-Woelki 2003, *passim.*

highly diverse. Universally, religions underlie and have set the tone of family law, and diversity of religions has continued to foster diversity of legal rules.[54]

Evidence of this can certainly be seen if we take a worldwide perspective. Family law in Asian and African countries for example, often based on religious or customary norms, diverges substantially from European codes. Nevertheless, continuing globalisation and internationalisation of the law has recently begun to bring individual jurisdictions closer together worldwide. Some recent reforms in Arab and Islamic jurisdictions are quite in tune with fundamental principles of family law in the West, even if they are religiously informed, motivated and substantiated.[55]

Europe, however, has in recent years witnessed some unmistakable moves towards harmonisation of family-law codes, though how significant these are judged to be will depend on the prism through which they are observed – whether the focus is on commonality or difference and whether emphasis is placed on the intermingling of different systems or on cultural and national independence and distinctiveness. After an initial preponderance of comparisons focusing on harmonisation and integration, more recent assessments have tended to concentrate on differences, a phenomenon no doubt partly attributable to pluralisation and fragmentation as one aspect of globalisation and the general focus in discourse on cultural identity and distinctiveness.[56]

The debate as to whether family law in Europe is converging or diverging fails to address the issues involved in their entirety. The converging trends in European family law are largely the result of discourse on personal and human rights.[57] This is borne out by the evidence that the cultural dimension of family law is increasingly restricted to representing a core of convictions held by the majority of people in the context of significant differentiation within society. This in turn can be attributed to the shrinking area on which there is any basic normative consensus within society as a whole. As differences within society have proliferated, so the meaning of family law has diminished. Today, public interests are scarcely able to justify legal restrictions on the act of marriage, rules governing the internal structure of the marriage relationship or the sanctioning of its termination. As a result, family law in European countries is becoming less institutionalised and more contractual in its nature, and personal autonomy in individual and family existence is replacing legally designed family models.[58]

54 Krause 2006, 1099.

55 An example of this can be seen in the new Moroccan family law code, the *moudawana*, which came into effect in 2004.

56 For an extensive discussion of the debate on family-law harmonisation, see Antokolskaia 2006, *passim*.

57 For a detailed review, see Vlaardingerbroek 2002, 120.

58 Eekelaar 2003, 108.

The process of the state's withdrawal from the family area of life has not been consistently thought through by any means. While the drawing of borders between the public and private spheres has repeatedly been unmasked as an ideological conceit,[59] it remains a conviction which is intrinsic to liberal thinking. The borders between what is public and what is private must be revisited and redrawn, in the light of the plurality of cultural identities and expectations regarding family law.

Religion, Nation and the State

National identities and the relationship between religion and the state, as a national entity defined by its constitution, play an important part in determining how the border is drawn between the private and public spheres. The flows of migration which Europe experienced during the second half of the twentieth century, which served in no small part to rebuild the continent after the Second World War, and the subsequent evolution of the diaspora communities to which they gave rise as many migrants then stayed put, have also presented a challenge for the relationship between religion, nation and state. The term 'diaspora' is associated with migrants' ongoing ties with their countries of origin, with bridging distances and fostering transnational networks, all of which are processes in which religion plays an important role. Equally importantly, the migrant communities have established forms of organisation and solidarity in their adopted countries, and these have lent expression to their identities, their interests and their personal and collective motives. European countries, for their part, had, and still have, to reconsider their political traditions, their principles of nationality and citizenship in the light of this. Because national identity is rooted in history, countries with different state traditions have developed different strategies and attitudes for addressing the present situation. The challenge all European countries face is to define the relationship between state identity and minority rights, to address the conflict between cultural homogeneity and the vigorously professed, and distinct, collective identities of their various migrant communities, to rethink their notions of space, culture and nation, and to redefine their roles as nation-states. This is a necessary process, because the nation-state is by no means a neutral arena, but a territory which is keenly fought over.

There is a wide diversity of models upon which the relationships between religious and ethnic communities and the state are based. The identity of a nation as an imagined community[60] may be more ethnic or civic in its emphasis, depending

59 Cf. Geuss 2002, *passim*, in particular 21.

60 Anderson 1983. According to Anderson, a nation is a community whose construction is social, and is thus imagined by the people who perceive themselves as part of a particular group.

on whether the nation's sense of community is defined by a common ethnicity and culture or by its people being governed by a common set of political institutions.[61]

France, for example, has a concept of nationhood which is unambiguously civic, and national identity is based on citizenship and on the legal and political equality of its citizens. The French Revolution created a nation which is *une et indivisible*, 'a nation that understands itself as the sole source of sovereignty and legitimacy and demands absolute and undivided loyalty of its members who compose the nation as equal citizens'.[62] France has a policy of inclusion and assimilation, aimed at achieving a homogeneous society. Of course, there have always been counter-movements, as 'France moved bit by bit from the concept of an organic nation and adopted new aspects of liberalism'.[63] Yet one of the most striking features of the French nation remains the strict divide between state and religion. Church and state are clearly separated, and there is a constitutional commitment to the principle of *laïcité*.[64] In France, state neutrality in religious matters means that religion and its symbols are totally absent from the public sphere – in contrast to the United States, where a multiplicity of religious expressions are accepted in the public arena. Like other countries, however, France is also confronted by prescriptive or normative quasi-imperatives such as diversity, cultural identity and pluralism. While these may not challenge the concept of the state as the only frame of reference directly, they undoubtedly have an impact on family-law practices.

In contrast to France – indeed, at the opposite end of the spectrum from it – the concept of national identity in Germany is forged from the belief in a common ethnicity. This is because '[n]ation-building occurred in protest against and in conflict with the existing state pattern'.[65] In Germany, the predominant perception of the nation is as an ethno-cultural community striving for a state of its own.[66] Of course, the end of the German Reich necessarily required a reconsideration of national identity. Democracy and human rights are now crucial elements in Germany's self-definition as a nation. Despite this, in the German notion of nationhood, the line between inclusion and exclusion is essentially determined by ethnic affiliation.[67] In Germany, loyalty to the state and loyalty to a religion can co-exist, and the expression of religious themes in the public arena is permitted. To that extent, Germany is not a nation in which church and state are totally separated. In a landmark judgment, Germany's Federal Constitutional Court emphasised that there is no strict separation between church and state in Germany, and that the state's overarching attitude towards religious matters is one of neutrality and

---

61 Cf. Töpperwien 2001, 42.

62 Cf. Töpperwien 2001, 101, 110.

63 Cf. Töpperwien 2001, 129.

64 Article 1, Constitution de la cinquième république. The significance of this is paramount, cf. von Krosigk 2000, 33.

65 Töpperwien 2001, 141.

66 Ehringfeld 1997, 89, refers to Germany as an ethnic nation-state.

67 For an extensive discussion, see Töpperwien 2001, 152.

openness, promoting the freedom of religious belief for all religions equally.[68] That said, the nature of the relationship between the state and religious communities is one which clearly accords privileged treatment to the major Christian churches and to the Jewish religious community.[69]

The Swiss national identity is a compromise between these two positions. The Swiss nation is described as a *Willensnation*, a nation which relies on the will of its constituent groups to be Swiss. Switzerland is a nation based on communal civism.[70] It accommodates and incorporates a diversity of communities, as is apparent from the different languages and regions of which the country is composed. While diversity is an important element in Swiss national identity, not all religions are placed on an equal footing. Each canton has the authority to determine whether it wishes to confer the special status of *Landeskirche*, or official church, to selected religious communities. In most cantons the Roman Catholic and Evangelical Reformed church are recognised as *Landeskirchen* in public law and are accorded special privileges accordingly.

In England, unity between religion and state is incorporated in an established state church. The special relationship between the Crown and the Church of England is symbolised by the monarch, who is both the Head of State and the Supreme Governor of the Church of England.[71] The principal leader of the Church of England, the Archbishop of Canterbury, is nominated by the Prime Minister, in consultation with the Head of State.[72]

Since the change of regime in Spain in 1975, the relationship between church and state has been a troubled one.[73] Article 16, section 3 of Spain's 1978 constitution states that Spain has no state religion. This same provision does, however, then go on to place particular emphasis on the Catholic church. In 1992, Spain's parliament enacted a law whose purpose is to guarantee equality between religions.[74]

The public policy of accommodation of religious diversity differs depending on whether there is a clear separation of religion and state, whether there is some support for religious institutions or whether there is a state religion.[75] But despite all the various particular characteristics of the relationship between religion, nation and state in Europe's national jurisdictions, their links through international law have resulted in a degree of convergence in their treatment of religious minorities.

---

68 In German, 'Bundesverfassungsgericht', abbreviated as BVerfGE, BVerfGE 108, 282.

69 See detailed analysis in Rottleuthner 2006, 30.

70 According to Töpperwien 2001, 233.

71 Cf. Rosman 2003, 29.

72 Owen Hood, Jackson, Leopold 2001, 315, note 15–014.

73 For details, see Bernecker 1995, 129.

74 Ley 26/1992 de 10 de noviembre, por la que se aprueba el acuerdo de cooperaćion del Estado con la Comisión Islámica de España.

75 For comparative analysis for Europe, see Cesari 2003, 265.

Muslim Communities in Europe

The current Muslim presence in Europe has essentially evolved as a result of immigration to prosperous industrial nations during the second half of the twentieth century.[76] International migration has occurred in response to employment opportunities arising from post-war reconstruction and economic growth as Europe was rebuilt. In the European countries considered here, Muslim populations vary between four and ten per cent of the overall total and are constantly growing. The Muslim communities in individual European countries vary enormously in terms of origin, history and ambitions. The position of each of these communities is unique and specific to the circumstances of its adopted country.[77] Moreover, the individuals within Europe's Muslim communities exhibit great diversity with regard to their relationship to, and understanding of, their faith, so that many diverging opinions and forms of behaviour exist within these communities.

The history of the United Kingdom's Muslim communities can be traced right back to the activities of the East India Company.[78] The more recent employment-related migration from former British colonies and the New Commonwealth since 1945 has created many distinct ethnic minority communities, characterised by customs, religious beliefs and concepts of the family which are not infrequently very much at odds with those of the majority community.[79] Most Muslims in the UK, whether first- or second-generation migrants, are from the Indian subcontinent – from India, Pakistan and Bangladesh – and the remainder from the former Middle Eastern and African colonies of the British Empire. The immigration that has taken place since the 1970s has been characterised by new migrants joining family members already established in the UK. It is certainly true that many of their traditions and values have been modified to meet the expectations of the majority community, particularly in the case of those who were born and educated in the UK. Nevertheless, much has been preserved and maintained. One explanation for this may be that Muslims from the Indian subcontinent have always been a minority within a larger Hindu majority, that they have long been accustomed to this status and are thus particularly predisposed to the idea of delimitation between population groups, and are used to protecting and fostering their Islamic identity in enclosed communities. In the UK, these communities were quick to build mosques and secure supplies of their own specific food. The UK has a large and expanding network of Muslim organisations, with *imams* acting as religious intermediaries between their own communities and the state, a task in which they have been assigned a multitude of roles. In this regard, in the UK one can observe

76 For a comprehensive and differentiated, if somewhat older, picture of the Islamic presence in Europe, see Bistolfi 1995, 13.

77 See also the comparative analysis of the Muslim presence in various European countries in Hussain 2003, 215.

78 Cf. Yilmaz 2005, 55.

79 Poulter 1987, 589.

a communitarian and multicultural approach to the presence of Muslims, and the UK is tolerant towards expressions of religious diversity.[80] Further reasons for the establishment and maintenance of largely closed immigrant communities can be seen in the pressure exerted on them, both from within and from outside. Pressure from outside has taken the form of exclusion, discrimination and stereotypification, while that from within is exerted by means of transnational community structures: that is, close links between Muslims in the UK and relatives in their countries of origin.[81] The vast majority of Muslims living in the UK hold British nationality.

France's Muslim community is very large by European standards, a fact explained partly by its colonial past and partly by the policies it has used to address labour shortages. Muslims in France mainly originate from former French colonies – in the North, West and sub-Saharan parts of Africa, which are predominantly Muslim. After the Second World War, the majority of the immigrants from the Maghreb came to France as lone, male guest workers. They arrived without their families and with the firm intention of returning to their countries of origin. During the Algerian war, Algerians in France were subject to harassment and police raids. Despite this, many Algerian migrants stayed in France, both during and after the war. Indeed, in the war's aftermath, large numbers of entire families migrated to France. The arrival of whole families made for a significant change in the immigrants' needs, and religion resumed an important role in their lives. As in other countries, the challenges presented by the sheer number of immigrants were eminently practical in nature, with an urgent need for housing, employment and education. [82] France relies heavily on its state institutions, particularly its schools, as a secular environment in which to promote integration,[83] a circumstance closely linked to its profoundly held belief in the principle of *laïcité*, which is largely responsible for institutional blindness towards religious pluralism.[84] Immigrants to France are confronted with compelling arguments to assimilate.[85] Roughly half of France's Muslim population are French citizens.

In Germany, conversely, the acquisition of nationality is impeded by the idea of ethnic affiliation, and these restrictions have only recently been relaxed as a means of encouraging the integration of second-generation immigrants.[86]

80 These special factors are considered in Kepel 2006, 26.

81 Cf. Poulter 1987, 590.

82 Cf. Moch 2007, 136.

83 Cf. Moch 2007, 139.

84 For a fundamental discussion of *laïcité* in France, its evolution and its significance for the 'Islamic question' today, see von Krosigk 2000.

85 Cf. Kepel 2006, 28.

86 Cf. Germany's Nationality Act (in German, 'Staatsangehörigkeitsgesetz', abbreviated as 'StAG'). New regulations on this have applied since 1 January 2000: under section 4, para. 3 of the StAG, the children of immigrants who were born in Germany can acquire dual nationality. For this to apply at least one of the parents must have been legally ordinarily resident in Germany for at least eight years (subsection 1) and must have been

Even today, it is still only a minority of Germany's Muslim population who are German citizens. During Germany's post-war economic boom, migrant workers were recruited by the million.[87] Many of these people stayed in Germany and arranged for their families to follow them there. Despite this, until the late 1980s, Germany was unwilling to see itself as a migration destination, convinced that the migrants – the *Gastarbeiter* – would eventually return home. Islam was regarded as a foreign issue, rather than a domestic one, and the formative potential which a policy of active integration could have delivered remained untapped until fairly recently.[88] In Germany, the dominant Muslim community is formed by migrants from Turkey. The development of its specific Islamic identity is a comparatively recent phenomenon, and it is one which has played and will continue to play an important part in negotiations with its adopted country.[89]

Switzerland's economy has also derived great benefit from employment-related immigration since the Second World War. The Muslim community in Switzerland has evolved partly as a result of employment-related migration from former Yugoslavia and Turkey, and partly through the arrival of refugees from the Balkans and Africa. For many years, the status accorded to migrant workers in Switzerland was precarious, with foreign workers intended primarily to cushion fluctuations in the overall demand for the labour.[90] The current political situation in this regard is characterised by restrictive immigration and naturalisation policies and integration initiatives which are still in their infancy.

Spain's experience of an Islamic presence on its soil goes back a long way. Its first encounter with Islam occurred in the seventh century, with the southern part of the country remaining under Arab rule until 1492. For many years, Spain was a country characterised by emigration, and it was not until the economic upswing following the country's EU accession in 1986 that Spain experienced net immigration. The majority of Spain's Muslim migrants originate from North Africa, other Arab countries, Eastern and South-Eastern Europe.[91]

Recent migration from countries whose majority population is Muslim, which has principally served to reunite families and has therefore resulted in a feminisation of migration – and the subsequent generations of people who were born and have grown up in Europe – are key policy issues for European countries. European policy-makers must appreciate the transition of these migrants from mere transients to settlers and the growing self-awareness and sense of identity

granted a permanent right of residence (subsection. 2). Furthermore, in order to maintain their German nationality, the children concerned must renounce the nationality of their parents between the ages of 18 and 23 (section 29, StAG).

87 Cf. Bade, Oltmer 2007, 159.

88 For a detailed discussion of this, see Bade, Oltmer 2007, 161 and 168; Hussain 2003, 233.

89 Cf. Kepel 2006, 27.

90 See extensive discussion of this in Vuilleumier 2007, 200.

91 On the Muslim presence in Spain, see Hussain 2003, 240.

which this has brought about for these communities. Today's migrant communities are principally composed of families, with the result that policy-makers are confronted with family constellations which may differ from the traditional nuclear family model. The transnational character of contemporary migration is a challenge for national legal frameworks, since migrants often negotiate and adhere to multiple family ideologies and norms, sift through a multiplicity of cultural references, alternatives and compromises, and engage in relationships across national boundaries.[92] The marriages of Muslims living in Europe with spouses from their country of origin or the country of origin of their parents are significant in a number of different ways. Roger Ballard puts it as follows:

> It is not hard to discern why multi-generational corporate extended families are proving to be such resilient institutional features in the contemporary world, at least within communities of non-European origin. The economic advantages which can accrue to those who organize their domestic affairs on this basis can be substantial, especially when they are transnationally extended. Once it is taken for granted that family assets are held collectively, it follows they can and should be distributed (and redistributed) amongst family members according to the principle of 'from each according to their ability, to each according to their need'; the group can readily order itself as a miniature multinational corporation, shifting assets, ideas and personnel across borders in such a way as to maximize their collective advantages. Nevertheless interpersonal relationships within such collectivities are frequently far from egalitarian; superordinates are expected to offer support and guidance to their subordinates, whilst subordinates, typically defined in terms of gender, generation and age, are expected to respect and obey their elders. However membership of such a collectivity brings substantial benefits. The capacity to facilitate access to every potential resource of which any network member may become aware, no matter how spatially distant, enables extended networks to maximize members' material, financial and emotional security when times get tough ... . Transnational extension has in no way undermined established patterns of kinship reciprocity; indeed, their strength has for the most part been reinforced.[93]

92 Grillo 2008, 15.
93 Ballard 2009, 308.

Chapter 2

Real and Virtual Legal Spaces: The Scope and Limitations of Conflict-of-Laws Rules

The Starting Point: Conflict-of-Laws Rules

Investigation into the relationship between cultural diversity and family law in Europe principally centres around conflict-of-laws rules, the rules determining which law applies in family disputes involving foreign nationals.[1] Which family law is applicable to an Iranian married couple living in Europe? Will a European country recognise a marriage between minors rightfully concluded in a foreign country? Is a man who has repudiated his wife in his country of origin entitled to enter into a new marriage in a European country? How binding are bans on marriages between spouses of different faiths under the law of the parties' country of origin? Are the children born to a man's second wife in a polygynous marriage legitimate? Conflict-of-laws rules do not address cross-cultural family situations as such, since they apply only in family constellations in which at least one of the parties concerned is a foreign national. If one or more of the parties is a foreign national, conflict-of-laws rules then apply irrespective of whether cultural issues are at stake or not. Conversely, if none of the parties are foreign nationals, conflict-of-laws rules do not apply, irrespective of the extent to which the parties' understanding of family-law matters may be informed by convictions rooted in other cultures.

Law has a cultural dimension. Indeed, it is part of the fabric of every culture. It follows that the right to maintain cultural identity gives rise to an individual's interest in being judged according to the law to which he or she has the greatest cultural affinity.[2] Whether the individual's nationality or the cultural environment in which they live should be the determining factor is an issue which different European jurisdictions approach in different ways – as is readily apparent from the contradictions in the solution to this dilemma adopted by the private international law codes of Germany, France and Spain on the one hand, and Switzerland and England on the other.

On many questions of family law, the private international law codes of Germany, France and Spain adhere to the principle of nationality as the key factor in determining the applicable legal framework, whereas Switzerland and England adhere to the principle of residence or domicile.

1 See, *inter alia*, Foblets 2000, 11.

2 Cf. Looschelders 2001, 468; Von Hoffmann, Thorn 2007, 3, notes 12 *et seq.*

Nationality as the Determining Factor

Provisions under the laws of specific countries

In many European countries – Germany, France and Spain being prominent examples – the law which applies to many family issues continues to be determined by the nationality of the persons concerned. The idea appears to be that people have organised their lives based on one particular legal system and that their affinity to that system should be protected, even if the focus of their vital interests has shifted. Determining applicable law on the basis of a person's nationality is meant to pay heed to a person's right to cultural identity.

In Germany, each spouse in a couple wishing to marry is subject to the matrimonial law provisions of the country of which he or she is a national.[3] It is a principle of German law that the substantive-law requirements placed on each of the two spouses under the law of the country of which each is a national apply distributively and not cumulatively. Distributive applicability of several law canons means that the requirements relating to one and the same legal act, in this case marriage, are judged in accordance with those several law canons. One result of this is that, for example, a bride who, under the law of the country of which her husband is a national, is not yet of marriageable age, but who is already eligible to marry under the law of the country of which she is a national, is permitted to conclude marriage, under article 13, section 1 of the Introductory Act to the EGBGB.[4] German law will be applied, however, if disproportionate effort would be required for marriage to be effected through the application of foreign law and if one of the spouses habitually resides in Germany or is a German citizen.[5] The form of the legal act of marriage is, in principle, governed by German law.[6] The general legal consequences of marriage and, thus, also the statutory matrimonial property regime are, in principle, determined by the law of the state of which both spouses share nationality, or last shared nationality during the time of the marriage in the event of one of them still being a national of that state. Otherwise, the applicable law with respect to the statutory matrimonial property regime is that of the state in which both spouses habitually reside, or most recently habitually

3 Article 13, para. 1 of Germany's Introductory Act to the Civil Code (in German, 'Einführungsgesetz zum Bürgerlichen Gesetzbuch'). Hereinafter simply EGBGB.

4 Staudinger, Mankowski 2003, article 13, EGBGB, note 49; Von Hoffmann, Thorn 2007, 304, notes 2 *et seq.*

5 Article 13, para. 2, EGBGB.

6 Article 13, para. 3, sentence 1, EGBGB. A marriage between two persons engaged to be married, neither of whom is a German national, may, however, be celebrated before a person properly authorised by the government of the country of which one of the persons engaged to be married is a national, according to the formalities prescribed by the law of that country. A certified copy of the registration of the marriage in the Register of Births, Deaths and Marriages, kept by the person properly authorised therefore, furnishes conclusive evidence of the marriage celebrated in that manner (article 13 para. 3 sentence 2, EGBGB).

resided during their marriage, if one of them remains habitually resident there.[7] By way of exception, the spouses may choose the law which applies to their marriage, namely when the spouses have several nationalities, are not of the same nationality or are habitually resident in different countries.[8] In Germany, divorce is governed by the law that applies to the legal effects of the marriage at the time the divorce application is served.[9] Thus, the divorce law of a foreign country will apply in cases where both spouses either share the same non-German nationality or shared it during their marriage and one of the spouses still holds that nationality at the time of filing for divorce.[10] Only in cases where the marriage cannot be dissolved under the law of that country will the divorce be subject to German law, provided that the spouse petitioning for divorce is a German national at the time of making the petition or was a German national at the time the marriage took place.[11] Claims for maintenance, however, are governed by the substantive law applicable in the jurisdiction in which the former spouse entitled to such maintenance habitually resides, in as far as a right to receive maintenance is provided for under that law. The law of the state of which both spouses are nationals or, if necessary, German law applies in cases where the application of such law is the sole means by which a duty to provide such maintenance can be upheld.[12] The parentage of a child is governed by the law of the state in which the child habitually resides and may also be governed by the law of the state of which the relevant parent is a national.[13] The legal relationship between a child and his or her parents is – as a rule – governed by the law of the state in which the child habitually resides.[14]

France does not have a specific law on matters of private international law. The *Code Civil* does, however, stipulate conflict-of-laws norms. The prerequisites for a marriage are governed by the law of the country of which each spouse is a national, subject to *ordre public* constraints. A distinction is made between *condition de fond* and *condition de forme*. The former is based on the law of the state of which each of the future spouses is a national and is derived from

7 Article 14, para. 1, EGBGB and article 15, para. 1, EGBGB.

8 Article 14, para. 2 and 3, EGBGB; article 15, para. 2, EGBGB.

9 Article 17, para. 1, sentence 1, EGBGB in conjunction with article 14, EGBGB.

10 Cf. article 14, para. 1 subsection 1, EGBGB; this may also apply in cases under article 17, para. 1, sentence 1, EGBGB in conjunction with article 14 para. 2, subsections 2 and 3, EGBGB, particularly under the law of the country in which both spouses are habitually resident or were last habitually resident during their marriage, if one of them is still habitually resident there. The choice of applicable law under article 14, para. 2 to 4, EGBGB also extends to the applicable divorce law, cf. Kropholler 2004, 362. Article 17, para. 2, EGBGB does, however, set forth the procedural limitation that divorces in Germany may be pronounced only by a court.

11 Article 17, para. 1, sentence 2, EGBGB.

12 Article 18, para. 1 and 2, EGBGB.

13 Article 19, EGBGB.

14 Article 21, EGBGB.

article 3, paragraph 3 and article 171–1 of the *Code Civil*.[15] If the future spouses are not both of the same nationality, this means that each spouse has to meet the requirements of eligibility to marry provided for under the law of the country of which he or she is a national, without also having to meet the requirements imposed by the law of the country of which his or her future spouse is a national.[16] There are exceptions to this arising from specific provisions in French law which have *ordre public* character and therefore are bilateral requirements which both future spouses have to meet.[17] *Conditions de forme*, the formal requirements of a marriage, are regulated by the law of the country where the marriage ceremony takes place.[18] A ceremony which takes place in France produces a formally valid marriage if it complies with the formal requirements of French law. For spouses sharing the same nationality, the legal consequences of marriage derive primarily from the law of the state in question, for those of different nationalities it is the law of the state in which they jointly live and have their domicile which primarily defines these.[19] Since 1992, the Hague Convention on the Law Applicable to Matrimonial Property Regimes has applied in France. Article 4, paragraph 1 of the Convention states that if the spouses have not designated an applicable law, their matrimonial property regime is governed primarily by the law of the state in which they establish their first *résidence habituelle* after marriage. If the spouses do not have their habitual residence in the same state, article 4, paragraph 2, section 3 of the Convention states that their matrimonial property regime is governed by the law of the state of their common nationality.[20] Similarly, foreign divorce law is applicable only if the spouses neither share French nationality nor have their shared domicile in France.[21] The law applying to maintenance obligations is determined by the Convention on the Law Applicable to Maintenance Obligations and is thus determined by the jurisdiction in which the spouse entitled to receive maintenance habitually resides.[22] Finally, the question of parentage is governed by

15 Devers 2010; Gutmann 2009, 156.

16 Revillard 2006, 46, note 86; Gutmann 2009, 156.

17 Revillard 2006, 48, note 88.

18 Devers 2010; Gutmann 2009, 159; Revillard 2006, 49, notes 91 *et seq.*

19 Cf. Gutmann 2009, 163 and Revillard 2006, 57. The application of French law to French spouses is explicitly mentioned in article 3, para. 3 of the Code Civil.

20 If the spouses do not have their habitual residence in the same state, nor have a common nationality, article 4, para. 3 of the Convention on the Law Applicable to Matrimonial Property Regimes states that their matrimonial property regime is governed by the law of the state with which, taking all circumstances into account, it is most closely connected.

21 Article 309 of the Code Civil, though French divorce law is also applicable in exceptional cases if no foreign jurisdiction claims competence and the French courts have international jurisdiction; this whole issue is discussed in Gutmann 2009, 167 *et seq.*

22 Article 4 of the Convention on the Law Applicable to Maintenance Obligations (applicable *erga omnes* under article 3).

the personal law of the mother on the day of the child's birth.[23] However, where the child and his or her parents have their habitual residence in France, the apparent status (the so-called *possession d'état*) has all the consequences resulting from it under French law.[24]

Under Spanish law, private international law matters are essentially governed by a small number of provisions of the *Código Civil* (articles 8–12). These state that applicable personal law is determined by a person's nationality.[25] In Spain, foreign nationals may marry under Spanish law or under the law of a country of which one of the spouses is a national.[26] Article 9, paragraph 2 of the 2 *Código Civil* governs the law applicable to the legal consequences of marriage. In the case of marriages between spouses sharing the same nationality, this will primarily be the law of the country of their common nationality at the time of marriage. If the spouses have no common nationality, the applicable law will either be the personal status law or the law of the jurisdiction of habitual residence of one of the two spouses, and which of these applies is required to be confirmed by both spouses prior to marriage by declaration before a notary public.[27] The spouses may also conclude matrimonial property agreements. The validity of such agreements depends on whether, at the time they were concluded, they were in accordance either with the law governing the legal consequences of marriage, or with the law of the country of origin or of the jurisdiction of habitual residence of one of the spouses.[28] For spouses sharing a common nationality at the time of filing, divorce and separation are governed by the law of the country concerned. Where no such common nationality is shared at the time of filing, the law of the jurisdiction in which the couple habitually reside applies. If the spouses habitually reside in different states at the time of filing, Spanish law applies, in as far as such jurisdiction rests with the Spanish courts.[29]

Congruence of cultural identity with nationality: a notion at odds with our times

Making nationality the connecting factor in international family law has the obvious advantage of providing a firm point of reference which can be reliably ascertained.[30] However, it is difficult to justify the very premise on which it rests

---

23 Article 311—14 of the Code Civil.

24 Article 311—15 of the Code Civil; regarding maintenance, see article 311—18 of the Code Civil.

25 Article 9, para. 1 of the Código Civil.

26 Article 50 of the Código Civil.

27 Article 9, para. 2 of the Código Civil.

28 Article 9, para. 3 of the Código Civil.

29 Article 107, para. 2 of the Código Civil.

30 It has been argued that a further advantage of making nationality the connecting factor is that this will help to ensure consistency between court decisions in different countries, particularly since courts in migrants' countries of origin are likely to see nationality as the connecting factor. Consistency in court decisions, it is argued, is of paramount importance here, since it is particularly vital that limping legal situations be

– namely that there is a close cultural affinity between the individual and the nation granting nationality, and that questions relating to the personal status of an individual should therefore be answered in accordance with the law of the nation concerned.[31]

First, people's legal convictions can be greatly at odds with the legal rules in their country, as is evidenced by marriages performed by imams in Turkey or by forced marriages in some South Asian cultures, both being invalid under the law of the countries concerned. Moreover, the cultural imprint of the legal system does not necessarily equate with the cultural identity of the individual. Indeed, ethnic or religious minorities such as members of the Baha'i in Iran or Kurds actually define their cultural identity in contradistinction to the societies representing the majority in 'their' states.[32] This is also illustrated by the case of the Iranian woman who fled from Iran to Europe after the Revolution in order to get away from Iran's theocratic state and its Islamic law, only to find, decades later, that her cultural identity resulted in her divorce proceedings being subjected to that very same Islamic law. Furthermore, the principle of applying the law of a person's nationality may often fail to capture the customary laws which are both influential and often applied in practice in many African and Asian countries.[33] Ultimately, religion rather than nationality is the basis for cultural identity among Muslims, as is evidenced by the splitting of family law by religion seen in Islamic countries.

Second, if private international law requires that Muslim residents in European countries have to be judged according to the law of their foreign nationality, they will then not be permitted to benefit from the possibly more favourable provisions of the European code. Not least in order to benefit women from Islamic countries, Spain has therefore decreed that Spanish law will prevail in cases where the law of a woman's country of origin does not permit divorce or permits it only in a manner which discriminates against her.[34] Empirical studies indicate that a majority of

avoided in personal matters, cf. Von Hoffmann, Thorn 2007, 189, note 16. For a discussion of the argument that democratic considerations justify the principle of nationality being the connecting factor, see Mansel 2008, 165.

31 Intense and extensive debate is being conducted in Germany regarding the connecting factor in family law. For continuing argument in favour of the nationality principle, see Rauscher 2004, 719; Jayme 2003a, 224; Kegel, Schurig 2004, 446. Differentiated assessments can be found notably in Mansel 2008, 154 and 164; for a critique of nationality as the connecting factor Basedow 2001, 414; Siehr 2007, 391; Henrich 2001, 443. For arguments against the nationality principle, see Kropholler 2004, 269. For a European perspective, see also Foblets 1999, 32.

32 Cf. Mankowski 2004, 286.

33 Cf., for example, Chaïbou 1998, 157; Foblets, Reyntjens 1998, 1.

34 Article 107, para. 2, subsection c of the Código Civil. This provision is remarkable when one considers that Spain did not grant the right to divorce until 1982. Article 61 of Switzerland's Federal Code on Private International Law (in German, 'Bundesgesetz über das Internationale Privatrecht', abbreviated as 'IPRG') contains a similar rule. The principle here is that where both spouses share the same foreign nationality, the law of their

Muslim women living in Europe would like to be granted the protection of their position under the law of their European country of residence.[35]

A third major objection to applying law based on an individual's nationality is that it is opposed to the dialectic of integration. It does not pay adequate heed either to those who are in the process of integrating in the country to which they have emigrated, but who have not acquired the nationality of that country yet, or to those who, despite having acquired the nationality of their new country, have grown up in – and had their identity formed by – other cultures. Indeed, several European countries expect foreign nationals to meet very stringent requirements for citizenship. Whether, and when, immigrants achieve legal integration by means of naturalisation thus depends on how liberal the nationality laws of the country in question are. It is certainly true that the problems arising from linking applicable law to nationality have been mitigated by the trend towards liberalisation seen over the last decade, which has made acquisition of the nationality of their country of residence easier for immigrants, particularly those of the second generation. The life of immigrants is often one of continuing transition. Furthermore, cultural identity is not a self-contained phenomenon. Cultural identification based solely on nationality can often overshadow the dialogue and dialectic of an individual's relationship to that which is other, masking the contradictions and simultaneity of the different elements in their cultural conditioning.

Fourth, applying law based on an individual's nationality with the objective of protecting cultural identity becomes unworkable in cross-national and cross-cultural contexts.

Finally, the lack of congruence between applicable procedural and substantive law – with substantive law being determined on the basis of nationality while procedural matters are determined by the *lex fori* – has numerous other ramifications, especially since the substantive and procedural aspects of family-law matters certainly are dovetailed – both in the East and the West – and in some instances are even fused.[36] Does *talaq*, for example, constitute grounds for divorce, on the basis of which a court can decree divorce by application of foreign divorce status, or is it a private procedure, in which case it is hard to reconcile with the German courts' monopoly[37] in divorce matters? The other problem, frequently discussed in Germany, that it is completely at odds with the function of a German

country of origin is applicable, unless such law does not permit divorce, or permits it only under exceptionally strict conditions, and one of the spouses is also a Swiss citizen or has lived in Switzerland for two years.

35 Cf. Foblets 2001, 42; Foblets 2000, 17. Foblets conducted interviews with Moroccan women living in Belgium. See also Silvestri 2008, 7, 63.

36 For a discussion of these highly complex constellations in the German context, see Gärtner 2008, 71.

37 See section 1564 of the German Civil Code (in German, 'Bürgerliches Gesetzbuch', abbreviated as 'BGB') and article 17, para. 2, EGBGB. For extensive discussion on this, see Gärtner 2008, 46. French law also requires that all divorces pronounced in France have

court to apply religious law (*wesensfremde Zuständigkeit*), also results from this split between procedure and applicable substantive law, between form and content.[38] This is a fundamental problem arising from the application of Islamic, that is, religious, law by courts in Europe:

> Thus, when a religious rule is applied by a secular tribunal, 'out of context', by secular judges with no religious training or loyalty, in a different procedural setting and with different rules of evidence, it is divorced from its authoritative source and is, in some sense, at the mercy of an alien power.[39]

It is not only because courts are not properly trained for such tasks that the application of foreign, religious law in Europe has proven to entail difficulties, but also because this practice effectively applies law outside of its usual context, implying that the law is an idiopathic manifestation, and that jurisdiction is simple to perform and infallibly leads to a given result. It ignores the fact that, in reality, the law is able to develop its content, its meaning and its effect only in a given cultural context, and that these are also susceptible of transformation.

The erosion of the principle of applicable law based on nationality

The concept of nationality-based jurisdiction in private international law hails from the era of the 'guest worker', when it was wrongly assumed that the immigrants brought in to rebuild Europe would eventually leave their host countries again, so that their 'distinctness' had to be preserved.

Not least as a result of the new and enduring presence of migrants and their families and the efforts being undertaken to facilitate their integration, the concept of applying law based on nationality is now being eroded in a number of ways. To some extent, this erosion is a result of reform of the private international law of several European countries,[40] but it is also partly attributable to international treaties and the emergence of European conflict-of-laws rules.

The EU legal framework in family-law matters currently in place under the Brussels IIa Regulation governs only matters of international judicial jurisdiction in divorce issues and the recognition of member states' decisions in marital matters.[41] Applicable law in such cases has so far been determined on the basis of national conflict-of-laws norms. Significant changes to this practice are, however,

---

a judicial character, cf. Gutmann 2009, 174. Regarding England, see Family Law Act 1986 (c. 55), section 44, subsection 1.

38 See, however, the German Federal Court of Justice's judgment of 6 October 2004, XII ZR 225/01.

39 Wasserstein Fassberg 2005, 40.

40 Cf. Kohler 2006, 11; Mansel 2008, 168.

41 Council Regulation (EC) No. 2201/2003 of 27 November 2003 concerning jurisdiction and the recognition and enforcement of judgments in matrimonial matters and in matters of parental responsibility, repealing Regulation (EC) No. 1347/2000.

imminent.[42] The basis for establishing uniformity of private international law in family-law matters in the European Union is now article 81 of the Treaty on the Functioning of the European Union of 9 May 2008, which provides for conflict-of-laws regulations to be promulgated by the European Union. On 17 July 2006 the European Commission put forward a proposal 'amending Regulation (EC) No. 2201/2003 as regards jurisdiction and introducing rules concerning applicable law in matrimonial matters'. The proposal aimed to harmonise conflict-of-laws rules in matters relating to divorce. Under the proposal, in cases where an effective choice of applicable law had not been made[43] divorce proceedings were to be conducted in accordance with the law of the state in which the spouses have their common habitual residence, or, failing that, in accordance with the law of the state in which the spouses had their last common habitual residence, provided that one of them remains habitually resident there, or, failing that, with the law of the state of which both spouses share nationality, or – in the case of the United Kingdom and Ireland – with that of their common domicile, or, failing that, with that of the state in which a filing for divorce was submitted.[44] The conflict-of-laws norms of this proposed regulation also impinged on the European Union's relations with non-member states. Since the proposal has so far failed to obtain the required unanimous approval by all European Union member states, a common regulation for conflict of laws in matrimonial matters currently remains a *desideratum*.[45]

Conventions and rules on mutual recognition also have the potential for further progress in this area. In order to avoid the numerous clashes which can arise from the multiplicity of existing conflict-of-laws rules, in certain areas of law several jurisdictions simply recognise legal situations which have been established in other countries, without consideration and reassessment of the applicable or applied law.[46]

---

42 For detailed discussion of this, see, for example, Kohler 2008, 1673.

43 Article 20a of the proposed Regulation. This provided that in cases of divorce and of separation, the spouses could determine the applicable law by mutual consent and choose between the law of the state in which the spouses had their last common habitual residence, provided one of the spouses was still habitually resident there, or the law of the state of which the spouses were nationals (or, in the case of the United Kingdom and Ireland, either spouse was domiciled), or the law of the state in which the spouses had a common habitual residence for at least five years, or the law of the member state in which the petition was submitted.

44 Article 20b of the proposed Regulation.

45 In the meantime, the Council of the European Union issued a decision authorising enhanced cooperation in the area of the law applicable to divorce and legal separation (Council Decision of 12 July 2010).

46 For a review of the fundamental issues involved, see Coester-Waltjen 2006, 392; Kohler 2006, 22; Gärtner 2008, 373. See also article 45, para. 1, IPRG, which states that a marriage concluded abroad is recognised in Switzerland.

Residence or Domicile as the Determining Factor

In the majority of areas of family law in Switzerland, applicable law is determined on the basis of a person's domicile or their place of habitual residence,[47] and it is for this reason that Swiss law is generally applied to people from migrant backgrounds living in Switzerland.[48] It is only for Iranian citizens that Switzerland applies the law of a person's primary nationality, that is Iranian law, in matters of international personal, family and inheritance law.[49] Also, in cases where both spouses share the same foreign nationality and only one spouse is domiciled in Switzerland, applicable law is determined on the basis of nationality in matters relating to separation and divorce and the law of the state of which both spouses are nationals is applied, unless the law of the country concerned would either not permit divorce or permit it only under extraordinarily restrictive conditions.[50] This alternative method of determining applicable law on the basis of nationality rarely comes into practice, however. Furthermore, the substantive law prerequisites for marriage to be celebrated in Switzerland are also subject to Swiss law. However, if the requirements under Swiss law are not met, a marriage ceremony in Switzerland may be conducted between two foreign spouses, provided the prerequisites under the law of the country of which one of them is a national are met.[51] There are also plans for a reform to current law, which will ensure that all future marriages performed in Switzerland are governed solely by Swiss law.[52] In matters relating to child law, the determining factor is essentially the habitual place of residence of the child.[53] Finally, in exceptional circumstances, the law referred to in international family-law matters may be declared to be inapplicable if consideration of all the

47 A person has his or her domicile in the state in which he or she resides with the intention of remaining there permanently, while his or her place of habitual residence is the state in which he or she has resided for a considerable length of time, even if the duration of such residence has always been subject to limitation; cf. article 20, para. 1 subsections a and b, IPRG.

48 Cf. Schnyder 2006, 48, notes 137 *et seq.*

49 Convention d'établissement du 25 avril 1934 entre la Confédération suisse et l'Empire de Perse.

50 Article 61, para. 2 and 3, IPRG.

51 Article 44, para. 1 and 2, IPRG.

52 Memorandum of the Federal Council of Switzerland, Gesetzliche Massnahmen gegen Zwangsheirat, Bericht mit Vorentwurf, November 2008, at the instigation of Parliamentary motion no. 06.3658, Heberlein, 20 and 25.

53 Articles 68, 72 and 82, IPRG and article 4 of the Convention on the Law Applicable to Maintenance Obligations (applicable *erga omnes* under article 3). On 1 July 2009, the Convention on Jurisdiction, Applicable Law, Recognition, Enforcement and Co-operation in Respect of Parental Responsibility and Measures for the Protection of Children (Hague Convention on the Protection of Children) came into force in Switzerland; regarding the link to the child's habitual place of residence, cf. article 5, para. 1 and article 15, para. 1 of this Convention (applicable *erga omnes* under article 85, para. 1, IPRG).

relevant circumstances clearly demonstrates that the issue at hand is only very loosely connected with the law in question, while simultaneously being much more closely connected with the law of another jurisdiction relevant to the case.[54] This last provision is something of a safety valve, and is used only in exceptional circumstances to permit deviation from the applicability norms stipulated in private international law. The Federal Supreme Court has been very restrictive in its application of this provision and has used it only for the sake of justice in individual cases,[55] such as those in which the persons concerned have been living in Switzerland for only a very short time and close ties exist with the law of another country.

In English law domicile is the main determining factor in conflict-of-laws rules.[56] Domicile refers to the place and jurisdiction with which the person concerned is connected. Everyone has a domicile, and no one has either several or none. For a person to change their domicile by acquiring a new one – a so-called domicile of choice – they must settle in their new domicile permanently or indefinitely.[57] As a general rule, the marriage ceremony must be valid under the *lex loci celebrationis*.[58] While the substantive law prerequisites for a marriage are those applying under the law of the domicile, rules under the *lex loci celebrationis* may also have an effect. For example, future spouses can be prevented from marrying in England if one of them is aged 15 or less, even if marriage at that age would be permissible under the future spouse's *lex domicilii*.[59] Unless the parties have agreed otherwise, matrimonial property rights are governed by the law of the matrimonial domicile.[60] Parental responsibility is determined solely on the basis of English law, the domicile and nationality of the parties being irrelevant

54 Article 15, para. 1, IPRG.

55 As an example of many such instances, Swiss Federal Court Decisions 131 III 289; 128 III 346.

56 Briggs 2008, 22.

57 Briggs 2008, 24.

58 'A marriage is formally valid when (and only when) any one of the following conditions as to the form of celebration is complied with (that is to say): (1) if the marriage is celebrated in accordance with the form required or (*semble*) recognised as sufficient by the law of the country where the marriage was celebrated; (…)', Rule 66 in Collins 2006, 789.

59 Briggs 2008, 245.

60 'In the absence of a contract or settlement, the rights obtained by the husband and wife in each other's movable property as a result of the marriage, whether that property is possessed at the time of the marriage or acquired afterwards, are determined by the law of the matrimonial domicile. Where, at the time of the marriage, both parties are domiciled in the same country, the matrimonial domicile is (in the absence of special circumstances) that country.' Rule 156 in Collins 2006, 1280; cf. also Briggs 2008, 235; Collier 2001, 281. It should be noted, however, that English law does not recognise the concept of 'matrimonial assets', see Welstead 2008, 72.

in this regard.[61] Divorce or judicial separation in England is governed by English domestic law.[62]

Admittedly, applying law on the basis of an individual's place of residence does not ensure that the individual's cultural identity is safeguarded either. One problem arising from linking applicable law to a person's centre of vital interests – and this applies particularly to Muslims – is that the legal conditions prevailing in different jurisdictions are not attuned to each other and can result in limping legal relationships. Thus, legal practices established in Europe might not be recognised in the countries of origin of the parties concerned, either because their country of origin insists on its own laws being applied, or because the provisions of European law would contravene *ordre public* conventions in their country of origin.

Despite this, the concept of determining applicable law on the basis of the parties' domicile is certainly a viable starting point for any discussion about the accommodation of cultural diversity, insofar as it is regarded as desirable to foster cohesion between people living in the same country by providing them all with a uniform legal framework. Only when parties' lives exhibit genuinely transnational attributes is the application of the legal norms of other countries justified.

Better Law and Party Autonomy

Certainly, there are other approaches which may be taken to determining applicable law.

Basing applicable law on the individual's closest social and cultural ties – called the 'better law' or 'proper law' approach – permits a case-by-case determination, though this places considerable undirected and unstructured powers in the hands of the courts.[63] Such an approach can also impinge considerably on the predictability of the outcome, since the territorial and personal coverage of a law is open to judicial discretion.

Possibilities for allowing the individual to choose the law which is applied do, however, constitute a promising alternative approach in this regard. The concept of party autonomy is gaining increasing support,[64] particularly as a means of constraining the nationality principle and of precluding any unpredictability and

61 'The responsibility of a parent as regards the person and upbringing of his minor child is not affected by the domicile or nationality of the parties, but is governed wholly by the law of England.' Rule 95 in Collins 2006, 969.

62 Collier 2001, 320: 'the English courts have always applied the English law of divorce exclusively. […] The Domicile and Matrimonial Proceedings Act 1973 contains no such provision, but the Law Commission had said that its omission was not intended to change the law; on this matter', see also: Rule 77 (1) in Collins 2006, 878: 'In proceedings in England for divorce or judicial separation, the court will apply English domestic law…'.

63 Cf. Foblets 1999, 37.

64 Cf. also the extensive scope for choice of law in article 20a of the proposed Rome III Regulation.

uncertainty with respect to the conflict-of-laws rules and legal norms to which the parties are expected to comply.[65] Giving the parties the freedom to choose applicable law relies on their will and their willingness to exercise that freedom and trusts that they will autonomously reach the best decision as to which legal system is appropriate for governing their relationship. However, there are also limits to what can be achieved with party autonomy. First, it is necessary to establish that the parties have chosen a particular law of their own free will and that their choice is compatible with the fundamental principles and values of the law of the jurisdiction which has the task of applying the law so chosen. Furthermore, party autonomy does not permit any law to be chosen. Rather, the freedom of choice must be confined to a choice of either the law of the state of which the parties are nationals or the law of their domicile.

Party autonomy in determining applicable law is partly a reflection of the increasing contractual freedom applying in family-law matters.

Switzerland's Code on Private International law accords priority to the spouses' choice in matrimonial property matters.[66] The spouses may choose between the law of the state in which they both reside, or will reside after marriage, or that of one of their countries of origin.[67]

In Germany, as far as the general legal consequences of marriage are concerned, spouses may choose for their marriage to be governed by the law of a state of which one of them is a national, provided that either neither of the spouses is a national of the state in which they both habitually reside or that the spouses do not habitually reside in the same state.[68] This option is, however, available only to spouses who do not share or subsequently obtain the same nationality, or shared the same nationality during the marriage if one spouse still possesses that nationality.[69] Spouses may also choose the law which will apply to their matrimonial property. Here, the spouses may choose the law of the state of which one of them is a national, the law of the state in which one of them habitually resides or, as far as immovable property is concerned, the law of the state in which the property is located.[70]

Spanish law provides extensive scope for the choice of applicable law, permitting spouses to choose the law applicable to the legal consequences of marriage, provided they do not share a nationality.[71]

---

65 Cf. Foblets, 1999, 37; Mansel 2008, 174; Henrich 2004b, 327; Kohler 2006, 14. A plea for choice of law can be found in Basedow 2001, 413.

66 Article 54 in conjunction with article 52, para. 1, IPRG.

67 Article 52, para. 2, IPRG.

68 Article 14, para. 3 subsections 1 and 2, EGBGB.

69 Article 14, para. 1 subsections 1 and 3, EGBGB.

70 Article 15, para. 2, EGBGB.

71 Article 9 para. 2 of the Código Civil, scope for choice of law being, however, restricted to either the law of the country of origin of one of the spouses or that of the country in which one of the spouses habitually resides.

In France, spouses are permitted to determine, prior to their marriage, which law will apply to their matrimonial property rights. They may choose between the law of the state of which one of them is a national, the law of the state in which one of them habitually resides or the law of the state where one of the spouses establishes his or her first habitual residence following their marriage.[72] Once they are married, spouses are also permitted to change the law applying to their matrimonial property rights.[73]

English law, by contrast, is relatively aloof to the principle of choice of applicable law and provides practically no scope for exercising such choice in family-law matters.[74] The only way in which influence can be exercised on the applicable law is through the flexibility inherent in the principle of domicile of choice.[75]

Ordre public and Self-Affirmation: Alien Traditions and Received Moral Values

Ordre public – also referred to as public order or public policy – is a key element in private international law. Indeed, it is often the concept of *ordre public* – in individual cases and where a particular affinity to the country of residence is given – which limits the applicability of Islamic family law, particularly in countries which determine the law applicable to an individual on the basis of nationality and therefore often have to consider Islamic family law.[76] In this process, it is not the legal systems of other countries themselves – which, as a matter of principle, are all treated equally – that are being measured against the cardinal principles of European law canons. Rather, it is the result of applying those other countries' legal

72 Article 3 of the Hague Convention on the Law Applicable to Matrimonial Property Regimes, 14 March 1978.

73 Article 6 of the Hague Convention on the Law Applicable to Matrimonial Property Regimes, 14 March 1978. The scope for choice of law is limited to the law of the country of origin of one of the spouses or the country in which one of the spouses has his [or her] habitual residence at the time of designation. In the case of real estate, the law of the country in which the property is located may also be chosen.

74 Collins 2006, 4.

75 Briggs 2008, 24.

76 For Switzerland: article 17, IPRG (applicable law); article 27, para. 1, IPRG (recognition and enforcement); for Germany: article 6, EGBGB (applicable law); section 328, para. 1 subsection 4 of the German Code of Civil Procedure (in German 'Zivilprozessordnung', abbreviated as 'ZPO') (recognition), Rohe 2004, 21; for Spain: article 12, para. 3, Código Civil (applicable law); for France: article 3, Code Civil (applicable law and recognition); for England: 'English courts will not enforce or recognise a right, power, capacity, disability or legal relationship arising under the law of a foreign country, if the enforcement or recognition of such right, power, capacity, disability or legal relationship would be inconsistent with the fundamental public policy of English law.' Rule 2 in: Collins 2006, 92.

systems which is being put to the test. The same applies to a decision reached by the application of the law of another country which should then be recognised in a European country. If the result of applying this foreign law or the decision requiring recognition are at odds with fundamental principles of law or fundamental values of the European country concerned, the foreign law will not be applied and the decision made under it will not be recognised. Furthermore, specifically from the standpoint of German legal practice, *ordre public* considerations are considered to be relative not only with regard to substance, but also with regard to place and time. In this context, relativity with regard to place effectively means that the more tenuous the connection to Germany, the more significant the principles of German domestic law which are infringed must be. As a result, a more stringent yardstick is applied in cases where the connection with Germany is close, as would be the case where a party was habitually resident there or indeed held German nationality, than in cases where the connection to Germany is weaker or more distant.[77]

From a comparative law standpoint, there is little evidence of coherent or substantial legislative pronouncements on *ordre public* matters. This descriptive and empirical, sometimes even random, invocation of *ordre public* stands in stark contrast to the major normative significance which the concept has. In this respect, *ordre public* is an elusive concept which confers a great deal of discretion upon the judiciary. The following section will nevertheless illustrate a number of discernible trends based on specific individual examples.

The Protection of Individual Rights

Ordre public arguments are consistently used to protect individual positions. This can be seen in the prohibition of child marriages or of forced marriage, and this is undoubtedly correct with regard to fundamental legal principles.

It is a principle of the private international law codes of European nations that marriages concluded in other countries are recognised as valid.[78] Indeed, some countries permit or even require marriages to be celebrated under the law of the state of which the spouses are nationals.[79] *Ordre public* considerations set the limits to the recognition of a marriage concluded abroad or according to foreign law.

---

77 For Germany cf. Gärtner 2008, 90; German Federal Court of Justice (in German, 'Bundesgerichtshof') judgment of 4 June 1992, BGHZ 118, 312 (349). Similarly, an unusual judgment resulting from the application of the law of another country may prove easier to accept in cases where the same decision has already been duly reached by a court abroad than when a German court makes the decision by direct application of foreign legal norms, cf. Kropholler 2004, 667.

78 For Switzerland: article 45, para. 1, IPRG; for France: article 171—1 of the Code Civil; for England: cf. for example Briggs 2008, 242; for Germany: article 13, para. 3, EGBGB; for Spain: article 49 of the Código Civil.

79 For Switzerland: article 44, para. 2, IPRG (a revision in favour of Swiss law is currently in preparation); for France: article 3, para. 3 of the Code Civil and article 171—1

Forced marriages have been the subject of wide debate for some years. Coerced marriage is a violation of human rights and a form of violence which infringes the individual's right to freedom in entering into marriage. The Universal Declaration of Human Rights of 1948 states that marriage may be entered into only with the free and full consent of the intending spouses.[80] This principle is reaffirmed in a whole series of further international conventions.[81] Forced marriage occurs when the marriage takes place against the will of at least one of the spouses, when their refusal is ignored or when they do not dare to resist because the psychological, social and emotional pressure exerted by the family is too great, or even because physical coercion was applied or threatened. A marriage is considered to be arranged, conversely, if, while it may often have been initiated or intermediated by relatives, the future spouses have consented to it. Although the borderline between forced and arranged marriage is very significant, it is also fluid and difficult to pinpoint, and it cannot be determined solely by the application of enlightened concepts of free will, but must take the applicable cultural context into account.[82] Arranged marriages are also often advocated by young men and women from immigrant backgrounds who have grown up in Europe and, though their own involvement in the search for and selection of future spouses and in the various negotiations between the families varies considerably, it is in many cases substantial.[83]

Public debate often identifies forced marriage and patriarchal codes of honour with Islam. This discursive link is both misleading and problematical, since, although forced marriages occur in the Islamic world and are regarded as part and parcel of the cultures of various regions of the world, notably in South Asia,

---

of the Code Civil; for Germany: article 13, para. 1 and 2, EGBGB; for Spain: article 50 of the Código Civil.

80 Article 16, para. 2 of the Universal Declaration of Human Rights of 1948.

81 Cf. article 23, para. 3 of the International Covenant on Civil and Political Rights of 16 December 1966; article 10, subsection 1, sentence 2 of the International Covenant on Economic, Social and Cultural Rights of 16 December 1966; article 16, para. 1, subsection b of the Convention on the Elimination of All Forms of Discrimination against Women of 18 December 1979; see also article 12 of the European Convention on Human Rights.

82 Cf. also Renteln 2004, 122, which cites examples, and the enquiry by the Fondation Surgir 2006, 12. Those interviewed referred to the difficulties involved in distinguishing between coercion and arrangement. This centres on the understandings of the idea of consent, of which there are certainly many. Terms used in discussing arranged marriage included 'cultural norm', 'habit', 'absence of coercion'. Conversely, the coerced marriage was identified with the following characteristics: a family decision to which there was no alternative; the inability of one or both parties to refuse the marriage; decision by father rather than husband; bride did not know groom prior to wedding; marriage was planned a long time in advance, possibly when the child was born; economic ties exist between the families.

83 See the clear analysis in Cesari, Caerio, Hussain 2004, 20.

the overwhelming majority of expert opinion regards them as inadmissible under Islamic law.[84]

Some European countries have responded to the phenomenon of forced marriage by enacting reforms to various parts of their law. These reforms are principally intended to demonstrate that forced marriage is not acceptable to European cultural and legal values. In England, the *Forced Marriage (Civil Protection) Act* of 2007 created a special legal framework for the protection of those concerned. France has in recent years also enacted numerous reforms to its civil code in order to prevent forced marriages. As a result, no marriage can enter into effect if there is no concurring will on the part of both parties for it to take place.[85] In Germany, too, where the legal principle prevails that the prerequisites for marriage are subject to the law of the state of which the spouses are nationals, and where marriages concluded abroad are recognised, forced marriage infringes *ordre public*.[86] The same effectively applies in Switzerland, since forced marriages can also not be recognised as valid there.[87]

Marriageable age under Islamic law is generally below that applicable in European countries.[88] Hanafitic teaching holds that a person reaches marriageable age with puberty, but that for men this cannot be before the age of 12 and for women not before the age of nine. A marriage may, however, also be validly concluded between spouses below those ages, even between young children, though in these cases the conclusion of marriage and its consummation are separated in time.[89]

Recognition of these marriages performed abroad and the application of the law of other countries both require a determination of the minimum marriageable age stipulated by *ordre public*. The practice of the Swiss authorities is to refuse recognition of marriages involving people aged under 16 on the basis that such recognition would be contrary to the interests of *ordre public*. This practice is in alignment with the legal age of consent to sexual acitivity set out in the Swiss Penal Code.[90] German doctrine teaches that recognition of marriages involving people aged 15 or under should be prohibited on *ordre public* grounds.[91] In France legal scholars are hesitant to acknowledge marriages involving minors (those under the age of 18), though no specific judgments on this appear to have been recorded.[92] In Spain recognition of a marriage involving people aged under 14

---

84 Pearl, Menski 1998, 143.

85 Lemouland 2010; Ferrand 2006, 1318; article 146 of the Code Civil.

86 Scholz 2002, 327.

87 Cf. Büchler 2007, 747.

88 This applies both to classical Islamic law and to the current law of many Islamic Arab states, Pearl, Menski, 1998, 141; Nasir 2009, 50; Welchman 2007, 61.

89 Büchler 2003, 27; Pearl, Menski 1998, 141 and 143.

90 Cf. Büchler, Fink 2008, 60.

91 Cf. Staudinger, Mankowski 2003, article 13, EGBGB, note 203; Rohe 2006, 95.

92 Cf. Revillard 2006, 47, note 87; Loussouarn, Bourel, de Vareilles-Sommières 2007, 405.

is refused.[93] In England, a marriage between persons either of whom is under 16 may be recognised as valid provided that the marriage is valid by the law of each party's domicile and neither of the spouses' domicile is in England. If either party is domiciled in England, the marriage will be recognised provided that both spouses are over 16.[94]

Analysis of the question of recognition must begin with the internationally agreed standards currently in place, specifically the Universal Declaration of Human Rights mentioned above, the Convention on the Elimination of All Forms of Discrimination against Women,[95] more broadly the Convention on Celebration and Recognition of the Validity of Marriages[96] and the Convention on Consent to Marriage, Minimum Age for Marriage and Registration.[97] On the last of these, the Office of the United Nations High Commissioner for Human Rights has published a recommendation that the minimum age for marriage should be 15, though also acknowledging that autonomy in legislating on this rests, in principle, with individual member states.[98] The Council of Europe Parliamentary Assembly has also examined this issue and passed a resolution recommending that the minimum marriageable age be raised to 18 and that marriages concluded abroad not be recognised – except with regard to the legal consequences of marriage – if one of the spouses was under 18 at the time of the marriage.[99]

This last initiative clearly goes beyond the objective of protecting children. A balance needs to be achieved between, on the one hand, the danger of abuse and coercion, the danger of undue influence being exerted and the protection of sexual integrity and, on the other hand, freedom of marriage, the respect of other jurisdictions and the objective of avoiding limping marriages. In principle, setting a minimum marriageable age at 16, in accordance with the Swiss Penal Code, appears a tenable approach.[100] In individual cases, recognition of a marriage

93 Giménez Costa 2004, note III, 3.1 b); cf. Huzel 2006, 1201, note 8; cf. also article 48, para. 2 of the Código Civil.

94 Collins 2006, 817; cf. also Murphy 2000a, 80.

95 Article 16, para. 2 of the Convention on the Elimination of All Forms of Discrimination Against Women.

96 Article 11, para. 1 subsections 3 and 4 of the Hague Convention on Celebration and Recognition of the Validity of Marriages of 14 March 1978, though none of the countries discussed here is a signatory.

97 Articles 1 and 2 of the Convention on Consent to Marriage, Minimum Age for Marriage and Registration of Marriages, UN General Assembly, 7 November 1962; Switzerland is not a signatory, while Germany, France, Spain and the United Kingdom are.

98 Principle II of the Recommendation on Consent to Marriage, Minimum Age for Marriage and Registration of Marriages, UN General Assembly, 1 November 1965.

99 Resolution 1468 (2005), Forced Marriages and Child Marriages, Council of Europe: Parliamentary Assembly, 20 June 2005, Doc. 10590.

100 Article 187 of the Swiss Criminal Code (in German, 'Strafgesetzbuch', abbreviated as 'StGB'). The Swiss Criminal Code aims to ensure that children are free to

involving a 15-year-old spouse may be justifiable, specifically when refusal of such recognition would create more problems for the person in need of protection than it would solve, by, for example, denying the basis for the right to maintenance. Recognition is also justified in cases where, at the time of recognition, both spouses have reached an age which no longer poses any *ordre public* problems and both freely declare their intention to continue the marriage which came into effect when they were very young. *Ordre public* should not stand in the way of that intention in such cases.[101]

Many Islamically influenced jurisdictions impose an absolute ban on Muslim women marrying non-Muslim men, and these jurisdictions will also declare a marriage to be dissolved if impediment caused to it by differences in religion occurs after the marriage has been celebrated.[102] As far as recognition of marriage is concerned, this is in principle not relevant, since the impediment to marriage resulting from differences in religion means that no marriage may be entered into abroad or that such a marriage ceases to exist. Notwithstanding that, it is worth considering whether a marriage celebrated abroad, which is invalid as a result of an impediment to marriage on religious grounds according to the law of the country concerned, should nevertheless be recognised by a European state. The spouses' joint wishes and, in particular, the fundamental human right to freedom of religion and marriage should be sufficient in such cases for the impediment to marriage on religious grounds under foreign law to be deemed unworthy of consideration and for the marriage therefore to be recognised. Prohibitions on inter-religious marriage and forced divorces under foreign law should certainly not be applied in European countries on the grounds that upholding them is contrary to the interests of *ordre public*,[103] even though the price of protecting the fundamental human rights at issue in these cases will necessarily result in cumbersome, limping legal situations, in as far as such marriages may not be valid in the countries of origin of the spouses concerned.

---

develop without interference and are protected until they have reached sufficient maturity to decide for themselves whether to consent to sexual acts.

101 Cf. also Rohe 2006, 95.

102 Nasir 2009, 69; Büchler 2003, 33.

103 In the case of Germany, cf. article 13, para. 2, subsection 3, EGBGB, which states that the conditions required for the conclusion of marriage are governed by the law of the country of which the future spouse is a national. However, if the future spouse fails to meet a requirement under the law of that country, German law shall apply in cases where it would be incompatible with the principle of the freedom of marriage to refuse to allow the marriage.

The Defence of Family-Law Dogmas

Inconsistencies and variations in emphasis between different countries are, however, apparent in the assessments of enduring traditional Western family-law dogma such as monogamy in the context of *ordre public*.

Polygamy is probably the Islamic law institution which has given rise to the greatest amount of debate, both in the Islamic world and the West. While monogamy has become the established norm in several countries, polygamy remains permissible in many Islamic states. *Sura* 4, verse 3 of the Qur'an limits the number of wives a man may have to a maximum of four, and requires him to treat them all equally,[104] and this requirement has prompted some jurisdictions to stipulate that certain prerequisites have to be met before second marriages can be entered into.[105]

There is little doubt that no polygamous marriages may be entered into in European countries and that any such marriages would, if they occurred, be null and void.[106] There is, however, some controversy, both in the literature and in practice, with regard to the recognition of polygamous marriages validly entered into in non-European countries. The essential question here is whether the principle of monogamy is fundamental to European law and values. Recent developments indicate the emergence of a consensus that polygamous marriages validly entered into abroad enjoy a ubiquitous status and that certain legal consequences arise from

104 *Sura* 4, verse 3 of the Qur'an: 'If ye fear that ye shall not Be able to deal justly With the orphans, Marry women of your choice, Two, or three, or four; But if ye fear that ye shall not be able to deal justly (with them), Then only one, or (a captive) That your right hands possess. That will be more suitable, To prevent you From doing injustice.' *Sura* 4, verse 129 of the Qur'an: 'Ye are never able To be fair and just As between women, Even if it is Your ardent desire: But turn not away (From a woman) altogether, So as to leave her (as it were) Hanging (in the air). If ye mend your ways And practice self-restraint, Allah is Oft-Forgiving, Most Merciful.'

105 Cf. Büchler 2003, 35; Welchman 2007, 77; Nasir 2009.

106 For France: Cadet 2005, 75; for Spain: Cadet 2005, 76, for England: Shah 2005, 97, and, implicitly, Private International Law (Miscellaneous Provisions) Act 1995 (c. 42), section 5. In many countries, polygamy is even a criminal offence, cf. for Switzerland: article 215 StGB; for Germany: section 172 of German Criminal Code (in German, 'Strafgesetzbuch', abbreviated as 'StGB'); for France: article 433—20 of the Code Pénal; for England: Offences Against the Person Act 1861 (1861 c. 100 24_and 25 Vict), section 57; and polygamy also results in a marriage being or void, cf. for Switzerland: article 105 para. 1 of the Swiss Civil Code (in German, 'Zivilgesetzbuch', abbreviated as 'ZGB'); for Germany: section 1314 in conjunction with section 1306, BGB; for France: article 184 in conjunction with article 147 of the Code Civil; for Spain: article 73 para. 2 in conjunction with article 46 para. 2 of the Código Civil; for England: Matrimonial Causes Act 1973 (c. 18), section 11, subsection b.

them, particularly with regard to maintenance, inheritance and social security.[107] Partial recognition also affords protection to the second wife and there appears to be some reluctance to intervene in actual relationships which have not been questioned by any of the parties concerned. This is also justified since confidence in a given legal situation should be protected as a matter of principle.[108] There are, however, certainly some nuances in the way this is put into practice. In Germany, a polygamous marriage entered into abroad has wider-ranging legal consequences than in France. Conversely, many countries appear to deviate from this open approach when it comes to their legislation on foreign nationals. Immigration to the country of residence of the spouse for the purpose of family reunification is generally granted only to one wife.[109] This differentiation can hardly be justified, either on equality grounds or with regard to the need for protection of married women, of their children, or of family life generally.[110]

A general point here is that the refusal to recognise polygamous marriages usually serves to protect public order and morality rather than personal rights. Whether this is legitimate with regard to the recognition of legal arrangements established abroad – a cardinal principle here being equality between jurisdictions – is at least debatable.

---

107 For Germany section 34, para. 2 of the German Social Security Code I (in German, 'Sozialgesetzbuch I', abbreviated as 'SGB I'); Mansel 2008, 198; for France, Cadet 2005, 185. Cour de cassation, Chambre Civile 2, 14 Feburary 2007 (05-21.816), where pension and insurance claims were granted to a second wife in a polygamous marriage which was not recognised; for Switzerland: Büchler, Fink 2008, 59.

108 For France: Gutmann 2009, 158, on the so-called 'effet atténué de l'ordre public'; for Switzerland: Büchler, Fink 2008, 56.

109 France has specific regulations on this: article 30, para. 1, loi n° 93-1027 of 24 August 1993: 'Lorsqu'un étranger polygame réside sur le territoire français avec un premier conjoint, le bénéfice du regroupement familial ne peut être accordé à un autre conjoint. Sauf si cet autre conjoint est décédé ou déchu de ses droits parentaux, ses enfants ne bénéficient pas non plus du regroupement familial.' For Germany: section 30, para. 4, of the Residence Act (in German, 'Aufenthaltsgesetz', abbreviated as 'AufenthG'). Article 6 of Germany's Basic Law (in German, 'Grundgesetz', abbreviated as 'GG') provides no fundamental protection to bigamous marriages, particularly since the principle of monogamy is one of Germany's basic cultural values and is thus one of the principles informing the structure of its constitution (German Federal Constitutional Court judgment of 30 November 1982, Federal Constitutional Court, judgment of 4 May 1971, BVerfGE 31, 58, with further references). For Switzerland: Büchler, Fink 2008, 58, with numerous references; for England: Immigration Act 1988 (c. 14), section 2, Shah 2005, 110. Finally, article 4, para. 4 of the Council Directive 2003/86/EC of 22 September 2003 on the right to family reunification reads as follows: 'In the event of a polygamous marriage, where the sponsor already has a spouse living with him in the territory of a Member State, the Member State concerned shall not authorise the family reunification of a further spouse.'

110 Cf. also Kälin 2000, 203.

Shi-ite jurisprudence allows for temporary marriages, so-called *mut'a* marriages. The duration of such marriages must be defined or at least definable. Temporary marriages do not bring with them all the legal consequences of indefinite marriage. Specifically, they do not commit the husband to support the family financially and they do not give rise to any inheritance rights. The groom is, however, required to provide the bride with a dower. A *mut'a* marriage is generally dissolved through the lapse of time, without a divorce.[111]

Although hardly any judgments in the matter are recorded,[112] it can be assumed that a temporary marriage would not be recognised in European countries, since it contravenes the model of marriage entered into for as long as the spouses shall live. It should of course be noted that this principle of Christian marriage exerts little normative effect, as current divorce rates attest, and it is also somewhat undermined by the fact that contractual elements now incorporated into family law effectively make divorce a matter which can depend solely on the will of one spouse only.

In many Sunni Muslim countries, the number of *misyar* marriages is increasing. In a *misyar* marriage, husband and wife do not live together and the husband has no obligation to provide for the material needs of the wife. Such marriages can, but need not, be limited in time, and can in any case be dissolved by divorce. '*Urfi* marriages, which are particularly widespread in Egypt, also do not impose any financial obligations on the husband. The prevalence of all these forms of marriage is attributable to the fact that young men are often not able to afford the obligations arising from 'full' marriage, but that couples wish to pursue a sexual relationship, and this is permitted only within a marriage. The treatment of *misyar* marriages in private international law has not yet been discussed. This form of marriage contravenes the principle of a comprehensive life partnership, although that principle no longer obliges couples to live together in European countries either. Provided this form of marriage is valid in the country in which it was entered into and whose law is applicable to it, nothing should stand in its way in European countries.

Imposed Primacy of the Substratum of Domestic Law and the 'Manifest Destiny' Concept of Culture

Ordre public considerations do not always serve to protect the rights of the individual or family-law dogmas. It is not uncommon for *ordre public* discourse to be deployed solely to ensure primacy for the substratum of a country's own

---

111 For *mut'a* marriage and the practice of *mut'a* in Iran see Haeri 1989, 49.

112 See, however, for England: Asylum and Immigration Tribunal, LS (*Mut'a* or *singhē*) Iran [2007] UKAIT 00072: 'The Islamic institution of mut'a or singhē is in its essence neither permanent nor exclusive. It is not marriage within the meaning of the Immigration Rules, and its existence does not imply a relationship continuing or intended to continue beyond its termination.'

family-law norms and to support its self-affirmation. This occasionally takes the form of an *apologia*. The *ordre public* approach also raises fundamental problems, because it is often unable to abstract from foreign law as such and must therefore limit itself to deciding the case, thus focusing solely on the legal situation which has been created or on the result of applying the foreign law.

The theoretical inadequacy of its approach to limiting cultural autonomy is most evident when arguments are put forward which concern violation of equality of rights between the sexes. Islamic family law as a whole is based on the attribution of specific functional roles between the two sexes,[113] which, incidentally, cannot in and of itself be contrary to *ordre public* principles, since only the result of applying or recognising specific foreign norms or judgments and not the foreign law itself can be subjected to scrutiny. A contradictory position to this can be seen in a more recent decision by Switzerland's highest court, which decided that allocating child -custody rights solely on the basis of the parents' sex and the child's age was not compatible with *ordre public*, even if, as was the case in this particular instance, there was no evidence that awarding sole custody to the father – which Iranian law required – posed any threat to the child.[114]

Ordre public discourse runs the risk of evoking memories of the 'manifest destiny' concept of culture and of the idea that Western morality is inherently superior to that of other cultures. This danger becomes particularly apparent, for example, in discussions about valid and inopportune grounds for divorce. Debate becomes heated when it comes to discussion of the Islamic law institution of divorce by unilateral pronouncement by the husband, the *talaq*, which according to classical Islamic law may be obtained extra-judicially and against which the wife has no right of recourse. The limited scope available to the wife to apply for divorce is a similar bone of contention in this regard. There are different forms of *talaq*. The variation between them lies in the number of times the declaration has to be made and in the period of time which has to elapse between each declaration for them to be valid. A maximum of three *talaq* need to be pronounced for divorce to become effective, the first two being revocable, the third being irrevocable.[115] It is also possible for the marriage contract to delegate the right to divorce to the wife, so that, should certain specific events set out in the contract occur, she is entitled to pronounce *talaq* on her husband's behalf. These events usually include the husband treating his wife abusively or entering into another marriage.[116] Muslim law also permits a divorce by *khul'*, which is generally a divorce by mutual consent, instigated at the wife's behest. The parties can agree that the wife releases herself from the marriage contract by having to return the *mahr* and forfeiting her

---

113 Welchman 2007, 89; Büchler 2003, 39.

114 Swiss Federal Court decision 129 III 250; regarding this same problem, see also Yassari 2006, 202.

115 Cf. Nasir 2009, 111.

116 Cf. Pearl, Menski 1998, 283.

maintenance rights.[117] Conversely, a *faskh,* or unilateral divorce instigated solely by the wife, must be obtained from a court and requires the wife to prove and apply for the court's recognition of a specific reason for divorce. The catalogue of possible grounds for divorce is more or less comprehensive depending on the school of law and the jurisdiction concerned. The standards of proof are stringent and a conciliation process has to take place prior to divorce being granted.[118]

A number of legal systems of the Islamic world permit divorces to be obtained extra-judicially. In some countries a husband can divorce his wife by simply pronouncing the word *talaq* three times. No reasons need be given, the wife in some instances need not be present, and no further formality is required.[119] In some jurisdictions the divorce would usually be registered with a court, notwithstanding that this is not necessarily an essential requirement for its validity.[120] As a matter of principle, European countries generally recognise divorces pronounced in other jurisdictions, provided that there are no objections to this on *ordre public* grounds.[121] Each of the multiplicity of extra-judicial means by which a divorce may be obtained raises the question of whether it would qualify for recognition in Europe. The approaches taken by individual European countries with regard to recognising divorce effected abroad by means of unilateral repudiation by the husband vary.[122] Courts in some countries take into account the circumstances surrounding the repudiation and whether the divorce resulting from it is in fact unacceptable to the values of the country in question, while other jurisdictions simply note, irrespective of the circumstances of the individual case, that the institution of divorce by repudiation contravenes the principle of equality between the sexes or procedural principles. For example, the *Cour de Cassation*, France's highest court, is restrictive in its approach, ruling that unilateral repudiation is generally contrary to the interests of *ordre public.*[123] The Swiss Federal Supreme

117 Cf. Pearl, Menski 1998, 283; Büchler 2003, 50; Nasir 2009, 115.

118 Cf. Pearl, Menski 1998, 285; Büchler 2003, 53; Nasir 2009, 118.

119 Cf. Pearl, Menski 1998, 282; Büchler 2003, 44.

120 Cf. Pearl, Menski 1998, 279 and 286; Büchler 2003, 44; Welchman 2007, 53.

121 For England: Family Law Act 1986 (c. 55), section 51 para. 3 subsection c (cf. 2006, 912; Briggs 2008, 257); for Switzerland: article 27, IPRG; for Germany: section 328, para. 1 subsection 4, ZPO); for France: article 3 of the Code Civil; for Spain: articles 21 et seq., especially article 22, subsection a of Council Regulation (EC) No. 2201/2003 of 27 November 2003 (Brussels IIa Regulation).

122 For an extensive discussion of the problems arising when procedural recognition for private divorces in third-party states cannot be carried out under the EU's Brussels IIa Regulation, both because article 21, para. 1 of Brussels IIa states that the regulation covers decisions made by member state courts only, and because, in the absence of a judgment by a member state court, no 'decision' as defined in Brussels IIa can be said to exist, see Gärtner 2008, 310.

123 Cf. Cour de Cassation, Chambre civile 1, 25 October 2005, (03-20845); for a discussion of the evolution of this restrictive view, from 'ordre public subjectif' to 'ordre

Court, by contrast, did recognise a private divorce performed in another country, a divorce where neither spouse appeared before a court, the couple's wish to divorce was documented in writing only and the parties were represented by their respective counsel.[124] Conversely, this same court did not recognise a divorce merely pronounced during a meeting of relatives and without the knowledge or against the will of the spouses.[125] Furthermore, a Swiss court of second instance recently upheld the recognition of a Moroccan divorce judgment based on repudiation, on the grounds that in this case the wife had agreed to the divorce.[126] In England, the law defines clear procedural prerequisites which divorce judgments must meet in order to be recognised under English law. These state that recognition of a divorce performed in another country can be refused, if it was obtained

> without such steps having been taken for giving notice of the proceedings to a party to the marriage as, having regard to the nature of the proceedings and all the circumstances, should reasonably have been taken; or without a party to the marriage having been given (for any reason other than lack of notice) such opportunity to take part in the proceedings as, having regard to those matters, he should reasonably have been given.[127]

In Germany, repudiation of the wife will not necessarily be ruled null and void on *ordre public* grounds. While it is true that repudiation contravenes the principle of equality between the sexes if such right of repudiation is granted to one spouse only, the crucial factor is not the nature of the divorce act, but only any actual violation of the wife's interest which may have occurred as a result. Divorce by repudiation is thus regarded as discriminative if the wife does not have the same right of repudiation as the husband. However, should the wife also wish to be divorced from her husband, there would then be no reason to declare the divorce ineffective.[128]

Divorce by repudiation is nevertheless in principle contrary to the interests of *ordre public* if the repudiation itself is pronounced in a European country, and

---

public objectif', see Cadet 2005, 82 and Gutmann, 2009, 170. On similar developments in Spain, see Cadet 2005, 90.

124 Swiss Federal Court decision 131 III 182.

125 Swiss Federal Court decision 122 III 344.

126 Cour suprême du Canton de Berne, 806/96, of 20 December 1996. Somewhat differently still Swiss Federal Court decision 88 I 48, but also Swiss Federal Court decision 126 III 327.

127 Family Law Act 1986 (c. 55), section 51 para. 3 subsection a; for a critical appraisal, see Mayss 2000, 65.

128 Cf. Von Hoffmann, Thorn 2007, 347; but also the decision by the Higher Regional Court (in German, 'Oberlandesgericht') in Stuttgart of 3 December 1998 – 17 VA 6/98, where infringement of the right to be heard – irrespective of the outcome – was judged to be contrary to German *ordre public* principles.

European courts which are asked to apply foreign law on conflict-of-laws grounds in such cases will neither grant divorce based on repudiation nor uphold such a pronouncement.[129]

There are numerous reasons why divorce by repudiation is subject to such strict legal assessment. Violation of the principle of equality between the sexes is frequently cited. This is problematical, because it is not the law itself, but rather the result of its application, in this case dissolution of the marriage through divorce, which must be shown to be at odds with the interests of *ordre public*. Another approach is to reject the possibility of instant dissolution which repudiation would provide, though given the trend towards unilateral divorce being permitted after ever shorter periods of separation in Western countries, this carries little conviction. Spain, for example, already now permits unilateral divorce without requiring any prior period of separation.[130] Divorce by repudiation does, however, violate the wife's procedural rights in a quite spectacular fashion, because it does not involve her in any legal procedure, it does not require her consent and even the acknowledgement that the marriage has been dissolved is not required in principle. It should, however, be noted that not all Islamically oriented jurisdictions recognise divorce by repudiation without the wife's involvement.[131] Moreover, should she so wish, a wife must also be able to choose to dispense with the legal protection which non-recognition of divorce by a European court provides – and thus avoid the effort involved in (new) divorce proceedings in a European country.[132] Finally, it is apparent that the courts' monopoly in divorce matters is also under threat in Europe, as is demonstrated by the many initiatives undertaken to permit administrative forms of marriage dissolution.[133]

There have in fact been instances in which German courts have decided that divorce on the basis of Islamic law and by means of *talaq* does not contravene *ordre*

129 For France: Gutmann 2009, 170; for Spain: Cadet 2005, 81. Domestic private divorce proceedings often fail because of the courts' monopoly in divorce matters.

130 Article 81 para. 2 of the Código Civil: unilateral divorce without a prior period of separation is possible under Spanish law, provided at least three months have elapsed since the marriage was celebrated.

131 Under classical Islamic law, the wife need not even have knowledge of the repudiation. Many Islamic Arab countries have, however, introduced a requirement that repudiations be officially registered. Cf. Büchler 2003, 44; Pearl, Menski 1998, 280 and 282.

132 Cf. Bucher 2008, 38.

133 In Europe, divorce is today obtained in an administrative procedure in Denmark, Norway and Russia. In the Netherlands, in principle, a divorce can be obtained only by a judicial proceeding. However, the possibility of obtaining a divorce without the intervention of the courts does exist. To do this, the spouses must first transform their marriage into a registered partnership. Subsequently, the registered partners can dissolve their partnership by mutual consent. The competent authority for both steps is the civil registry office. Theoretically, this 'lightning divorce' can be carried out in one single day. See Boele-Woelki, Braat, Sumner 2003, 117.

public, provided the wife agrees to the divorce or provided that the prerequisites for divorce under German law have been met, particularly in cases where the prescribed period of separation has elapsed. A private divorce which has already been pronounced and which is effective under the law of the spouses' country of origin can also be presented as evidence of severe hardship in upholding the marriage. In such cases the repudiation itself is taken as the grounds for a European court decision to grant divorce.[134]

Classical Islamic law and the law of several Arab and Islamic countries recognise marriage by proxy. The parties to the marriage do not need to be present at the marriage ceremony. Notably, the bride is often represented by a male relative.[135] European family laws, by contrast, do not allow marriage by proxy and consider the presence of both spouses to be mandatory. Whether a proxy marriage conducted abroad in compliance with the applicable law contradicts the *ordre public* of European countries and therefore cannot be recognised is an issue on which there has been considerable debate. The view that having a spouse represented, rather than physically present, at a marriage or divorce is contrary to the interests of *ordre public* is, however, indefensible in cases where such representation merely serves to present the statement which the spouse would have made, rather than appropriating the spouse's freedom to decide.[136] Such an approach would in fact give precedence to simple notions of domestic family law over foreign law without invoking, or protecting, any fundamental European legal principles. The physical presence of the spouse and the spouse's declaration of intent in person can hardly, in and of themselves, be regarded as fundamental principles of European law. Any further rights requiring the protection of the law, such as the right to the exercise of free will, are not affected by a marriage by proxy.

A similar problem arises in the law on parentage. Classical Islamic legal teaching and many Arab jurisdictions hold that it is not possible for a child to establish a paternal relationship to his or her father if the father is not married to the child's mother.[137] In France, parentage is governed by the personal law of the mother on the day of the child's birth.[138] French courts have, however, applied 'objective' *ordre public* reasons not to uphold alien law when this would make it

---

134 Cf. Andrae 2007, 1731; Gärtner 2008, 71 and 92 with references to case law.

135 Welchman 2007, 68; Büchler 2003, 26. According to some schools of legal thought and jurisdictions not only is the bride represented by the guardian and does the guardian (*wali*) conclude the marriage contract on her behalf, the bride may also not marry without the guardian's consent.

136 For a discussion of the legal position in Switzerland, see Büchler, Fink 2008, 52.

137 Pearl, Menski 1998, 399.

138 Article 311—14 of the Code Civil.

impossible for the child to establish a paternal relationship to his or her father and when the prerequisites for such a relationship are met under French law.[139]

Restraint in Recourse to an Ordre public Rationale

Current discussions of the *ordre public* dimension in the private international law context show contradictory trends. France, on the one hand, supports development away from a subjective appreciation of the interests of *ordre public* towards an objective definition. This means that there is an increasing tendency no longer to consider the circumstances of an individual case or the result of applying alien law or of recognising a decision made in another jurisdiction, but rather that the alien law *per se* is assessed and subject to a summary value judgment. German courts, conversely, seem to be sparing in their use of *ordre public* arguments, or at least to use them in their traditional function as instruments deployed only in exceptional circumstances in order to correct a result which would be unacceptable to the values of German law in every respect and not simply as a means of disempowering an alien law which would in principle be applicable.

Certainly there is increasing reason to doubt whether the Christian, middle-class concept of marriage as a monogamous union concluded for a lifetime can be granted primacy in the international context. There are several reasons for this. First, for many years marriages in Europe took numerous different forms, resulting in many different types of partnership. The present form and meaning of marriage is based on the model of nineteenth-century middle-class society. Second, the current institutional interpretation of marriage has been intensely questioned in recent years, and the exclusivity and privileges of marriage are being eroded. Third, and as a concomitant to the second point, the forms taken by families in the Western industrialised world have been subject to rapid change in recent decades and are becoming pluralised. The same applies to family values. Furthermore, many institutions, such as a child's full paternal relationship to a father who is not his mother's husband, or equality of child-custody rights between mother and father, are recent developments in Europe, so that the argument that they constitute elements which are fundamental to the values underpinning European jurisdictions at least lack any significant historical foundation and depth. Other institutions have developed so quickly that they can hardly be regarded as established, divorce being a case in point. Within one generation, Spain, for example, has seen the canonical prohibition of divorce replaced by the possibility of unilateral dissolution of marriage without a prior period of separation. Fourth, and most importantly, there is the question as to who or what should be protected. Protection of the weaker spouse certainly requires recognition of marriage, particularly in cases where the weaker spouse derives certain claims from being married and conjugal union is what he or she wants. Non-recognition often results in such marriages

---

139 For an account of the developments leading up to this 'objective' understanding, see Cadet 2005, 93.

being driven into illegality, which is at odds with the need of women and children for protection.

Finally, *ordre public* discourse also appears somewhat paradoxical because it effectively involves including what is excluded, by first using nationality as the basis for creating a border within a nation or even a person – between the self and that which is other – in order then to use *ordre public* as the basis for creating a superior form of the self, to which, given sufficient evidence, all that is other must be subject. *Ordre public* thus serves, particularly in its objectivised manifestation, to modify or undermine in a fairly basic way the decisions underlying the conflict-of-laws rules of certain jurisdictions.

Recourse to an *ordre public* rationale should be restrained both in a concrete sense – by searching instead for solutions which are valid within the framework of the foreign norms – and also in an abstract sense – by returning to values which transcend all societies, values enshrined in the fundamental human rights embodied in constitutions[140] and international law, which include the respect of human dignity which is inherent to some procedural pronouncements. Social integration and cohesion within a society, by contrast, is best achieved by determining applicable law primarily on the basis of a person's centre of vital interests.

The Ineffectiveness of the Private International Law Approach

To summarise, serious misgivings apply to determining the family law applicable to an individual on the basis of their nationality, particularly since this is an approach based on exclusion. It amounts to nationalist legal pluralism. It is an approach which anticipates a difference, which it then re-emphasises with every decision. It is thus a performative act, engaging in the binary logic of the self and that which is other. On the other hand an approach combining a greater role for party autonomy with regard to applicable law, harmonised conflict of laws, multilateral agreements and the recognition of other countries' decisions, and a view of *ordre public* derived from international sources should provide a great degree of legal certainty to those moving between countries. That said, the determination of applicable law based on nationality is in decline, ceding ground to a determination of jurisdiction based on shared living space and choice of laws, the objective being to find common ground.

140 For a discussion of the basic-rights aspects of the *ordre public* objections in the German legal context, see Looschelders 2001, 463. In its 1971 leading judgment (the so-called 'Spanish decision') BVerfGE 31, 58, Germany's Federal Constitutional Court concluded that the private international law norms and the foreign legal norms which were presented as being applicable should both be assessed entirely on the basis of the basic rights enshrined in German law. For a comprehensive review of this subject, see Coester-Waltjen, Kronke, Kokott 1998.

Indeed, legal pluralism is embedded in private international law. Conflict of laws is, however, structurally unable to protect cultural identity. In any case, any handling of cross-cultural cases of family law caught up in the binary opposition between an individual's nationality and country of residence will always produce undifferentiated results, since the person is included or excluded from a given legal community regardless of his or her individual cultural circumstances or beliefs. When Muslims have no formalised relationship with a country other than that in which they live, conflict of laws is not even applicable, regardless of a foreign cultural imprint, that is their culture being foreign to that of their country of residence. To put it more pointedly: conflict-of-laws discourse, by creating its own order and by the way it links people to legal systems, participates in creating the self and that which is other, but it does not shape the encounter between the two.

Chapter 3
Accommodation and its Scope: The Respect for Cultural Identity in the Application and Promulgation of Substantive Family Law

The Superseded Legal order

Where private international law does not refer to the law of the country of origin of those concerned in a case, the question then arises as to how the legal system of that country, having been superseded under conflict-of-laws rules, should or can be taken into account within the scope of the interpretation of substantive law. In the German literature the two-step approach (in German 'Zweistufenlehre')[1] and the date theory (in German 'Datum-Theorie')[2] address this issue. The two-step approach in private international law theory generally takes account of the foreign element insofar as the superseded jurisdiction is taken into consideration at a second stage. The date theory, on the other hand, holds that there are special circumstances in which the law of a foreign country, while its direct applicability is ruled out by conflict-of-laws rules, should play some part in judicial consideration, either as a locally relevant fact (local data), or as a morally relevant yardstick (moral data).[3] It is certainly true that these approaches lend significant flexibility to conflict-of-laws determinations, since they are informed not solely by substantive law anchor points, but take the expectations placed on the law by those concerned into account as well. However, they have only a heuristic value in the context of norm-based references to laws of other countries. These approaches cannot provide any normative integration of purely culturally connotated perceptions of the law if a formal link to the law of a foreign country is missing.

---

1 Cf. Jayme 2003b, 84; Von Hoffmann, Thorn 2007, 37, note 129; Dannemann 2004, 114.

2 For a fundamental discussion, see Schulze 2003, 155; cf. also von Hoffmann, Thorn 2007, 37, note 129.

3 An example mentioned in the literature is the case where the assessment of the obligation of a parent to maintenance takes into account the maintenance towards a child whose adoption is not recognised in the forum state; cf. Schulze 2003, 159.

We must therefore leave the field of private international law and ask ourselves whether and how the substantive family law of European countries is able to take account of the multiplicity of cultural ties which exist.

The normative integration of diverse, culturally connotated perceptions of law can be described by reference to different levels.

Narratives on the Equality of Differences

First, the codes of several countries include norms which require the authorities to pay due heed in their actions to religion, ethnic origin, cultural background and language, examples in areas relating to children being the *Children Act* in the England[4] and the *Code de Procédure Civile* in France.[5] However, such commitments to cultural diversity, sometimes also referred to as narrative norms,[6] merely lend concrete expression to principles which are generally applicable in any case, the more so as consideration is regularly accorded to individual circumstances in the way in which specific cases are decided. These norms nevertheless have considerable significance, not only because of their programmatic content, but also because they require justification, and such justification implies reflection on and disclosure of the decision parameters used and cultural imperatives applied by those determining the case. As a result, consideration is given not only to the 'foreign', culturally connotated, expectations placed on the law, but also to the values-based premises and understandings inherent in the applicable European code. In specific cases, it is preferable for the focus here to be on commonalities rather than on assessments which imply the attribution of specific characteristics to 'domestic' and 'foreign' law and thus emphasise differences.[7]

General Clauses, Normative Terms and the Balance of Interests

Consideration of Cultural and Religious Identity in Interpretations of Substantive Law

Second, general clauses, normative terms and the balance of interests all offer potential to take different perceptions of family law into consideration. The

---

4 Section 22, para. 5, subsection c, Children Act 1989: '(5) In making any such decision a local authority shall give due consideration (...) (c) to the child's religious persuasion, racial origin and cultural and linguistic background'.

5 Article 1200 of the Code de procédure civile: 'Dans l'application de l'assistance éducative, il doit être tenu compte des convictions religieuses ou philosophiques du mineur et de sa famille'.

6 Cf. Jayme 1993.

7 Cf. also the interesting case review by Jivraj, Herman 2009, 288, which explores judicial representations of non-Christian beliefs in English child-welfare cases.

interpretation of substantive law is open to evaluations of foreign law as well as to expectations, cultural practices and cultural understandings.

For example, an assessment of whether the prerequisite of 'extraordinary circumstances' in Swiss family law necessary for granting visiting rights to third parties[8] is met must be made with due regard to the cultural significance of family ties between relatives.[9]

To take another example, an assessment as to whether a wife has been forced into marriage, which would give grounds for a case for nullity,[10] can be made only with reference to practices within a culture. Of course, this does not mean that forced marriages are justifiable on the grounds of cultural considerations, but merely that the conduct of those concerned can only be understood and their intentions can only be assessed, if the cultural context is known and its implications appreciated.

Or, again, in deciding whether, by living apart for a certain amount of time, a couple acquire the right to divorce,[11] it is necessary to consider that it is usual under Islamic family customs for couples to live apart in different households only when a marriage has ended in divorce and not because it has failed. For that reason, to interpret the prerequisite of 'living apart' as physical distance is ill-suited to integrating a culturally and religiously diverse society. In fact, in the Islamic context, the failure of a marriage is indicated by the efforts at reconciliation which precede a divorce.[12]

Similarly, to assess whether the continuation of a marriage can be construed as constituting intolerable hardship, and thus justify an immediate divorce at the unilateral instigation of one spouse only,[13] it is necessary to consider the difficulties

---

8 Article 274a, ZGB.

9 Members of the extended family are bound together by the necessary relationships of mutual reciprocity, rendering them far less individualistic; regarding Asian communities in England, see Ballard 2008, 46.

10 For Switzerland: article 107, ZGB; for Germany: section 1314, para. 2, subsection 4, BGB; for France: article 146 and article 180 para. 1, of the Code Civil; for England: Matrimonial Causes Act 1973 (c. 18), section 12, subsection c and section 13, Forced Marriage (Civil Protection) Act 2007 (c. 20); for Spain: article 73, para. 1 of the Código Civil.

11 For Switzerland: article 114, ZGB; for Germany: section 1565 *et seq.*, BGB; for France: article 237 *et seq.* of the Code Civil; for England: Matrimonial Causes Act 1973 (c. 18), section 1, para. 2, subsections c, d and e; for Spain: article 81, para. 2 of Código Civil and article 86 of the Código Civil. Unilateral divorce without a prior period of separation is possible under Spanish law, provided that at least three months have elapsed since the marriage was celebrated, unless it is proven that there is a risk to the life or to the physical integrity of the spouse requesting divorce, or of the common children or of the children of either of the spouses. In such cases, the requirement that three months have elapsed since the marriage was celebrated does not apply.

12 Pearl, Menski 1998, 286; Büchler 2003, 43.

13 For Switzerland: article 115, ZGB; for Germany: section 1565, para. 2, BGB; for England: Matrimonial Causes Act 1973 (c. 18), section 1, para. 2, subsections a and b; for France: article 242 of the Code Civil.

facing a woman living in an Islamic socio-cultural context who has been deserted or repudiated but remains married.

A decision made by a Frankfurt district court was the subject of considerable public debate in this area. The case involved a German woman of Moroccan origin who applied for public subsidy of her legal costs in a petition for divorce from her Moroccan husband 'under duress', a unilateral petition for divorce before the usual one-year separation period had elapsed. Her petition was based on her assertion that her husband was abusing her. The district court judge in the first instance case refused to grant immediate divorce, citing *sura* 4, verse 34 of the Qur'an. The judge's argument was that this passage provided that men from countries such as Morocco had a right to chastise their wives if they were disobedient[14] and that the woman should have been aware of this eventuality when she married her husband. Jurisdiction in this case was subsequently withdrawn from the judge.[15] Rightly so, since inviolability of the person is a fundamental right of every individual and cannot be impinged upon in any way on cultural grounds.

Another case which was also the subject of intense public debate, this time in France, is less clear cut.[16] The court appealed to in the first instance ruled that a bride's false pretence of virginity entitled her husband to petition for the marriage to be annulled. The key issue here is how the law regarding deliberate untruths, specifically where one future spouse has the intent of deceiving the other future spouse about his or her essential attributes,[17] are understood and interpreted by legal authorities and courts in marital law matters. If the applicable law is interpreted to mean that only substantive grounds from an objective point of view would entitle the deceived party to petition for annulment, then in European countries the bride's non-virginity would probably not (or no longer) be considered to be sufficient grounds for an annulment of the marriage. If, however, purely subjective grounds are also deemed admissible, then deceit with regard to virginity would constitute grounds for a petition for annulment in the same way as would, for example, deceit with regard to personal financial circumstances, provided that the deceitful party

---

14 *Sura* 4, verse 34 of the Qur'an. For a discussion of differing interpretations of this verse, see Zentrum für Islamische Frauenforschung und Frauenförderung 2005, 25.

15 Press release by the Frankfurt am Main Local District Court (in German, 'Amtsgericht Frankfurt') on 21 March 2007; cf. also Gärtner 2008, 122, note 419, which states that the decision was incorrect in any case, because the judge had incorrectly based her decision on the Qur'an and not on Moroccan family law, which was in fact applicable in this case. Under Moroccan family law, the husband has no right to chastise his wife.

16 Tribunal de Grande Instance de Lille, 1 April 2008, JCP 2008 (N° 26) 35; see decision of 17 November 2008 of the Cour d'Appel de Douai [Online, 17 November 2008], available at: http://blog.dalloz.fr/files/ca-douai.pdf [accessed: 9 November 2010].

17 For Switzerland: article 107, subsection 3, ZGB; for Germany: section 1314, para. 2, subsection 3, BGB; for England: Matrimonial Causes Act 1973 (c. 18), section 12, subsection c; for France: article 180, para. 2 of the Code Civil; in Spain: article 73, para. 4 of the Código Civil.

was at least able to recognise the essential nature, in the other party's eyes, of the attribute concerning which deceit was practised.

The Concept of the Best Interests of the Child as a Gateway to Culturally Determined Values

The greatest potential for consideration of culturally determined value systems undoubtedly arises by applying the maxim of the child's best interests, a principle also firmly established in international law.[18] It is these which form the paramount consideration in child-related cases. It is of course also true that a child has a right of his or her own to cultural and religious identity, and this can be at odds with the parents' duty to bring up their child, thus forming his or her identity.[19] Thus, cultural and religious identity is not the only element determining a child's welfare, but it is certainly an important one.

Child custody

Child-custody decisions in family law in Europe are directed by considerations of the best interests of the child,[20] and these must also include consideration of the cultural context and of the expectations placed on the law. Of course, decisions on the child's custody should not be made solely on the basis of the sex of the parent and the age of the child,[21] even though such an approach remains an integral part of Muslim legal understanding.[22] That said, pursuit of a strict dogma of equal rights between the parents, and without any heed to the context of the case, is equally inappropriate in an Islamic cultural context.[23] Expectations placed on the law, family resources, the self-image and understanding of those involved, and

---

18 Article 3, para. 1 of the Convention on the Rights of the Child, 20 November 1989.

19 On the conflicts arising in the areas of adoption and religious education, see Scolnicov 2007, 251.

20 For Switzerland: article 133, para. 2, article 298a and article 307 ZGB; For Germany: section 1627, 1671, para. 2, subsection 2 and section 1672, BGB; for France: article 373–2 of the Code Civil; for England: Matrimonial Causes Act 1973 (c. 18) section 25, para. 2; for Spain: article 92, para. 4 of the Código Civil.

21 Cf. Swiss Federal Court decision 129 III 250; and, still somewhat differently, the Swiss Federal Court decision of 27 December 2001, 5P.324/2001.

22 Cf. Pearl, Menski 1998, 410; Büchler 2003, 57. Developments in the personal status laws of many countries are, however, tending to extend the period of custody normally assigned to the mother over her children following divorce beyond the age limits contemplated in classical Islamic law. In addition, there is an increasing number of references to the concept of the interest of the child which affect how the judge may allocate custody rights; cf. Welchman 2007, 134; Nasir 2009, 158.

23 For a detailed review of German jurisprudence and jurisdiction in this area, see Yassari 2006, 197; Ehringfeld 1997, 188.

social and cultural perspectives are all factors to be considered in determining the child's best interests.

Adoption

Adoption is unknown in Islamic law, and is indeed forbidden by the Qur'an,[24] a prohibition which European legislators heed. Consideration of the child's best interests has prompted French legislators to forbid adoption if the child or the adoptive parents are nationals of a country which recognises the prohibition of adoption promulgated in the Qur'an, unless the child was born in France.[25] Swiss law, conversely, will not grant an adoption in Switzerland if the adoption would not be recognised by the adoptive parents' country of origin or domicile and this would therefore be severely prejudicial to the child's interests.[26] Switzerland's legislation also requires the consent of both the child's biological parents and the child's country of origin, before a child who has so far lived abroad can be given into foster care to a couple in Switzerland who intend subsequently to become the child's adoptive parents.[27] Notwithstanding this, a Swiss Federal Court judgment handed down in 2004 states somewhat apodictically that cultural considerations are not relevant to adoptions under Swiss law. This was in a case where a childless married couple

24 *Sura* 33, verse 4 of the Qur'an: 'Allah has not made For any man two hearts In his (one) body: nor has He made your wives whom Ye divorce by *Zihar* Your mothers: nor has He Made your adopted sons Your sons. Such is (only) Your (manner of) speech By your mouths. But Allah Tells (you) the Truth, and He Shows the (right) Way.' *Sura* 33, verse 5: 'Call them by (the names Of) their fathers: that is Juster in the sight of Allah. But if ye know not Their father's (names, call Them) your Brothers in faith, Or your *Mawlas*. But there is no blame On ye if ye make A mistake therein: (What counts is) The intention of your hearts: And Allah is Oft-Forgiving, Most Merciful.' Quoted from Yusuf 'Ali 1999. The background to these revelations from the Qur'an is explained thus. There existed a so-called father/son relationship between the Prophet and Said, the freeman. As was usual in pre-Islamic times, this had been legitimised through adoption. Later, the Prophet wanted to marry Said's divorced wife. This was not possible, however, because of the absolute prohibition against fathers marrying the former wives of their own sons. The verses were intended to resolve this dilemma. A further verse (33:37) explicitly authorises the Prophet's marriage to Said's former wife, Zaynab. Regarding the prohibition of adoption under Islamic law, see Pearl, Menski 1998, 408; Büchler 2003, 57; regarding the prohibition of adoption in various countries, see Nasir 2009, 145.

25 In 2001, France incorporated article 370–3 into the Code Civil. For a discussion of this provision and the courts' approach to it, see Fulchiron 2007, 816.

26 Article 77, para. 2, IPRG. Under this provision, where the adoptive parents live outside Switzerland or are nationals of a country other than Switzerland this has a decisive effect and is also taken into account in the application of Swiss law.

27 Article 11c, para. 2, subsections c and d of the Swiss Federal Ordinance on the Fostering and Adoption of Children of 19 October 1977 (in German, 'Verordnung über die Aufnahme von Kindern zur Pflege und zur Adoption', abbreviated as 'PAVO'). For a detailed review, see Siehr 2007, 373.

sought the right to take into foster care a niece or nephew, with a view to subsequent adoption, thus fulfilling their wish to have a child. The Federal Supreme Court emphasised that the institution of adoption under Swiss law was guided solely by the needs of the child.[28] In Germany, by contrast, courts have examined the question of whether, in the case of a child from an Islamic country, *kafala* might be a more appropriate alternative to adoption, which is forbidden under Islamic law, since the former would help to ensure continuity in the child's cultural development.[29]

Inter-ethnic and inter-religious adoption poses problems of a more general nature, too. Does the adoption of a child with a religious affiliation different from that of his or her adoptive parents infringe the child's right to protection of his or her religious and cultural identity? Where a child has already reached a certain age and has formed a degree of religious and cultural identity, then religious and cultural affiliation is undoubtedly a significant factor in determining whether adoption is in his or her best interests. Yet does this mean that inter-religious adoptions are also problematical in cases where the child has a cultural heritage but has not yet experienced his or her own religious identity? It often appears unclear what interests a restrictive approach to inter-religious adoption furthers, specifically whether such an approach is perhaps not always guided solely by the child's interests but also by those of his or her community of origin, which may not necessarily be the same.[30] The UN Convention on the Rights of the Child states that when considering adoption or other forms of care, due regard should be paid to the desirability of continuity in a child's upbringing and to the child's ethnic, religious, cultural and linguistic background.[31] The law[32] and practice[33] of a number of countries shows that continuity of religious affiliation is a cardinal consideration in the assessment of a child's best interests as far as adoption is concerned.[34]

---

28 Cf. Swiss Federal Court decision 5A.35/2004 of 4 February 2005; also, with a differing result, Swiss Federal Court decision 135 III 80.

29 In the light of article 6, EGBGB, cf. the judgment of the Higher Regional Court in Karlsruhe, of 25 November 1996, 11 Wx 79/96.

30 Cf. Scolnicov 2007, 254, see critically Murphy 2000b, 33.

31 Article 20, para. 3, sentence 2, UN Convention on the Rights of the Child.

32 For England: section 1, subsection 5, Adoption and Children Act 2002: 'In placing the child for adoption, the adoption agency must give due consideration to the child's religious persuasion, racial origin and cultural and linguistic background'; cf. also section 22, para. 5 subsection c, Children Act 1989; cf. also article 9, para. 2, subsection g of the European Convention on the Adoption of Children, to which Switzerland and Germany are both signatories; cf. also article 16, para. 1, subsection b of the Convention on the Protection of Children and Co-operation in Respect of Intercountry Adoption, whose signatories include Switzerland, Germany, Spain, France and the United Kingdom.

33 For a clearly critical assessment of English court decisions, see Scolnicov 2007, 256.

34 According to Scolnicov 2007, 254, 259. She concludes that 'The analysis of the legal approaches to the need for adoption of a child into the religion of birth uncovers a common underlying acceptance, that parents have a presumptive right to determine their

Child protection

When parents inflict serious harm on their children, an intervention by the state on behalf of the children is justified, even if the concept of state intervention in child upbringing can appear alien to families from countries where it is up to the extended family and its surrounding community to regulate behaviour and place sanctions on the transgression of boundaries.

Values held by parents and the values promoted by the state, as represented by its child-protection agencies, can also differ considerably. To implement child-protection norms and practices which are both aware of, and sensitive to, cultural considerations is a difficult undertaking. There are two main reasons for this. On the one hand, cultural and religious considerations occur in the triangular field of tension between the child's needs, the autonomy of the parents and the state's obligation to protect the child. The intervening authority has to balance the safety and welfare of the child against the autonomy – including its cultural aspects – of the parents. On the other hand, ethnological research has shown that perceptions of child well-being differ considerably between cultures. There is no consensus as to what constitutes the proper way of bringing up a child.[35] While people from Western cultures would quickly agree that immersing children in hot baths in order to imbue them with qualities which are highly prized in some other cultures places those children in jeopardy, and that the same applies to subjecting children to pain-inducing initiation rituals, it is equally true that such broadly practised Western customs as making small children sleep in their own beds and their own rooms, or ignoring their hunger pangs so as to induce them to adhere to fixed mealtimes, are met with astonishment and incomprehension by people attuned to certain African and Asian cultures.[36]

Addressing diverse cultural contexts is not optional. A key prerequisite for establishing a culturally sensitive child-protection practice is the awareness that perceptions of children's needs differ from culture to culture, and that they are culturally contingent, even though the principle of children's well-being transcends all cultures.[37]

The resolution of so-called conflicts of autonomy – those conflicts which potentially involve limiting parents' rights in bringing up their children (or their more general rights as parents) – poses particular problems. This is because the state intervention undertaken with a view to protecting the child tends to accentuate

offspring's religious identity, even when these are no longer part of their family unit, and to the protection of this connection.'

35 Cf. An-Na'im 1994, 62.

36 Regarding these examples, see Korbin 1981, 4; cf. also a case which occurred in the United States, where a refugee from Afghanistan was seen kissing the penis of his baby boy, a traditional expression of love by the father. To the neighbours and the police, it was child abuse. See Crossette 1999.

37 Cf. the British study in Brophy, Jhutti-Johal, Owen 2003.

tensions with the child's parents and can result in an irreparable break between the child and his or her family.[38]

To define legitimate criteria for legal intervention is a difficult task. Parents may invoke cultural considerations in defending their conduct, asserting that their actions are consistent with, and required by, cultural traditions. While any extension of normative prescriptions will necessarily have some arbitrary elements to it, particularly since the only conceivable approach is one carried out on a case-by-case basis, the standards for intervention by the state set out below are worthy of particular mention.

Parents' personal responsibilities should be respected, and these include the handing down of cultural values, traditions and religious beliefs. The UN Convention on the Rights of the Child requires signatory states to respect the responsibilities, rights and duties of parents or members of the extended family or community as provided for by local custom, as well as those of legal guardians or other persons legally responsible for the child, to provide, in a manner consistent with the evolving capacities of the child, appropriate direction and guidance in the exercise by the child of his or her rights.[39] Accordng to the Swiss Federal Court, the state should intervene only when the parents' conduct can no longer be regarded as compatible with their task of caring for and bringing up their children. Only where the observance of religious precepts substantively and materially impinges on a child's well-being is it justifiable to place the interests of the child above the rights of his or her parents.[40]

Intervention by the state should not focus primarily on parental faults or deficiencies, but rather on the needs of the child, and any decisions taken should enhance the bond between the child and his or her parents and deploy existing family and community resources wherever possible. This also means that extra-legal solutions should be sought wherever this is possible and reasonable.

The UN Convention on the Rights of the Child guarantees the child's right to freedom of religion.[41] However, the same provision refers explicitly – and in so doing goes beyond the general norm – to the signatory states' obligation to respect the rights and duties of parents to provide direction to the child in the exercise of his or her rights.[42] This position is justified because the child's right to religious identity and the protection of that right serve primarily not to protect the child's freedom of decision, but to protect his or her affiliation and ties to his or her family.[43] It is neither necessary nor indeed even desirable for parents to raise their child by granting him or her open options regarding his or her own future

38 Regarding the legal nature of parents' rights, cf. Kälin 2000, 207. Regarding German case law, see Ehringfeld 1997, 169.

39 Article 5, CRC.

40 Cf. Swiss Federal Court Decision 119 Ia 178, 194.

41 Article 14, para. 1 of the UN Convention on the Rights of the Child.

42 Article 14, para. 2 of the UN Convention on the Rights of the Child.

43 Cf. Scolnicov 2007, 253.

religion. Rather, parents should give their child the experience of belonging to a community.[44] However, out of respect for their children's autonomy, parents have obligations not to force their religious beliefs upon their children once they are old enough to express their own considered judgments on religious matters. Moreover, even if, in his or her early years, a child's right to freedom of religion strengthens the protection provided by family control, that right is still perceived as an individual right of the child's in the sense that it is the child who holds the right, and the right acknowledges the importance both of the child's cultural and religious ties and, by extension, of the religious cohesion of his or her family.

State intervention is both justified and required to prevent irreparable and irreversible harm to the child, so as to protect his or her integrity and preserve his or her freedom of choice.[45] Indeed, no right to inflict bodily harm on cultural grounds will ever be accepted,[46] even though there is still no consensus in society that corporal punishment cannot legitimately be used in a child's upbringing and despite the fact that some sort of punishment seems to exist in all cultural traditions.[47] The right to physical integrity is a non-negotiable and indispensable human right. The imminent circumcision of a young girl[48] can – according to a more recent German Federal Supreme Court decision – result in the parents' right to decide where the child resides being rescinded.[49]

Ultimately, the general legal requirement in child-protection cases that due account be taken of the various conflicting interests involved can, as the child grows older, lead to a decision in favour of the child's own autonomy, if the child has grown apart from the culture which has been passed on to him or her and is shaping his or her own life by integrating into a new societal environment.

---

44 Cf. Mills 2003, 502. She criticises the well-known premise of 'the child's right to an open future', notably put forward by Joel Feinberg. Feinberg sees the child's right to an open future as a guarantee that the child be able to grow up to be the adult which he or she would have been, if his or her options had not already been restricted during childhood, observing that 'in any case, that adult does not exist yet, and perhaps he never will. But the child is *potentially* that adult, and it is that adult who is the person whose autonomy must be protected now (in advance).' Feinberg 2007, 78.

45 Cf. also Renteln 2004, 67.

46 Cf. also Kälin 2000, 210, 214. Taking a somewhat more differentiated approach, and providing examples, also Renteln 2004, 54.

47 Cf. also Bainham 1995, 236; conversely, in Germany, section 1631, para 2, BGB.

48 Regarding this practice, its cultural logic and the approach taken to it in Western countries, see Renteln 2004, 51.

49 Decision of the German Federal Court of Justice of 15 December 2004, XII ZB 166/03. For Switzerland, see Cottier 2005, 698, in particular 707. There are no Islamic origins to the practice of 'female circumcision'. To what extent the Islamification of wider geographical areas helped to propagate the practice has not been established. Regarding the practice and the current policies of Islamic states towards it, see Badry 1999, 211.

The Translation or Transposition of Islamic Family Law

Islamic law institutions can have a bearing on the courts' application of domestic law in Europe. Such foreign norms can be translated or transposed if – to simplify somewhat – there are institutions in family law in Europe which are comparable in their function and legal consequences.

The most commonly discussed example is the *mahr* or dower paid by the groom to the bride under Islamic law.[50] The *mahr* forms an indispensable part of every Islamic marriage[51] and consists of either money or other assets. Although the *mahr* is agreed at the time of betrothal, disbursement of a portion of it is often deferred and made conditional on events such as divorce or the groom's entering into a second marriage.[52] While the amount of the *mahr* and its nature are largely at the discretion of the spouses, some Arab and Islamic countries have passed laws regulating this.[53] In the absence of a specific agreement, the customary *mahr* is payable.[54] There is some controversy regarding the function of the *mahr*. Modern authors see it as a form of participation in the economic status of the husband, as well as a means of granting the wife financial independence during marriage, an element of financial protection should the marriage be dissolved (an important consideration since the matrimonial regime under Islamic family law is one of separate property) and, finally, a deterrent against ill-considered repudiation of the wife by the husband. Particularly in cases where the wife is entitled to ask for payment of the entire *mahr* at any give time, this strengthens her position considerably.[55]

50 For an extensive discussion of the dower, see Pearl, Menski 1998, 178; Büchler 2003, 31; Nasir 2009, 83; Wurmnest 2007, 531; for extensive discussion of the Judaic law parallel, *the kettubah*, see Herfarth 2000, 34.

51 *Sura* 4, verse 4: 'And give the women (On marriage) their dower As a free gift; but if they, Of their own good pleasure, Remit any part of it to you, Take it and enjoy it With right good cheer.' Quoted from Yusuf 'Ali 1999. The question of whether the *mahr* forms a constitutive part of the marriage ceremony is answered differently by the various schools of Islamic jurisprudence, cf. Pearl, Menski 1998, 179; Wurmnest 2007, 528. It should, however, be noted that it is very rare for the absence of a *mahr* agreement to result in a marriage being declared null and void.

52 Cf. Pearl, Menski 1998, 180; Nasir 2009, 86.

53 In principle, no upper limit is defined, but only a very modest minimum, which the various schools of jurisprudence define differently. Cf. Nasir 2009, 85, regarding the various regulations on this. Prosperous Arab states have witnessed very substantial dowers being demanded, and legal restrictions on the maximum amount have therefore recently been enacted, cf. Esposito, DeLong-Bas 2001, 85.

54 Cf. Pearl, Menski 1998, 180; Büchler 2003, 31.

55 Cf. for example article 1085 of the Civil Code of the Islamic Republic of Iran; article 31, para. 2 of the Morrocan Family Code, the *Moudawana*.

Since the *mahr* is so deeply embedded in Islamic legal thinking, it is common among Muslims in Europe as well,[56] which raises the question of how a court should treat such an agreement in the context of divorce proceedings, for example.

The legal classification of the *mahr* relevant in the context of private international law is highly controversial. Which conflict-of-laws norms apply depends on what type of agreement the *mahr* is deemed to be. Whether the law of the country of origin of the parties or that of their country of residence or domicile applies can ultimately depend on whether the *mahr* is considered to be financial support during marriage or maintenance after divorce, whether it is a contractual obligation, a property right or – in the event of a dissolution of a marriage as a result of death – an inheritance.[57]

However, the essential point here is a different one. The real question is whether and, if so, how, a European court should apply domestic law in its treatment of a *mahr* contract between a Muslim married couple, irrespective of their nationality. Let it first be noted that, in the context of an Islamic marriage, the *mahr* constitutes a contractual obligation, and the trust placed in this obligation deserves the protection of the law in the European legal context, too.[58] Of course, payment of a *mahr* will have an effect on the financial claims of the spouses in the event of divorce, by, for example, diminishing the wife's material needs when the amount of any maintenance is determined. In England, what has been agreed between the parties can be taken into consideration as one of the factors in determining any ancillary relief, but this is not binding on the judge.[59] However, whether, over and above that, the agreement of a *mahr* should be interpreted as meaning that bride and groom have opted for the separation of property regime, the view taken by French courts,[60] or whether indeed payment of a *mahr* should rule out any claim by the bride for maintenance after divorce from the groom remain questions to be determined on a case-by-case basis by assessment of the agreement itself. Both cannot be assumed to apply by default, however, since it is not evident that the *mahr* is functionally equivalent to these institutions. The *mahr* is independent of how assets are accumulated during marriage and of the degree of need at the moment of divorce. Indeed it is even independent of divorce as such.

56 Cf. for France: Fulchiron 1999, notes 93 *et seq.* and notes 588 *et seq.*

57 This has notably been discussed in Germany, where all the variations listed here can be found. For a comprehensive and differentiated review, see Wurmnest 2007, 546. A recent judgment by the German Federal Court of Justice qualified the entitlement to the *mahr* as a general legal effect devolving from marriage. See German Federal Court of Justice, judgment of 9 December 2009, XII ZR 107/08.

58 Cf. Wurmnest 2007, 555; Wurmnest 2005, 1879; German Federal Court of Justice, judgment of 28 January 1987, IV b ZR 10/86 and the judgment by the Higher Regional Court in Saarbrücken of 9 March 2005, 9 UF 33/04.

59 Cf. Matrimonial Causes Act 1973, section 25.

60 Cf. Henrich 2004a, 393; cf. Gannagé 1998, 632–7, on the decision of the Cour de cassation of 2 December 1997.

However, any assessment and interpretation must take account of the fact that the *mahr* has a specific function in the context of an Islamic divorce and that the parties and Islamic scholars may regard it as not being payable in certain cases, such as in the event of a so-called *khul'* (redemption) divorce, where divorce occurs at the wife's behest, but no evidence of specific grounds on which a women can obtain a judicial divorce – the so-called *faskh* – is given.[61]

A generally applicable principle should be that agreements concluded in the context of an Islamic marriage should always be protected when under the applicable laws of the European country the object of the agreement is at the disposal of the parties concerned, be it either as an ordinary contractual agreement or as part of a proper marriage contract. The family law applicable in European countries may, however, set out certain stipulations with regard to the form of marriage contracts.

A Broader Range of Institutions under Family Law

A final step towards incorporating Islamic legal expectations into the context of European law which could be considered would be to broaden the existing catalogue of family-law institutions, by adding variations based on different religious and cultural traditions.

Guardianship

Spanish family law, for example, has introduced the option of child protection based on the Islamic law concept of *kafala*, a form of legal guardianship or sponsorship.[62] This institution commits the guardian to protect, look after, support and maintain a child without, however, creating a full parental relationship between child and guardian as would be the case with adoption, which the Qur'an forbids.[63] *Kafala* affords a firm foundation for a lifelong relationship of care and belonging. The UN Convention on the Rights of the Child explicitly lists the *kafala* in accordance

61 Pascale Fournier analyses the case law of several different Western jurisdictions, namely Germany, France, Canada and the United States. She shows different understandings of *mahr* that all produce inconsistent and unpredictable results. She identifies three main approaches: one based on legal pluralism, one based on formal equality and one based on substantive equality. The legal pluralist approach views *mahr* as central to cultural and religious recognition; the formal equality approach considers *mahr* to be merely a secular contract; and the substantive equality approach projects feminist principles into its regulation. See Fournier 2009, 1.

62 Article 173 *bis* of the Código Civil.

63 Regarding the prohibition of adoption under Islamic law, cf. Büchler 2003, 57; Pearl, Menski 1998, 408; regarding the institution of *kafala* cf. Mitchell 2001, 200.

with Islamic law as one of the possible forms of child guardianship.[64] English law provides a similar legal institution. The *Adoption and Children Act 2002* introduced a new type of court order, special guardianship, intended to provide another option for legal permanence in addition to adoption. It is open, *inter alia*, to carers from minority groups who may wish to offer a child a permanent family and to have parental responsibility for the child, but have religious or cultural difficulties with adoption as it is set out in law.

Marriage

In addition to civil marriage, Spanish law also recognises marriage ceremonies according to canon law, and indeed places both forms of marriage – the religious and civil one – on an equal footing. Spain has also introduced the possibility of conducting an Islamic marriage with compulsory state registration.[65] This means that, under Spanish law, an Islamic marriage ceremony in Spain has all the civil law effects and consequences of any other recognised form of marriage. England does not require a civil marriage ceremony either. It is also now possible for mosques in England to be authorised to register marriages themselves, in the same way as synagogues and Sikh temples have already been able to do for many years.[66] Conversely, in Switzerland and France the law continues to require a civil marriage ceremony to be performed before a religious wedding may be celebrated,[67] while German law has recently abolished this requirement, albeit without also decreeing that religious marriage ceremonies in and of themselves have any effect in civil law.[68]

64 Article 20 para. 3 of the UN Convention on the Rights of the Child.

65 Article 59 of the Código Civil. Regarding religious marriage ceremonies in Spain, cf. Martinez-Torrón 2000, 56. The basis for this reform is the 'Acuerdo de cooperación con la Comisión Islámica' of February 2005. Article 7 of this convention states: 'Se atribuye efectos civiles al matrimonio celebrado según la forma religiosa establecida en la Ley Islámica, desde el momento de su celebración, si lo contrayentes reúnen los requisitos de capacidad exigidos por el Código Civil … '.

66 See Marriage Act 1949 (c. 76), Parts III and IV; Welstead, Edwards 2008, 24.

67 For Switzerland: article 97, para. 3, ZGB; for France: cf. article 165 and article 191 of the Code Civil.

68 Cf. the reform of German Law on Civil Status (in German, 'Personenstandsgesetz', abbreviated as 'PStG') of 19 February 2007, which has been in force since 1 January 2009. Sections 67 and 67a of the old PStG had stated that anyone celebrating a church wedding or other religious marriage ceremony, without the bride and groom having previously declared their intention to marry at a civil registry office, was infringing the law. These provisions were removed from the revised version of the PStG, giving rise to considerable controversy in the media.

Scope and Limits for Accommodating Cultural and Religious Identity in Substantive Family Law

One thing which all approaches to cultural diversity based on substantive law have in common is that they avoid abstraction and seek to find justice in individual cases, deciding each case on its own merits. The acknowledgement of religious and cultural imperatives in interpreting substantive law is part of an individualised approach to justice. These approaches do, however, lay themselves open to criticisms of normative ambiguity and confusion. The resulting overall picture is eclectic, a mosaic of cultural considerations which hardly constitutes a systematic view.[69] It is also certainly the case that the extent to which Islamic expectations of the law are being accommodated in the application of European substantive law does not go nearly as far as conflicts-of-laws rules under private international law would in fact allow. The legal framework applied is uniform, with only isolated instances in which cultural considerations are allowed to bring about differences in the results of interpretations of a specific norm. In this context, it is also necessary to consider that there is a significant danger, not easily controlled, of culture and its attendant arguments and claims becoming standardised attributes stereotypically ascribed to each individual based on his or her cultural background and then being regarded as intrinsic to the individual concerned.

69 With regard to the situation in England, see Yilmaz 2005, 54.

Chapter 4

Legal Pluralism: Justification and Dangers of a Lack of Common Ground

Legal Pluralism: Normative Dimensions of Pluralistic Social Structures

Ethnic polarisation has intensified.[1] There is some evidence that European systems of family law do not take sufficient heed of certain interests that are presumed to be cultural; reports from numerous countries lament the existence of segregated societies, of ethnic and religious enclaves, self-conscious and more-or-less well organised communities operating according to their own laws particularly in matters relating to the family.[2] The impression gained is that migrants from Asia and Africa tend to reconstruct their own legal worlds in their diaspora communities. Family disputes are sometimes settled in the context of informal conciliation processes, and the decisions of community leaders are heeded and put into effect without the parties concerned having recourse to official legal authorities or procedures.[3]

The literature employs the concept of legal pluralism to define the normative dimensions of pluralistic social structures, in other words to describe the 'presence in a social field of more than one legal order'[4] and how these orders interact with each other.[5] Legal pluralism refers to a plurality or multiplicity of norms within one legal order and to norms which coincide in the same social sphere and overlap in their approach to the same issues, people and territory. This multiplicity of legal understandings and aspirations within a nation-state can lead to culturally based conflicts. A more elaborate and conceptually developed definition of legal pluralism is provided by Chiba, who sees it as 'the coexisting structure of different legal systems under the identity postulate of a legal culture in which three combinations of official law and unofficial law, indigenous law and transplanted law, and legal rules and legal postulates are conglomerated into a whole by the choice of a socio-legal entity'.[6]

---

1 Ballard 2009, 309.

2 For France: Rude-Antoine 1991, 93; for England: Pearl, Menski 1998, 77; regarding the development of these 'ethnic colonies', see Ballard 2008, 38. For references to the discussion in Germany, see Schiffauer 2008, *passim*, in particular 48.

3 For England cf. Yilmaz 2005, 161 and 171.

4 Griffiths 1986, 1.

5 Cf. Hinz 1990, 124.

6 Chiba 1998, 242.

Legal pluralism is thus both an analytical framework and the cypher determining the simultaneous fragmentation, pluralisation, superposition and fusion of legal systems. It is the result not only of the transnationalisation of law and the growth in the number of authorities operating globally, but also of the legal fragmentation which migration is inducing within Western nations. Both phenomena are clearly at odds with the legal positivism identifying the law with the state.[7] They question many of the core assumptions on which the dominant jurisprudence of the modern nation-state is based.

Different disciplines have different notions of law and therefore of legal pluralism. Indeed, defining law for the purposes of legal pluralism poses a conceptual challenge.[8]

In the strictly legal conception of legal pluralism, the only law is that made and recognised by the state. There may be multiple bodies of law which coexist or overlap on a local and a global level, but the reason why their norms are seen as having the force of law is because they enjoy the legitimacy which results from their having been either promulgated or recognised by the state. This description has sometimes been criticised as being too narrow, conceptually inadequate and not borne out by experience.[9] The theoretical questioning of the primacy of the state and its implicit criticism of the positivistic concept of legal pluralism goes hand in hand with criticisms of the dominant modern idea of a single, homogeneous, coherent and unified legal order. As Menski sees it: 'This statist approach still privileges state-made laws over all other forms of laws and simply denies, in effect, a rightful place in the North for the legal systems of the South.'[10]

The concept of legal pluralism proposed by cultural anthropology is based on a notion of law which, contrary to the prevailing one – in which monistic state authority is implicit – instead evolves, almost in a genetic sense, in the social planes of human communities.[11] This understanding of legal pluralism conceptualises multiple forms of order. The idea here is that normativity springs from a number of different sources and, in particular, that the family is a locus for self-regulation, and that the interactive dynamism between various normative systems makes it indefensible to heed only the law of the state. The concept of legal pluralism is therefore a criticism of the dominant legal centralist approach to legal theory. Legal pluralism takes the view that people's very cultural identity demands that the whole structure of the law as an aspect of culture should include all regulations, however apparently different from state law, which specific population groups observe as law in their cultural tradition. Thus, the entire structure of the law appears pluralistic, consisting of different systems of norms

7 Cf. Fischer-Lescano, Teubner 2007, 37.
8 Cf. Tamanaha 2008, in particular 390.
9 Shah 2005, 2.
10 Menski 2006, 17.
11 For a fundamental discussion, see Griffiths 1986, 1.

interacting with one another – either harmoniously or conflictingly.[12] We can thus observe pluralistic legal structures within European states, if, in addition to state law, our observations also take into account other, empirically identifiable quasi-legal frameworks which manifestly also exert authority, even if state law does not recognise other normative systems. Such an approach effectively amounts to normative pluralism or empirical legal pluralism.

Indeed, pluralistic legal structures where state law, religious and customary law have co-existed and competed with each other[13] are a long-established feature of non-European countries with a colonial past. In many Asian countries we encounter a characteristic legal pluralism in which Islamic law coexists with modern state law and other customary and transplanted laws. The same applies to countries with an indigenous population defending the right to have their own laws.[14] Justice Marshall's words at the end of the 1970s in the US Supreme Court decision *Santa Clara Pueblo v. Martinez*, which acknowledged the right of Indian tribes to promulgate and enforce their own laws, even though they do not enjoy all the attributes of sovereignty, have become almost legendary in this regard.[15]

A legal theory analysis of pluralistic normative structures will also identify instances of 'transplanted law', that is to say law which large-scale migration has brought to Europe in its wake.[16] Various terms have been coined to describe this process, including that of 'reverse colonialisation'.[17] In fact, colonial migration from the North to the South, and the colonial subjugation of a large part of the world by European powers, also resulted in the transplantation of Western laws all over the world by a variety of reception methods.[18] What we are currently witnessing is perceived in some quarters as the same process in reverse. Migration from the South to the North is influencing the law in European countries in many different ways, even though the ideology of legal monism has meant that they are seldom immediately apparent. Alien legal concepts and understandings can be effective as customary law in European countries without needing any recognition by state authorities. The result is that normativity is seen as adhering to individuals, and, by extension, becomes polycentric. This in turn reflects the two main outcomes of globalisation – fragmentation within the state on the one hand, and, on the other hand, the erosion of nation-based borders and the concomitant evolution of transnational social spheres.

12 Chiba 1986, 4.

13 Legal anthropology assumes that the old legal pluralism is characterised by the incorporation of customary law and other forms of law into the legal system, cf. Tamanaha 2001, 171.

14 For a general view, with specific references to Canada, see Hinz 1995, 75.

15 Santa Clara Pueblo v. Martinez, 436 U.S. 49 (1978). Regarding this same case, see also Shachar 2001, 18.

16 Chiba 1998, 241.

17 Menski cited in Shah 2005, 4.

18 Menski 2006, 13.

Migration does not transplant law as a self-contained, de-contextualised entity, however. Rather, it subjects law to new interpretations and re-contextualises it, in a process which can result in values being transformed, hybrid structures emerging and normative systems becoming syncretised. Legal institutions and practices are thus not so much being transplanted as translated. The arrangements lived out in diaspora communities exhibit complex forms of translocalism[19] or – if one adopts the not always sound nation-oriented perspective – transnationalism.

Ethnographic Evidence: 'Entangled histories'[20] as Exemplified by Muslim Communities in England

One example which has been well examined is that of the partially autonomous legal culture prevailing within the Islamic community in England.

Even though persons domiciled in England are subject to English family law, since in English international family law domicile is the connecting factor, the family lives of many Muslims are in fact governed by unofficial Islamic law. That is to say that many Muslim men and women in England deliberately resort to Islamic law when it comes to regulating family-related matters and place little trust in what English law has to offer. Thus, in effect, they do not recognise the authority and legitimacy of secular English law where the family is concerned. A number of Islamic law arrangements and institutions have developed over time. Numerous Islamic or Muslim law *sharia* councils have existed in England for more than twenty years. The various existing bodies represent the different schools of thought in Islam. These institutions provide alternative modes of dispute resolution based on Islamic law and were established to meet the needs of a large part of the community of Muslims living in England. The community believes that Muslims must to a large extent be regulated by Islamic legal norms, appropriately interpreted and applied by the most knowledgeable scholars among them.

These *sharia* councils have appropriated for themselves the role of parallel quasi-judicial institutions. They enjoy substantial jurisdictional authority within the Muslim community and perform functions similar to those of a court: they conduct arbitration and reconciliation, mediate in intra-family conflicts, give legal opinions about family-law rules and legal procedures, advise in matters of family law, assist in the negotiation of Islamic marriage contracts, resolve disputes in family-law matters, pronounce Islamic divorces, and issue divorce certificates.[21]

England's Muslim community thus observes its own set of family-law rules: couples are wed in the Islamic marriage ceremony of the *nikah*, and the civil marriage ceremony is regarded as a sort of engagement, which does not in itself

---

19 Regarding 'translocalism', see Shah 2007, 178.

20 Randeria 2002, 284. The term 'entangled histories' refers to approaches which transcend traditional national history and assume a transnational perspective.

21 Cf. Bano 2007, 45.

allow a marriage to be consummated, even though it can be dissolved only by a divorce pronounced by an English civil court. As a result, some Muslim couples living in England marry twice. It is, however, estimated that about one third of couples marrying under the Islamic *nikah* ceremony do not become legally married under English law by having a civil marriage ceremony as well. This number includes many polygamous marriages concluded under the *nikah* ceremony.[22] As a result, many couples are not regarded as being married in the eyes of English family law and they therefore lack the protection which English law affords both during marriage and in the event of divorce. The reasons why Muslim couples choose to wed under religious law only and not under English law are complex. A religious wedding forms an important part of a person's religious identity. In the words of a young Muslim woman born and living in England:

> I have been divorced twice, and a civil marriage never took place [on either occasion]. I married [my second husband] two years ago … he didn't want to marry me in English law … [a] blessing in disguise because I would have had to pay thousands to get the decree nisi … . [23]

The immense significance of the religious act is also voiced by this woman's statement:

> At the end of the day I am a Muslim and for us Muslims a nikah is the most important thing, for us the civil marriage means, well, it is not until you have had the nikah that your marriage is acceptable, we can have a civil marriage but they're not going to accept that until we have the nikah done. For a Muslim a nikah is more important than a civil marriage … I'd be quite happy just to have a nikah […] I wouldn't go through a civil marriage … there is no need for me to go through that.[24]

This refusal to have recourse to English law can be seen not only as a reassertion of religious and cultural identity, but also as evidence of a lack of trust in official law and of a form of 'inner migration'.[25] An empirical study has, however, also shown that in a majority of cases the bride had expected her marriage to be registered under English law following the religious ceremony and the consummation of the marriage, but that the groom had then refused, a finding demonstrating the gender-specific nature of authority within a family,[26] as evidenced by this testimony:

---

22 Cf. Yilmaz 2005, 74 and 76; Shah 2003, 398. Another study found that less than half the sample who had married a partner domiciled in England had registered their marriage, cf. Bano 2007, 51.

23 Shah-Kazemi 2001, 32.

24 Shah-Kazemi 2001, 33.

25 Cf. Menski 2009, 34.

26 Cf. Bano 2007, 51.

> I think a lot of people are naïve, they just trust their husbands in that they will get a registered marriage. It's not that they don't know about registry or that they don't want it, they are just naïve in believing their husbands. I tell all my friends now that you must have a legal marriage first because if you have an Islamic marriage first then they will not agree to do a civil marriage. I mean you can do it on the same day there's nothing stopping you doing that. Because I really think that guys would begin to take marriages more seriously.[27]

In other cases, however, failure to have the marriage registered under English law is simply the result of the parties' ignorance of the legal situation:

> Well to tell you the truth I honestly thought that the Muslim marriage certificate would be recognised. I was quite shocked when I found out that it wasn't. I thought, hold on a minute we got married didn't we? I had a massive wedding; I've got the wedding photos to prove it, the wedding cassette to prove it. I have all this to prove it so how can they turn round and say to me that, sorry, no, it's not recognised. The only difference is … the only thing that we didn't do is swap some vows in the registry office. I mean that's the only difference.[28]

Limping marriages[29] in which women are disadvantaged[30] have been the main catalyst encouraging the establishment of religious arbitration bodies. This is because civil divorce is regarded by Muslims as a mere formality and often occurs before a religious divorce. There are different forms of divorce in Islamic law, the main one being the unilateral pronunciation of the *talaq* by the husband. Thus, if a civil divorce is pronounced by an English court and the husband then refuses the

27 Reproduced in Bano 2007, 52.

28 Bano 2007, 52.

29 The term 'limping marriage' refers to a marriage which has been dissolved through a civil divorce but not according to religious precepts or a marriage which is legal in one country but not recognised in another.

30 Cf. Keshavjee 2007, 170. He describes the case which originally led to the *sharia* councils being established: 'Its founder, the late Dr Zaki Badawi, a knowledgeable mufti and a charismatic individual, responded to the entreaties of a desperate Muslim woman who had attained her divorce in an English court but was unable to remarry Islamically, as her divorce was not recognised under Islamic law and consequently she was undergoing great hardship. Calling upon two imams, Dr Badawi pondered her predicament and, drawing on the philosophy and principles of the eponymous founder of the school of jurisprudence, Abu Hanifa, to which both parties belonged, he called upon the husband to come forth and explain why he was refusing to grant his wife the divorce … . Dr Badawi invoked the principles of classical Islamic jurisprudence *darura* (necessity) and *maslaha* (public interest) and followed Abu Hanifa's advice that in a non-Muslim country, it would be absolutely in keeping with the principles of Islamic law for the wise among the community to constitute themselves as a *qadi* court and mete out the necessary justice where public interest so warranted.'

talaq, he would be entitled, both under English law and Islamic law – since the latter allows polygamy – to enter into a new marriage. The wife, however, does not have this right. According to Islamic law she would be committing adultery by entering a new relationship or remarrying in those circumstances.[31]

Under Islamic law divorce is not an entirely unilateral prerogative of the husband, however. A Muslim woman seeking divorce has to make an application to a *sharia* law judge, citing and proving a specific reason for divorce or – if she reaches an agreement with the husband and he consents to divorce – renounce her financial claims. She would therefore take her case to the *sharia* council and request that it intervene in the family dispute in order to help her dissolve the Islamic marriage, and that it pronounce a divorce. In such cases, a civil court divorce may be considered as indicating that grounds for divorce also exist under Islamic law, provided that the husband has agreed to it.

Empirical studies show that the need to obtain a religious divorce certificate is the most common reason behind appeals to a *sharia* council made by women.[32] However, to obtain a divorce they must first take part in a reconciliation process. The Islamic *Sharia* Council leaflet states:

> The majority of these cases concern divorce, where the wife has obtained a British divorce which is not accepted by the husband, who considers such a divorce to be unacceptable with no bearing upon his right as a husband. As a result, the wife does not feel completely free to enter into another marriage before obtaining the Islamic Talaq. If there is a positive response from the husband, the Council will reason with him assuring him the return of his financial claim under the agreement of Khul'a, after which the Islamic divorce is granted. A great relief for the wife who is now free Islamically, to start a new life.[33]

The same happens when the husband refuses to pay the deferred *mahr* upon divorce. This is an excerpt from a letter by a Muslim woman to the Muslim Law *Sharia* Council:

---

31 Yilmaz conducted a survey of the Muslim communities in England. He notes that 'Talaq is still very important for the Muslim mind and for the community. In both Islam and Judaism, in order to remarry, a woman must obtain a religious decree of divorce. Under Jewish law, the wife must obtain a get, in Islamic law, a religious divorce must be accomplished in one of the ways of talaq, khul or mubaraat. If the woman is not religiously divorced from her husband, it does not matter that she is divorced under the civil law, in the eyes of the community her remarriage will be regarded as adulterous and any possible offspring will be illegitimate since it is not allowed under the religious law. So, in reality, until the religious divorce is obtained, the civil divorce remains ineffective because one party is unable to remarry.' Yilmaz 2003, 130.

32 Cf. Bano 2007, 48.

33 Islamic Shari'a Council of Great Britain and Northern Ireland, *An Introduction*, 7.

> Further to my recent visit to your office I would like to confirm our conversation about asking you to act on my behalf regarding my divorce. My marriage has been unacceptable to me since the day I got married. The marriage was a forceable [*sic*] one where parental pressure and force was used against my wishes. [...] It must be against Islam's teachings to force someone to live with someone who they do not consider as a partner in life. [...] I therefore need your assistance to help me break free of this bondage. I was born and brought up in England and therefore I could say that because I do not consider this marriage as valid, I could just forget everything and start fresh elsewhere, but I do respect my religion and its teachings and I need your guidance so that I do not lead a life in sin. My marriage was not registered in the Registry office so by English Law I am not considered married. [...] I look to you to resolve my life for me and give me the strength to live my life because if I cannot get divorced then I would destroy myself because life has become unbearable to me ....[34]

Empirical findings and women's testimony both confirm the existence of dynamics of authority within the family on the one hand and conservative interpretations of Islamic law and the assignment of traditional roles to women on the other hand. There is, however, evidence that women also use the *sharia* councils to challenge conservative views and cultural practices and to negotiate favourable agreements. Bano sums it up thus:

> as this study demonstrates, women feel the contradictory pulls which these forces exert, but their narratives must be heard. Some are happy to conform, others are not, some trade identities, but for others there is the primacy of a Muslim identity. Many are suspicious of state intervention challenging cultural norms deemed oppressive because the state has not historically acted as the neutral arbiter of disputes. Furthermore some women see themselves strictly bound to submit to the dictates of Islamic law and the commands of the authorities charged with its execution and we must recognise this as their lived experience.[35]

The *sharia* councils have no powers of enforcement and rely on their religious authority and the Muslim community's identification with Islamic law. Since the enactment of the *Divorce (Religious Marriages) Act* of 2002, English courts can require the dissolution of a religious marriage before granting a civil divorce. In other words, an English court can declare that a religious act, to which it ascribes no normative effect whatever, is a prerequisite for its own actions. A tangled web has indeed been woven here, with the global entangled histories postcolonial studies often refer to mapped onto local realities.

The expectations created by this Islamic family-law order, which in England is both normatively effective yet not officially recognised, have the effect of

34 Shah-Kazemi 2001, 47.

35 Bano 2007, 62.

preserving certain aspects of Islamic law, but also of providing them with new interpretations which are adapted to the social environment concerned. Islamic law is thus reconceptualised, reinterpreted and reconstructed,[36] in a complex process for which Islamic legal teaching provides various methods, most notable of which is *ijtihad*, deducing the meaning of law according to one's own best judgment, by personal reasoning.[37] Further important instruments to which current legal discourse in this field often refers are *darura*, which seeks to ascertain the necessity of a particular course of action, and *maslaha*, the concept of common good, which means considerations of the public interest.[38] In making their judgments, *sharia* councils also draw on the teachings of various different schools of jurisprudence and legal scholars.[39]

The overall result is a legal system exhibiting hybrid structures and content, which is why it is often referred to as '*angrezi sharia*', or English *sharia*.[40] It is perhaps best described as a postmodern answer to legal modernity, though it is a reality which clearly illustrates the relative insignificance of the law to which Ehrlich[41] refers.

Parallel Systems of Family Law? The Dangers Posed by Postcolonial Continuities

Traditions of Legal and Normative Pluralism in Family Law

Islamic communities in England sometimes claim the right to control communal and private life, to be afforded protection from the influence of mainstream practices in areas of social life and the right to formulate and apply their own family-law codes. They have become assertive and more vocal in demanding autonomy.[42] These efforts began in the 1970s, when the Union of Muslim Organisations of UK and Eire promulgated a formal resolution seeking the official recognition of a separate system of Islamic family law which would automatically be applicable to all British Muslims.[43] A more recent survey among British Muslims shows that a significant minority of Muslims is in favour of some implementation of *sharia*,

---

36 Cf. Yilmaz 2003, 118.

37 Regarding *ijtihad*, cf. Kamali 2003, 468.

38 Regarding the significance of necessity and considerations of public interest in Islamic legal theory, cf. Kamali 2003, 334 and 351.

39 Cf. Yilmaz 2005, 172. For an extensive review of this method of Islamic jurisprudence, termed *talfiq*, see Krawietz 2002, 3.

40 Pearl, Menski 1998, 58, 74 and 393.

41 Ehrlich 1989.

42 See Yilmaz 2005, 59.

43 Poulter 1998, 201.

with younger people more likely to prefer *sharia* and more reluctant to accept reform of traditional scholarly interpretations of Islamic law.[44]

More recently, the justness of this demand has been the subject of considerable debate, not least with regard to the right to cultural and religious identity. Muslim groups base their case on the historical fact that in many former colonies, Muslims were governed by their own religious family laws. In India, it is noteworthy that it was the British Parliament during the days of empire which gave statutory force to a pluralistic system of family law, under which different religious communities had distinctive systems of personal law administered by their own courts. Colonialism has left its mark on group rights to this day, since, when India gained independence, those laws were kept on the statute book. If this was acceptable to the British in India, Muslims in England see no reason why the state should not accommodate the communities of new immigrants and the coexistence of different family laws should not also be feasible in the UK.[45]

Furthermore they argue that, as members of the Islamic community, they are duty-bound to follow the precepts of *sharia* in organising their family lives rather than heeding the provisions of established English law. They view the right to adhere to *sharia* law as an essential part of their religious freedom.[46] What this illustrates is that in different cultural contexts different aspects of religious freedom are seen as paramount. While, in the context of human rights as they are traditionally understood in the West, the right to choose one's religion, to change religion and to abandon a religion is often central to the concept of religious

44 Mirza, Senthilkumaran, Ja'far 2009, 46.

45 See the references to this line of argument in Poulter 1990, 148. See also the jurisprudential view supporting this position by Muslim communities in Menski 2006, 25: 'we are heading towards reintroduction of personal law systems in Europe and North America as a result of South–North migration, one way or the other, officially or unofficially. European legal systems manifestly do not like this, because it reminds us of allegedly medieval models, but we are totally wrong in this. Almost the whole of Asia and Africa continue to have personal law systems today, and we could not reasonably argue that this concept itself is outdated and inappropriate for our day and age. If we accept that Roman law devised a personal law system and we have grown out of this ancient model in Europe, and the post-Ottoman Turks have developed beyond the *millet* system, this does not mean that the world as a whole has followed suit.'

46 This differs from the position taken by the Central Council of Muslims in Germany (in German, 'Zentralrat der Muslime in Deutschland'), which has published an 'Islamic Charter', article 10 of which states that Muslims can live in any country they choose, so long as they are able to observe their principal religious obligations. The charter goes on to say that Islamic law commits Muslims living in the diaspora to adhere in principle to local laws. The granting of visas, residence permits and naturalisation are thus contracts to which the Muslim minority must adhere. According to article 13 of this same charter, this acceptance of European laws extends to the area of family law. [Online, 22 Feburary 2002] Available at: http://www.zentralrat.de/3035.php [accessed: 9 November 2010].

freedom, the Islamic understanding of religious freedom principally relates to a person's right to observe their religious duties in their public and private life.

There is strong pressure for transition from the unofficial to the official, to Islamic family law explicitly recognised by the state, though not promulgated by it. In 2004, the Association of Muslim Social Scientists (UK) held a conference entitled 'Incorporating Muslim Personal Law into UK Domestic Law'. The following is an extract from Thomson's notes on its proceedings:

> At present Muslims in the UK face hardship in that their personal law is not recognised by the secular civil courts. Marriages and divorces conducted in accordance with the *Shari'a* of Islam are not recognised as valid by the law of the land even though they are acceptable in the sight of God. This state of affairs leads to difficulties, especially as regards the duties and rights between the spouses and divorcees, the legal status of their children, ownership of property, eligibility to state benefits and dealing with public authorities in general, especially when travelling abroad and when death occurs. Similarly, if a Muslim dies intestate, his or her estate is not distributed in accordance with the *Shari'a* of Islam. This leads to difficulties as regards the entitlement to and ownership of shares in the deceased's estate.[47]

Thomson goes on to cite the right to religious freedom, before proposing the following:

> What is being proposed is the recognition by the law of not only the personal law of the bona fide religious groups but also legal recognition of the decisions and rulings of their religious courts ... There should be a system of registration of bona fide religious courts, including civil Shari'a Courts for the Muslims, in order to ensure that standards are maintained and imposters are excluded. Once registered as a religious court, the decision of any of these courts should be recognised as legally binding on the parties and legally enforceable in the County Courts and High Courts. Given the differences between Sunni and Shi'a *fiqh*, and also the differences of *fiqh* between the different madhhabs within these two main groupings, ideally it should be possible to have *Shari'a* Courts which represent all the madhhabs. This would involve having a statutorily defined presumption that the fact that the religious court had dealt with the parties was conclusive proof that the parties had voluntarily agreed to submit to the religious court's jurisdiction and to be bound by its decision whether they agreed with it or not.[48]

There is also a body of committed opinion among legal scholars supporting the view that the Indian example could serve as a template for the reintroduction of

47 Thomson 2004, 1.
48 Thomson 2004, 2.

personal-law systems, legal systems in which a number of different laws of personal status co-exist, each being promulgated by a different religious community and recognised by the state.[49] Were normative systems such as Islamic law to remain officially unrecognised, the argument is that they would nevertheless continue to operate, albeit unofficially, thus creating tensions and legal uncertainties. Werner Menski, a prominent scholar in this field, concludes:

> We have to construct new culture-specific models that match the emerging socio-cultural and therefore legal pluralistic realities of our globally interconnected world today. At the end of the day, whether we choose the British model or the continental model, both appear to do the same thing, in that the official law takes limited but unsystematic account of cultural/religious/ethnic diversity as a matter not of foreign law, but of social difference within national boundaries. That, I am afraid, is not good enough for a sensible plurality-conscious legal approach. I therefore reiterate the point that the Indian model of accommodating complex legal pluralities needs to be studied in depth to investigate whether this is of use to European and North American jurisdictions.[50]

In short, what is being advocated is that religious communities should be granted their own autonomous spheres within the framework of secular state law, and the state law's authority to regulate family-law matters should be suspended in favour of norms based on religious-law principles. So far, the British government has rejected the idea of introducing a system of separate personal law for religious communities and the campaign 'One Law for All', launched in 2008, even aims to end *sharia* councils and Muslim Arbitration Tribunals on the basis that they work against equality and human rights.[51]

The Problems of Parallel Legal Structures

While an *apologia* for normative systems which are both autonomous and recognised by the state is comprehensible – given the collective experience of injury to the integrity of many groups within wider society – there are good grounds (both dogmatic and with regard to issues of legal practice and legal policy) for such postcolonial continuities[52] to be subjected to critical appraisal.[53]

---

49 For a robust view on this, see Menski 2006, in particular 24.

50 Menski 2006, 28.

51 Cf. One Law for All Campaign 2010.

52 For a discussion of the irony that the former colonies thus provide a vision of Europe's future, see Randeria 2003, 22.

53 For extensive discussion, see Rohe 2003, 409.

Multifarious communities and multifarious legal precepts
First, it can be argued that neither nineteenth-century imperial India, nor the tribal societies of postcolonial nations, nor areas within a nation-state inhabited by indigenous peoples are suitable models for the multicultural societies of twenty-first-century Europe.[54] Both the host nations and the migrant populations we find in Europe today are too multifarious within themselves. Europe's Muslim communities are characterised both by diversity of origin and by diverging levels of religious observance. The constant processes of adaptation, negotiation and challenges to the status quo which these communities have lived through have also resulted in a plurality of cultural understandings. A community-based system of personal laws amounts to an unwarranted restriction on plurality. It would replace cultural and religious diversity with a juxtaposition of more-or-less uniform and closed groups and would imply that fate has somehow bound the individual to a primordial cultural identity.[55] An enlightened pluralistic society cannot subject itself to an essentialist definition of culture, nor can it regard culture as a mere collective entity. Ballard generalises this as follows: 'Plurality is an endlessly dynamic phenomenon, not least because it is subject to a constant process of dialectical interaction between those who differ: in these circumstances any attempt to tie the resultant disjunctions down to an essentialised vision of permanently constituted difference by definition misses the point.'[56]

Moreover, it is not only the Muslim communities themselves which vary considerably, but also the legal precepts to which they adhere.[57] The Qur'an is not a legal canon, there is no one single 'Islamic law' and no systematically codified Muslim personal law. Rather, there is an Islamic legal tradition within which the Muslim world incorporates a number of different philosophical strands, schools of legal thought, and locally specific conventions. First and foremost, classical Islamic family law is subject to many different interpretations. Furthermore, there are discrepancies between the classical understanding of Islamic family law promulgated by the premises set out in the *sharia* and the specific local customs and conventions which migrant communities use to order their family lives.[58] Besides, unofficial law in the form of customs and conventions is inherently flexible and is continuously being rearticulated and renegotiated by the members of the community concerned. These processes are at their most intense when these communities are facing the challenge of a new environment which exerts social, cultural, moral and legal pressure on them.[59]

54 According to Pearl 1999, 111.
55 Cf. also Bielefeldt 2007, 105.
56 Bielefeldt 2007, 52.
57 Also according to Rohe 2009a, 101.
58 Cf. also Ballard 2006, 50.
59 Ballard 2006, 51.

There is always a question as to who would decide which particular appreciation of Islamic law would be applicable in a particular case.[60] There is certainly a danger that conservative members of communities, when endowed with authority, would claim the right to dictate which interpretation was correct. For England there is empirical evidence that women often have to struggle against the prevalence of conservative attitudes endemic within the *sharia* councils.[61] Moreover, the pitfalls which could result from inadequate guarantees of due process, of control, independence, transparency, representativeness and democratic legitimacy are real enough.

Finally, unlike the decision which the private international law systems of various European countries have made to subject foreign nationals – as far as family-law matters are concerned – to the law of their country of nationality, a pluralistic system of personal status law would not refer to the law of other countries but would effectively mean resorting to classical interpretations of Islamic law. However, in the Arab and Islamic countries, these classical interpretations, which were consolidated in the ninth or tenth century, have since seen significant further development. To what extent that further development would be taken into account under a pluralistic system remains unclear.[62]

Coherence and cohesion under threat

Second, pluralistic family-law structures pose a threat to social coherence and cohesion. The threat they pose in this respect is significantly greater than the one arising from the principle of nationality as a connecting factor common in conflict-of-laws discourse. This is because the pluralistic solutions envisaged, for example, by parts of the Muslim communities in England involve both the jurisdictions and the legal procedures concerned following rules of their own. Poulter describes the situation in England as follows:

> While English law should broadly approach other cultures in a charitable spirit of tolerance and, when in doubt, lean in favour of affording members of ethnic minority communities freedom to observe their diverse traditions here, there will inevitably be certain key areas where minimum standards, derived from shared core values, must of necessity be maintained, if the cohesiveness and unity of English society as a whole is to be preserved intact.[63]

Legal unity acts as a historically contingent dogmatic construction of the modern nation-state, it is predicated on the existence of a 'we' who either are able, or should be able, to encompass itself around cultural plurality.[64] A democratic and

60 Cf. also Poulter 1998, 211.
61 Cf. Bano 2007, 53.
62 Cf. also Poulter 1990, 158.
63 Poulter 1998, 391. For a critical discussion, see Menski 2006, 21.
64 Cf. Hicks 1991, 216.

secular society depends on a shared awareness and understanding of the law. Any pluralistic legal structures incorporating a variety of personal status laws would therefore have the effect of strengthening, sustaining and stabilising segregated community structures within society at large.

In *Refah Partisi v. Turkey*, a case brought as a result of the prohibition of one of Turkey's leading political parties, the European Court of Human Rights' argument – which admittedly oversimplified the issues at stake somewhat – was that legal pluralism was at odds with secularism, equality and democracy. The Court therefore decided that the dissolution of the party did not violate the European Convention on Human Rights. The *Refah Partisi* party's manifesto encompassed the introduction of legal pluralism. The Court held the *sharia* to be contradictory to fundamental democratic principles and stated that a secular state should confine religions to the sphere of private religious practice.[65]

All European countries are based on state-centred and centralist concepts of law. The nation-state as 'the state of and for one nation'[66] is a modern phenomenon. One of its core elements is the unity of the legal order.[67] This incorporates the idea that the state has exclusive legislative competence and that everyone is subject to the same law. While delegation of legislative competence to religious bodies in key areas which are central to the very structure of society is at odds with this idea, this objection does not apply to the provision of a wide range of possible legal constructs or the recognition, for example, of different forms of marriage ceremony, including religious ones.

The concepts of the secular state and the separation of powers are both arguments which are being advanced as objections to legal pluralism to this day. Indeed, a neutral state is not necessarily one which bans all affirmation of religious belonging and faith, and there are many different ways to reconcile the right to freedom of religion with the secular constitutional state. Nevertheless, the normative content of the legal order of European nations is largely secular, even if it is clearly linked to specific sets of values. The state cannot identify itself with any particular religion, it has to be impartial. Moreover, state policy and action should be based on reason and not be informed by religion. In a free and pluralistic society, a secular legal system – itself the product of a long and conflictual development process – forms the basis on which people live together.[68] A particular attribute

---

65 *Refah Partisi (The Welfare Party) and Others v. Turkey*, ECHR, Judgment of 31 July 2001, (Applications nos. 41340/98, 41342/98, 41343/98 and 41344/98), note 72; *Refah Partisi (The Welfare Party) and Others v. Turkey*, ECHR Grand Chamber, Judgment of 13 February 2003, (Applications nos. 41340/98, 41342/98, 41343/98 and 41344/98), notes 120 *et seq.*

66 Töpperwien 2001, 1.

67 For a portrait of the rich legal pluralism in medieval times and a description of how this pluralism was reduced as the state consolidated its power, see Tamanaha 2008, 377.

68 Cf. Bielefeldt 2007, 75, in particular 80.

of secularity, however, is that the spheres of the law, of politics, of science and of religion are differentiated. Of course, there are differing concepts of nationhood and different forms of self-description, and these themselves embody more or less cultural diversity and are either more ethnic or more civic in emphasis.[69] Nevertheless, the emergence of nation-states in Europe was closely linked with the splits between Christians of different doctrines, particularly since it was these very divisions which gradually deprived the political authorities of religion as a source of legitimacy, so that the secular state then had to legitimise itself on other grounds.[70]

Legal certainty, due process and the rule of law are also central attributes of today's European legal orders. The simultaneous existence of different family-law codes would create legal grey areas and could well impinge significantly on the legal order. Such pluralism puts into question the ties linking the state to law and justice. By being identified with a number of different legal orders, the state sees its authority undermined, because it leaves its citizens in doubt as to which course of ethical and legal conduct they are expected to follow. That is why the state is rightly expected to pursue an unambiguously identifiable law ethic.[71]

The Dangers of Collective Rights

Finally, pluralistic legal structures differ from observance of cultural identity based on the interpretation and concretisation of a unified substantive family law in that they are founded on the application of different law codes to different ascriptive groups, groups whose membership is not open-ended but mainly defined by religious or cultural affiliation, and in that these groups are then attuned to group-specific legal rules. Any discussion of collective or group rights in family law will inevitably give rise to numerous conceptual problems. Indeed, economic and political rights, but also property matters such as land rights, would need to be assessed separately since they pose different issues.

---

69 Cf. Töpperwien 2001, 42. He makes the distinction between the ethnic definitions of a nation, according to which a community is based on common descent or culture, and the civic definitions, according to which a nation is regarded as being a sovereign people (*demos*) living under a common political institution. The German national identity is based mainly on a shared culture and ethnicity. France, conversely, is a civic nation.

70 Cf. Habermas 1996, 135. Switzerland, for example, maintained systems of family law based on religious belief into the nineteenth century. At that time, the Confederation exerted regulation only over marriages and divorces involving couples of different Christian churches (through the Federal law on mixed marriages of 3 December 1850 and the Federal law of 3 February 1862, which made it possible for the Federal Court to pronounce the dissolution through divorce of mixed marriages in cantons where divorce was not possible). The Civil Code and its unifying civil family law came into force in 1912.

71 Cf. Bielefeldt 2007, 67 and 94.

Individual versus collective rights

To this day, the prevailing concept of human rights is – quite properly – one based on the rights of the individual. Moreover, rights in private law generally guarantee individual autonomy, choices and freedom of action. They are also essentially framed as legal positions of the individual. While it is true that the right to respect for family life does also have a relational aspect, it is still the right of each member of the family to choose their approach to family life, and international instruments phrase the right to family life as an individual's right. This is becoming increasingly important as family-law institutions themselves lose both credibility and authority. Likewise, recognition of cultural and religious identities and traditions comes from individual people themselves upholding and living by those traditions, not from those individuals merely belonging to a particular group. Recognition is owed not to a cultural tradition which needs protection, but to those people who observe that tradition or – as the case may be – no longer wish to do so. Both have a legitimate right to develop and change their identity, and group identity must remain a choice, an acquisition and not be an ontological imposition.[72]

What can certainly be said is that a more culturally aware interpretation of the rights of the individual is clearly preferable to an institutional representation and stereotyping of group identities.

The burden on the vulnerable

One crucial question concerns the position of individuals within protected minorities vis-à-vis their particular group, and the impact which the protection of religious and cultural minorities has on women. Traditional family-law systems often discriminate against women, and religious communities espouse practices which treat men and women differently, notably by depriving women of access to resources and family-law institutions. Particular religious groups may prize group obedience over individual autonomy. In fact, the recognition of collective rights can give rise to the 'paradox of multicultural vulnerability' described by Ayelet Shachar and often cited in Anglo-American discourse. In Shachar's words:

> well-meaning accommodation by the state may leave members of minority groups vulnerable to severe injustice within the group, and may, in effect, work to reinforce some of the most hierarchical elements of culture. I call this phenomenon the paradox of multicultural vulnerability. By this term I mean to call attention to the ironic fact that individuals inside the group can be injured by the very reforms that are designed to promote their status as group members in the accommodating, multicultural state.[73]

This paradox therefore states that the granting of group rights reinforces the structure of order within the family, with authoritarian structures within a

72 Cf. Bielefeldt 2007, 69.

73 Shachar 2001, 3, and specifically to matters relating to family law, 45.

community thus strengthening their hold, rather than having it dismantled. It is those whose position in a culturally motivated hierarchy is most vulnerable, especially women and children, who bear most of the burden of multicultural accommodation. The liberal political scholar Will Kymlicka[74] rightly argues that the aim of minority rights is to provide minority groups with external protections and to reduce their vulnerability to the economic and political power of wider society, not to afford protection to minorities so that they can then impose internal restrictions on their members in the name of tradition and cultural integrity. This argument has merit, since the protection of the context of life and the experience which goes to form cultural identity is not an end in itself, but serves the interests of the individual.[75] It is certainly true that a system of group-specific laws in family-law matters would make it even harder for women and children to maintain the equality of rights which international law guarantees. They would be worse off if their communities were accommodated by the state in this way, and it would be more difficult for vulnerable members of a group to assert their rights and for liberal institutions to alleviate oppressive traditions in their communities. Shachar is also right to conjure up the 'familiar specter of using family law as a tool for forcing a homogenizing and often conservative interpretation of what "loyalty" to the group requires, which is here defined in deeply gendered terms that revolve around women's roles as wives and mothers'.[76]

Private and public spheres

Discourse on the degree of cultural autonomy in the realm of family law regularly centres on where the line is drawn in the dichotomy between the private and the public sphere. In a legally pluralistic system of family law favouring group autonomy, the private sphere of the individual and that of the group are concentric – in the sense that individual rights are subsumed within those of the collective group. The often-stated argument that this need not be a major concern – provided that there is a right to exit, a right to turn away from cultural imperatives[77] – effectively places the burden of the conflict between group affiliation and personal freedom on the individual concerned. The very identity of each individual, however, has itself been formed through that individual's belonging to his or her community. Moreover, the individual in such cases often lacks the resources, equal access to the law and the freedom of subjective action which he or she would need in order

74 Kymlicka 1995, in particular 34. Kymlicka distinguishes between permissible external protection, for example the rights of a group to limit the economic and political power which the majority society exerts over them, and non-permissible internal restrictions, for example the rights of a group to limit the freedom of its members in the name of group solidarity or cultural affinity. For a critical assessment of this distinction, see Shachar 2001, 18.

75 Cf. Habermas 1993, 173.

76 Shachar 2007, 140.

77 Cf. Reitman 2005, 189.

to leave his or her community behind, particularly in a repressive environment, and he or she may therefore be compelled to use community-oriented privatised forums to resolve family disputes – as is apparent from numerous accounts of how marriages have come about. This is all the more true as autonomous group structures for their part can have the effect of consolidating oppressive family regimes. Individuals do not generally choose their religious affiliation, and the costs of choosing to abandon one's religious community or one's family can be very high. Indeed, a focus on exit can even worsen the situation of a vulnerable person since oppressive behaviour towards that person may be seen as ultimately being that person's choice, given that he or she has the option of leaving.[78] Effectively, therefore, the autonomy of the group results in its vulnerable members being left to fend for themselves.

Human rights at stake

A last but central objection to group-specific systems of family law relates to the content of such family law. That numerous aspects and interpretations of classical Islamic family law – though not of Islam *per se* – are incompatible with the constitutional and human rights upheld by European legal orders is not in dispute.[79] This applies, in particular, to the inequality of access granted to men and women with regard to certain family-law institutions such as polygamy, divorce and child custody. It also applies to the differences in the rights and duties of men and women in marriage, and to differences in the minimum marriageable age. One notable consequence of this is that those Islamic and Arab states which have ratified the Convention on the Elimination of All Forms of Discrimination against Women have entered reservations to article 16, which guarantees equality between the sexes in all matters relating to marriage and family relations.[80] In the Islamic legal tradition the dominant view is one of equal worth and equal dignity of men and women, most prominently in issues of moral and spiritual obligations towards God (*'ibadat*), but not one of identical positions and rights and duties in the social sphere (*mu'amalat*).[81] Conversely, it is a central and defining attribute of European societies, even if only a recent one, that men and women are seen not only as complementary and of equal value, but also that they are assured of equal positions and status in family-law matters. Nevertheless, tangible gender equality

78 The case is therefore sometimes made for a kind of 'reverse optionality', under which people are required explicitly to choose group law, with state law applying by default unless this explicit choice is made, cf. Mahajan 2005, 106.

79 The legal developments in different Arabic and Islamic countries and the diversity of views within and between those countries show that Islam and gender equality are not two fundamentally irreconcilable concepts. Indeed, as far as the status of women is concerned, rigidity and conservatism are dominant at the moment. Cf. Yahyaoui Krivenko 2009, 56.

80 Cf. also Poulter 1990, 159; Yahyaoui Krivenko 2009, 130.

81 Ali 2000, 37, with reference.

cannot yet be described as having been fully achieved – either in the Islamic world or in Europe.

The duty of the state to guarantee human rights prohibits it from relinquishing its authority over any central area over which it legislates. The European Court of Human Rights said in *Refah Partisi v. Turkey*:

> It is difficult to declare one's respect for democracy and human rights while at the same time supporting a regime based on *sharia*, which clearly diverges from Convention values, particularly with regard to its criminal law and criminal procedure, its rules on the legal status of women and the way it intervenes in all spheres of private and public life in accordance with religious precepts.[82]

Even if the essence of this statement is correct and justified, it should also be noted that the court is adopting a highly reductionist and misguided view of Islamic law, effectively portraying it as a self-contained, bound and unified construct, and thus not taking its diversity, dynamism and contextual attributes properly into account.

82 *Refah Partisi (The Welfare Party) and Others v. Turkey*, ECHR, Judgment of 31 July 2001, (Applications nos. 41340/98, 41342/98, 41343/98 and 41344/98, note 72). This judgment was then reviewed by the ECHR's Grand Chamber, which reached its decision on 13 February 2003. Cf. *Refah Refah Partisi (The Welfare Party) and Others v. Turkey*, ECHR Grand Chamber, Judgment of 13 February 2003, (Applications nos. 41340/98, 41342/98, 41343/98 and 41344/98).

Chapter 5
Beyond Cultural and Religious Identities: Introducing Discourse Ethics and Procedure to Family-Law Contexts

The Practice of Thinking in Discourses and Procedures

Parallel, religious-community-based systems of family law are not a realistic or desirable prospect for Europe. Nevertheless, simply ignoring existing patterns of normative pluralism is not a viable long-term approach either. The context-insensitive imposition of so-called civil family law in all realms of family life and the rejection of any form of culturally based variations in legal practice often leaves people, especially women, facing an unfair choice between their rights and their culture. Moreover, completely ignoring existing normative pluralism or the actual practice of family law which is current in certain communities today has the potential of both reinforcing existing informal, community-based procedures and of making them even less visible, often to the detriment of the most vulnerable.[1]

Resolving the culture-versus-rights conundrum requires an approach combining cultural and individual autonomy in the private sphere. 'Protecting choice, promoting inclusion'[2] must be the goal, reconciling the protection of cultural identity and autonomy on the one hand with the advancement of social and legal inclusion on the other hand.

This represents the final clue. The trail leads us away from thinking based on regulatory policy and institutions towards a view in which discourse and process play the key roles, the insight being that different family-law rationalities all exert their own normative authority, and that these influences cannot be reconciled simply by the application of a culturally sensitive interpretation of substantive family law. What is required instead is a system of family law with the potential to accommodate diversity.

The challenge is twofold. On the one hand, an appropriate theoretical framework has to be formulated. On the other hand, various legal institutions in the context of European family-law systems have to be reshaped. The following thoughts are mere outlines. They are an attempt to find solutions both *de lege lata*, using the legal framework in place, and *de lege ferenda*, with possible future initiatives and

---

1 Cf. Bader 2009, 52.

2 Boyd 2004.

the parameters of an integrative system of family law being outlined as a response to the tasks facing family law today.

Objectives and Theory

The objective of thinking about family law in discourses and procedures is to embrace openly the multiplicity of family-law discourses, with a view to directing these towards mutual understanding and consensus as set out in Habermas's discourse ethics.[3] In the field of family-law decisions, such thinking aims to provide the autonomous, culturally contextualised genesis of this multifarious discourse with a legitimating framework in which procedure holds its rightful place.

In principle, the approach based on discourse theory includes the trivial yet momentous observation that there is no such thing as a supra-cultural standpoint, that every opinion represents a portion of truth[4] and that, given the equivalence of every statement, as Taylor argues in his 'Politics of Recognition',[5] what should be sought is a shared compendium of family-law values. In contrast to genuinely pluralistic legal structures, what is needed here is some form of 'we' with the capacity to embrace and be embraced by plurality. A proceduralised and discursive approach to diversity in matters of family law will, of course, necessarily require a structure within which the different concrete issues arising can be systematically and coherently addressed.

Discourse

Discourses are a special type of argumentation situation.[6] Dialogue is central to any discourse theory. Appropriate actions are based on the deliberations of a number of individual discourse participants, with the various participants engaging in an unconstrained search for that which is right for all concerned, supporting consensus, yet recognising that that very consensus may always be modified as new arguments are advanced. Discourse as a rational concept thus seeks to gain insight from the deliberations of individuals arguing with each other in ideal circumstances. The 'truth' of the insights gained in this manner derives from the fact that the individuals involved are completely free from subjugation of any kind in the arguments they advance and that all are committed to the result that their deliberations eventually achieve, since it is the outcome of a process of free and reasoned deliberation among individuals. A further prerequisite for such discourse to succeed is that all those participating must do so on the same, equal footing and all must recognise human rights. The rationale for discourse is thus the practical insight or conclusion which is reached after the arguments of the various participants in a discussion have been heard and it is marked by a consensus

3 Habermas 1983, 53.

4 Cf. Glenn 1991, 213.

5 Taylor 1992, *passim*.

6 See Habermas 1985, 39.

between the participants.[7] Free discourse requires that its participants be free from constraint, free from subjugation, informed about the matters being discussed and committed to substantiating the arguments they put forward.[8] Autonomy and universality are both inherent to discourse theory.

Discourse-theory considerations may be applied for several normative purposes, both with regard to the way in which norms are substantiated and applied.[9] However, in the interests of each individual's freedom to determine his or her living arrangements, any family-law norms which are promulgated should serve, first and foremost, to protect the individual and ensure his or her autonomy. While the freedom to argue any case – which is itself so central to discourse ethics – is of particular significance where personal autonomy is concerned, it is nevertheless restricted by the laws currently in force. In a setting determined by the principles of discourse ethics, preliminaries, self-conceptions, lived expectations – all of which constitute a possible basis for substantive agreements – are all subject to discussion. This process should not be confused with bargaining based on individual narrow interests with a view to negotiating concrete contractual provisions. Discourse does, however, require participants to disclose their interests openly and to state and assert their positions.

It is, of course, quite possible that arguments which refer to culture will have a part to play in any consensus arrived at through discourse. Indeed this contributes to the strength and openness of deliberative models, since it is through the institutions of civil society that possible cultural objections can be voiced.[10] The discursive process provides a framework within which cultural stereotypes, expectations and projections can be openly declared, critically examined and subjected to new understanding. Discourse is a stage on which cultural notions and self-conceptions can be negotiated, mediated and ultimately modified.

Procedure

Proceduralisation is a more recent legal paradigm. Procedural theories of justice seek to substantiate justice on the basis of procedural considerations. As far as cultural identity and family law are concerned, it is of particular importance that procedural justice – and thus its correctness – is not prejudiced in any way by any prior assumptions. It does not, in other words, start from the premise of any

7 Tschentscher 2000, 101.

8 For a detailed review of the rules of discourse, see Tschentscher 2000, 222.

9 Habermas 1991, 138, for an alternative view, see Tschentscher 2000, 222.

10 For a groundbreaking discussion of this, see Benhabib 2002, 105. The deliberative model she proposes is based on the following theoretical commitments: 'The discourse theory of ethics; the dialogic and narrative constitution of the self; and the view of discourses as deliberative practices that center not only on norms of action and interaction, but also on negotiating situationally shared understandings across multicultural divides.' Benhabib 2002, 16.

particular religion, sense of status, tradition, assigned gender roles, cultural identity or any other social categories. A cardinal principle of procedural justice is that it is entirely unbiased in its content. In contrast to substantive justice, procedural justice thus represents justice of outcome, arrived at through procedures which serve to promote justice. Its outcome may be arrived at through agreement, or, in the absence of unanimity, through a decision made by a qualified authority. In the context of family law it is, of course, generally the case that feelings, shared history, responsibility and guilt run counter to disengaged rationality.[11]

In the context of family law, various forms of dispute resolution process have an important part to play in matters subject to autonomous regulation. It follows that these processes are of critical importance when it comes to negotiating cultural identity and incorporating different or foreign legal concepts and understandings. Glenn is right in observing:

> It thus becomes evident why the continuing, open use of foreign sources is one most closely associated with the dispute resolution process and not with affirmative forms of law-making. In refusing to decide that a given law is better than another an adjudicator refuses to generalize the effect of a decision he or she is required to make. The decision therefore addresses the particularities of the case to be decided, calling upon laws in the measure that they speak to the particularities of individual cases. Legal modesty is an essential element in the process. It is a modesty, however, which presupposes a perspective beyond that of any particular law or policy. It is a fundamentally immodest modesty – one which takes as possible the 'view from nowhere', the ability to abstract oneself from the turmoil of human endeavour and intelligently accomplish precise and useful tasks. Since the process of informal, non-functional reception is thus closely associated with dispute resolution, it is evident why it is so largely practiced in the world. Disputes continue to be the primary preoccupation of law, and their individual resolution is tolerant in the extreme of multiple sources of law. Multiple sources of law are opposed by those seeking to establish uniform policies, in other words seeking to establish the privacy of their own source of law. Effective dispute resolution is one which, however, takes no source of law as necessarily given, and no source of law as necessarily excluded.[12]

Thus a variety of dispute resolution processes provides a framework within which foreign legal concepts and understandings can be negotiated, since it is the parties involved in each case who will bring the norms to be applied with them and these norms will be characterised and supported by specific ideas, expectations and convictions.

---

11 Regarding the legal paradigm of proceduralisation cf. Tschentscher 2000, 245. Cf. also Taylor 1994, 262, who discusses the concept of disengaged rationality (in German, 'desengagierte Vernunft') which is part of Descartes' ethics.

12 Glenn 1991, 213.

Frameworks

This general theory and the important role it assigns to discourse and procedure not only implies, but also requires, both an external and an internal framework. The outer framework is concerned with the limits which should be imposed upon an individual's freedom to pursue his or her own religious and cultural convictions in family matters. The internal framework, for its part, addresses the question of what tasks family law has today. Of course, the limitations which both frameworks place on individual autonomy are closely interwoven. Their common purpose is to provide answers to the question as to the extent to which family law in European countries should allow culturally or religiously informed understandings and beliefs to be taken into account.

The Outer Framework: Human Rights and Constitutions

Human rights are integral to modern social orders and it is incumbent on those orders to uphold them. Although they are the result of a long history of learning, and of conflictual processes which societies have gone through, they must always be defended and negotiated anew. Moreover, because they serve to ensure that the dignity and freedom of every individual is acknowledged, they must also respect plurality within society and it is for this reason that their formulation will necessarily always be unfinished.[13] It is also true that the idea of universalism, itself closely linked to the concept of human rights, is constantly open to the criticism that it is ethnocentric.[14] Such criticism is often rooted in false generalisations about European and other cultures, in the misconception that each culture has its own homogeneous and uniform cultural identity and that its value systems are cohesive.[15] 'Cultures' are, however, plural within themselves. Moreover, human rights – as the outer framework of cultural and religious autonomy in the realm of family law – should be seen as normative claims and not as metaphysical imperatives. It is also true that as international conventions become ever more

13 Cf. Bielefeldt 2007, 48.

14 Ballard 2009, 325 raises the following objection, which deserves serious consideration: 'It is not my purpose to dismiss the utility of a discourse of human rights per se. My concerns … are threefold. Firstly to emphasize the profoundly emic character of the conceptual foundations of the current discourse; secondly to highlight the ease with which its non-universalistic deficiencies can be utilized as a means of doing injustice to those whose behavioural and conceptual premises are out of step with those underpinning Europe's Judaeo-Christian Enlightenment; and thirdly to underline how such alleged moral deficiencies are once again being used for hegemonic purposes: namely to de-legitimize, and in some instances actively criminalize, the familial strategies deployed by entrepreneurially minded migrants seeking to challenge established patterns of Euro-American privilege by engaging in strategies of globalization from below.

15 Cf. Benhabib 2002, 24.

numerous and more detailed,[16] they show an increasing convergence in values, and it is these conventions – as expressions of the horizon to the meaning of humanity – which provide the outer framework for cultural autonomy and plurality in family life. They therefore place limitations on so-called cultural rights: that is, on practices which are argued for primarily on the basis of cultural traditions.[17] The self-determination and equality which are understood as interdependent values are central here. They transcend the secular/religious dichotomy.

The European Convention on Human Rights of 4 November 1950, including its Protocols, the United Nations International Covenant on Civil and Political Rights and the United Nations International Covenant on Economic, Social and Cultural Rights, both of 16 December 1966, the United Nations Convention on the Rights of the Child of 20 November 1989, the United Nations Convention on Consent to Marriage, Minimum Age for Marriage and Registration of Marriages of 7 November 1962, the United Nations Convention on the Elimination of All Forms of Discrimination against Women of 18 December 1979 and the European Social Charter of 18 October 1961 all guarantee a number of individual rights. They represent the hard core of public policy in European countries. Family-law practices which would run counter to human rights provisions, and thus violate the rights of an individual which are protected by international law, cannot be recognised or accepted, not even if they are supported by recourse to claims of religious or cultural identity. Examples of such practices are forced marriage and female genital mutilation, neither of which, incidentally, is advocated by Islam.

An important international instrument in this regard is the one on the Elimination of all forms of Discrimination against Women adopted in 1979.[18] The convention is very adamant in its focus on strictly equal rights for men and women in family law. Article 16 is the most controversial article of the CEDAW and is considered to be a 'breakthrough in the area of human rights'.[19] It states:

> States parties shall take all appropriate measures to eliminate discrimination against women in all matters relating to marriage and family relations and in

16 Admittedly, the very density of human rights is itself a problem. So-called third-generation human rights contain far-reaching powers which either call their universality into question or at least give rise to some doubts about their content and scope.

17 For a fundamental analysis, see Poulter 1987, 598; for an extensive review, Poulter 1998, 68; a critical appraisal of this position can be found in Shah 2005, with further criticism on 16 and 54; Renteln 2004, 215. Her strongest argument is that the right to cultural identity itself has a number of the attributes of a human right, thus necessarily requiring that interests and rights be assessed and balanced in any case. Renteln draws the boundaries of cultural rights at the point where 'irreparable physical harm' is caused, though she concedes that 'there is no one analytic framework which is capable of solving all rights conflicts'. Renteln 2004, 218.

18 For a detailed discussion of the Convention, see Yahyaoui Krivenko 2009, 21.

19 Yahyaoui Krivenko 2009, 38.

> particular shall ensure, on a basis of equality of men and women: (a) The same right to enter into marriage; (b) The same right freely to choose a spouse and to enter into marriage only with their free and full consent; (c) The same rights and responsibilities during marriage and at its dissolution; (d) The same rights and responsibilities as parents, irrespective of their marital status, in matters relating to their children; in all cases the interests of the children shall be paramount; (e) The same rights to decide freely and responsibly on the number and spacing of their children and to have access to the information, education and means to enable them to exercise these rights; (f) The same rights and responsibilities with regard to guardianship, wardship, trusteeship and adoption of children, or similar institutions where these concepts exist in national legislation; in all cases the interests of the children shall be paramount; (g) The same personal rights as husband and wife, including the right to choose a family name, a profession and an occupation; (h) The same rights for both spouses in respect of the ownership, acquisition, management, administration, enjoyment and disposition of property, whether free of charge or for a valuable consideration.[20]

This means that the legal framework of countries which are signatories to this Convention must ensure that men and women have equal access to such family-law institutions as marriage, divorce and custody. A clear, and in my opinion over-zealous position in this regard is taken by the Council of Europe in its 'Women and Religion in Europe' resolution, which, among other things, calls on the member states generally to refuse to recognise foreign family codes and personal status laws based on religious principles which violate women's rights.[21]

As far as matters of family law are concerned, it is in fact regularly asserted that Islamic law is incompatible with the principle of equal rights for both sexes which is fundamental to human rights doctrine. As a matter of fact, Arab states which are signatories to the CEDAW have taken the opportunity to enter reservations to the articles of the Convention most relevant to marriage matters on the grounds of incompatibility with religion.[22] Classical interpretations of Islamic family law are based on the idea of a gender-segregated society in which specific roles are assigned to men and women,[23] as indeed was also the case in

20 Cf. also Council of Europe, Protocol No. 7 to the Convention for the Protection of Human Rights and Fundamental Freedoms (1984), article 5: 'Equality between spouses. Spouses shall enjoy equality of rights and responsibilities of a private law character between them, and in their relations with their children, as to marriage, during marriage and in the event of its dissolution. This Article shall not prevent States from taking such measures as are necessary in the interests of the children.' Finally, see also Council of Europe, Equality of Spouses in Civil Law (1978), which deals with the marital relationship in greater detail.

21 Council of Europe, Women and Religion in Europe (2005), article 7.1.2.

22 Cf. Tucker 2008, 80; Poulter 1987, 219; extensively Yahyaoui Krivenko 2009, 115.

23 Cf. Tucker 2008, 24 and 50.

Europe until comparatively recently. Classical interpretations of Islamic law grant ultimate authority and decision-making power to the husband and to the male members of a family. The respective roles of men and women are conceived of as being complementary. Egypt, for example, has registered reservations to articles 15 and 16 of the CEDAW refusing to accept formal equality between the sexes in family law and defending specific rights and duties for men and women. It argued that *mahr* under Islamic law and maintenance for the wife would institute 'an equivalency of rights and duties so as to ensure complementarity which guarantees true equality between spouses'.[24] It is of course true that the conditions actually prevailing in these countries are changing, with smaller family structures and women's participation in the workforce gradually replacing larger family groups, and these developments have certainly influenced family law in these countries.

The Islamic law institutions of *talaq* and polygamy pose particular challenges as far as equal rights between the sexes are concerned. Clearly, any legislation or legal practice which grants privileges to the husband in matters relating to marriage and divorce will infringe against the principle of equal rights for men and women, since it denies equal access to family-law institutions, and thus equality before the law.[25] This issue should not, however, be confused with the question as to the extent to which rituals such as *talaq* or the relationships between spouses in cases of polygamy generate legal consequences when it is not in fact the applicable law or its interpretation which maintains a traditional understanding of these institutions and which determines that only one of the sexes, namely men, do and can avail themselves of these practices, but rather that they are simply a product of their cultural context.

Talaq is deeply rooted in Islamic legal understanding. While it is certainly true that no legal effects can be generated by the *talaq* directly, the pronouncement of a *talaq* can nevertheless be taken into consideration in gender-neutral divorce law and legal practice. Similarly, polygamy, as a man's institutional right to enter into marriage with several women, cannot produce any direct legal effect. However, within the framework of a system of family law in which legal consequences do not derive from the institution of marriage itself but are instead functionally linked to the sharing of duties or to common children, legal outcomes cannot depend on the number of people with whom such relationships exist. Indeed, even in the context of the current law in European countries, it could be argued that second marriages constitute non-marital cohabitation, which in many legislations does have certain legal consequences.[26]

---

24 Cited in Yahyaoui Krivenko 2009, 139, footnote 446.

25 For detailed discussion, see Poulter 1987, 217.

26 Unlike other common law countries, England neither accords a particular legal status to cohabitation nor does it recognise 'common law marriage'. Nevertheless, in some legal contexts, cohabitation can result in the same treatment as that accorded to married couples. See the Law Commission, Cohabitation: The Financial Consequences of Relationship Breakdown (2007), 149, 164 and 174. In France, the PACS (pacte civil de

It can thus be seen that gender equality in law does not in fact prevent the expectations placed on traditional gender roles from being fulfilled. Autonomous decisions should be respected and agency recognised. Systematically unequal choices between men and women, however, largely derive from the gender regimes under which both sexes live and which create the backdrop of what seems possible and reasonable, rather than resulting from actual cultural coercion.[27] In this context it should not be forgotten that European states are obliged by international law to take appropriate steps to ensure equality of rights and responsibilities of spouses as to marriage, during marriage and at its dissolution.[28] The objective here is not only a law which treats both sexes equally, but also to ensure that equal rights for both sexes become part and parcel of everyday life – something which has not yet been achieved in Europe either. The concepts of gender equality enshrined in the constitutions of many European countries are comparatively recent phenomena and their everyday implementation in current legal practice still exhibits considerable gender stereotyping, with husband and wife often fulfilling the roles in family life traditionally ascribed to their gender.

Currently, although the general human rights instruments do not explicitly state that polygamy is unlawful, comments and recommendations clearly indicate that marriage must be monogamous, with a view to protecting vulnerable women.[29]

Finally, it is important to ensure that, by defining human rights as the outer framework, an inclusive perspective is being offered, in which shared values exist beyond cultural designations, in other words that human rights can meaningfully and productively be connected with different traditions.[30] Adopting this point of view does, however, require that human rights be immune from cultural appropriation, rather than being perceived as an exclusively Western concept and legacy.[31] This is a prerequisite for human rights to be fully recognised and accepted as inherent to culturally plural societies. Numerous approaches in Islamic studies support the compatibility of Islamic law with human rights principles, not least by stressing the philosophical foundation of the concept of human rights in the tradition of

solidarité), which gives a specific legal status to same sex-couples and couples of different sexes, requires formal registration (article 515–3 para. 4 of the Code Civil). See Bosse-Platière 2010a and Bosse-Platière 2010b. For examples of specific legal frameworks for non-married heterosexual couples, see New Zealand, Saskatchewan (Canada) or Sweden.

27 Regarding the significance of differentiating between choice and coercion, cf. also Phillips 2007, *passim*, in particular 37.

28 Article 23, para. 4 of the International Covenant on Civil and Political Rights GA Res. 2200 (XXI), UN GAOR, 21st Sess., Supp. No. 16, 52, UN Doc. A/6316 (1966).

29 Cf. article 14 of the General Recommendation 21: Equality in Marriage and Family Relations, UN GAOR, 1994, Doc. no A/47/38 (13th session, 1994); and the Human Rights Committee, General Comment 28: Equality of Rights between Men and Women (article 3), UN Doc. CCPR/C/21/Rev.1/ Add.10 (29 March 2000), article 24.

30 See, for example, Baderin 2005, 10.

31 For extensive discussion, see Bielefeldt 2007, 43.

Islam and advocating Islam's return to truly and purely religious questions and its abandonment of the quest for dominance over matters of law.[32]

One of the purposes of the constitutions of European states is to substantiate human rights on the national level. In so doing they create the common framework necessary to a pluralistic society. In no sense does that mean, as is frequently suggested, that they represent a systematic antithesis to *sharia*.

Internal Framework: Scope and Tasks of Family Law Today

The internal framework of autonomy in family law has to focus on the question of what tasks family law has, or still has, today. In a liberal society, the question as to what should be subject to regulation by the law is effectively an issue of justice. The premise of individual autonomy should therefore be the starting point of any discussion.

Autonomy and contract

Autonomy means that each individual chooses and puts into effect his or her own conception of what is right and just. Contractual autonomy is a key principle of the private law codes of liberal societies and it plays a central role in family law as well. Both the premise and the objective of modern family-law systems are to ensure that individuals are afforded freedom in determining their familial relationships. Reforms to family law in Europe in recent decades demonstrate how views of the law's role have evolved. Nowadays it is barely possible for legal restrictions on the celebration of marriage, prescriptions regarding the internal structure of a marital relationship or sanctions on the dissolution of marriage to be justified on public interest grounds. This is the result of the process of de-institutionalisation and contractualisation of family law seen in recent decades.

For a long time the only legal ties holding families together were those resulting from marriage. The idea was that the family which a marriage brought forth constituted an order of greater significance than the individual and should therefore be particularly safeguarded. The protection afforded to marriage as an institution largely came into effect through laws on divorce, but also through other sources, such as laws on parentage and descent. Constructionist accounts of family law have unveiled and questioned how traditional legal discourse about the family privileges certain family forms and individual behaviours. In recent decades family concepts have been broadened, focusing less on the institution of marriage and more on the function of a family unit and the tasks its various members fulfil. The erosion of the importance attached to marital status is clearly evidenced by, for example, the laws on divorce, which in European countries now allow marriage to be dissolved by mutual consent and which also make it possible for a marriage to be terminated unilaterally by either party, usually after a specified

32 As an example, see An-Na'im 1992, *passim*, in particular 10, 170. Regarding modern hermeneutic interpretations of the Qur'an, cf. Büchler 2009, 200.

period of time has elapsed, though in Spain such terminations require virtually no prior separation period.[33] Marriage is also losing its monopoly position, as some legislations now provide for certain legal rights and obligations to arise for couples who are not married.[34] Marriage is thus ceasing to be either the sole point of reference for regulating intimate partnerships or the only framework in which they are conducted.

As the state and the law lose their authority to define which relationships should enjoy their protection and should therefore be regulated by them, the protective aspect of family law has gained in importance. As a matter of fact, if family law were reduced to affording protection, marriage itself would no longer play any particular part in it and the legal consequences of a partnership would no longer be linked to the institution of marriage itself, but rather to the roles and shared responsibilities and the exchange of goods and services which very often occur when a couple have children together.[35] A second aspect of this is that in the event of a couple separating, family law now ascribes greater importance to negotiated, self-determined solutions, accords sovereignty in interpretation to the parties and concerns itself with the process of separation. As a rule, the response of family law to growing differentiation within society tends to be one of generalisation. Provided they are sufficiently abstracted, generalised values have the potential to provide society with a degree of binding force which will embrace individual differentiation and thus exert a certain integrating influence.[36]

---

33 For Switzerland: article 111 *et seq.*, ZGB (divorce by mutual consent possible at any time; divorce based on sole petition by one spouse after two years of separation); for Spain: article 81 of the Código Civil (divorce at any time by mutual consent and at any time without the consent of the other spouse if the marriage lasted at least three months); for France: articles 229 *et seq.* of the Code Civil (essentially provides for divorce by mutual consent or after having lived separately for two years); for England: Matrimonial Causes Act 1973 (c. 18), section 1 (divorce as a result of irretrievable breakdown of the marriage as indicated by adultery, unreasonable behaviour, desertion lasting at least two years, separation of at least two years with the agreement of the parties or separation of at least five years irrespective of agreement); for Germany: sections 1565 *et seq.*, BGB (divorce by mutual consent after separation for one year, or on the sole petition of one spouse after a separation of three years).

34 See, for example, Catalan Act 1998 on Stable Unions of Couples (Ley 10/1998 de 15 de julio d'unions estables de parella) or the PACS in France, article 515–1 of the Code Civil.

35 A view also put forward in Schwenzer 2006. Schwenzer's model family code bases the legal consequences of a relationship between heterosexual or homosexual partners on a legally defined partnership. This partnership includes marriages and non-marital relationships if (a) they have lasted more than three years, (b) there is a common child, or (c) one or each of the partners has made substantial contributions to the relationship or in the sole interest of the other partner.

36 A view expressed in Romano 2005, 229, referring to Parsons's concept of values in a differentiated society.

Admittedly, contemporary developments are not always straightforward. They are often contradictory, disordered or incoherent, and the perception of the family as an institution is still present, in many places even prevalent. While legislation in European countries is certainly progressing along the lines set out above, a genuinely new approach to family law is still far away, and transformation processes are complex and contradictory. Family law is, after all, an arena in which people's emotions, social life and expectations are all played out.

Proposals aimed at systematically reducing family law solely to its protective function, in other words to pursuing de-institutionalisation to its logical conclusion, have, however, already been put forward. The Model Family Code proposed by Ingeborg Schwenzer is a notable example. In her introduction she describes the central tasks of modern family law as follows:

> The first is a principle of non-interference of the state with respect to private individuals, to the extent that they are able to cooperate with one another and regulate their own most intimate relations and the best interests of children are not endangered. It is not the task of the state to dictate to individuals how they are to live their lives, be it in a marital or non-marital relationship, be it heterosexual or homosexual lifestyle. This corresponds to the fundamental principle of party autonomy, found in private law in the concept of freedom of contract. However, it is, secondly, the task of family law to ensure that no person may escape responsibility for the type of life he or she is living. The emphasis must be on the actual life lived, rather than on an empty shell.[37]

The Model Code's greatest potential lies in this very reduction of family law to these central functions, since this is what lends it the openness to incorporate a multiplicity of culturally connotated expectations in the family-law arena.

Contractualisation of family law is an expression of the fact that people should shape both their relationship and its aftermath themselves. The rationality of the contract lies in the self-legitimating balance which results from the trade-off between individual interests which occurs in the course of negotiation, which is marked by the approval of both parties and which forms the basis for mutual commitment for the future. The 'rightness' of the result – in an intersubjective sense – derives from the fact that the contract is freely entered into by both parties.

Integrating Islamic perceptions of family law in the manner envisaged here is part of the de-institutionalisation and contractualisation of family law. The focus here is not on Islamic law *per se*, or indeed its institutions, rules and directives, but rather on the question of how much autonomy European family-law systems should accord to the individual parties. How areas of autonomy are used, or whether the solutions agreed have been negotiated by reference to Islamic principles and values, is not the key concern. Besides, every set of family arrangements and norms chosen by every person – and not only those classified as Islamic – necessarily

37 Schwenzer 2003, 3.

has cultural connotations, and is an expression of the religious, cultural or socio-political convictions of the parties concerned.

Protection

A purely contractual viewpoint may overlook hierarchical patterns, dependency and inequality in relationships. For that reason, such arrangements need to be juxtaposed with both substantive arguments and an element of contractual justice. A primary characteristic of family-law frameworks should therefore be their protective function.

When reduced to its protective role, family law can be seen as having two essential types of task.

As far as the economic aspect is concerned, the cardinal principle is that, in a partnership, tasks are shared out between the parties. This results in shared responsibilities and interdependencies between the partners. Family law in the economic arena should ensure that the principles of private law which go along with the autonomy of the parties are also accorded particular respect within the intimacy of a couple. Those principles include ensuring an equitable compensation for contributions to family life, equitable sharing of its burdens, ensuring that legitimate expectations which have been created by the relationship between partners are protected and met, and that protection is afforded to the economically weaker party. The equitable compensation for contributions to family life and the sharing of its burdens should include, as its starting point, the agreement of the parties to share paid and unpaid work between them, and ensure that the party carrying out unpaid work for the good of the partnership, and whose career opportunities may suffer as a result, is appropriately compensated. The focus is thus on balancing the benefits and costs resulting from the partnership both during the relationship and in its aftermath. Particularly when one partner takes sole charge of looking after the children from a partnership, equitable compensation is clearly owed also after the relationship ends and it is the duty of the other partner to ensure a balance by making a financial contribution to the children's care. In some cases it is also a matter of simple justice to protect the trust placed in a particular constellation of circumstances or a particular standard of living, particularly where a relationship has lasted a long time. Protecting the trust placed by each party in the other aims to ensure that legitimate expectations which have been created by the relationship between partners may be met.

In the personal sphere, it is the children whose need for the law's protection is greatest. Their integrity should be defended, their rights upheld and their network of relationships protected – irrespective of the status of their parents. That the primary task of family law is to protect the well-being of the child is not in dispute. First and foremost, family law must protect the physical and psychological integrity and development of children and provide for protective measures which must be put into effect when the parents are unable, or no longer able, to carry out their duty of bringing up their children, or when parents abuse their parental privileges. Second, it is a cardinal duty of family law to provide a legal framework for the multiplicity of relationships between children and adults – be they social, biological or genetic – and for that framework to cover both the origination and the effects of such relationships. Finally – and this is a more recent development – family law also has the task of protecting children's rights of participation, by ensuring that they have a legally enforceable right to be heard in all matters concerning them.

Support and safeguards

Despite a family law that can and should be reduced to dogmatically convincing principles and refrain from making any moral judgments, the ending of a relationship often results in personal pain, feelings of loss, disappointment, feelings of guilt, reproaches, grief and fear. Furthermore, where the relationship which has or will be terminated has produced children, it will nevertheless continue in a modified form. The emotional ramifications of family-law disputes are of particular relevance to procedural law and practice. Since it is desirable for substantive law to be free of any irrational baggage, it follows that procedural law should be able to concern itself fully with the emotional complexities arising in cases of family-law disputes. Furthermore, in view of the fact that certain aspects of the partnership, namely, in particular, those resulting from parenthood, will continue following separation, family law must be conceived of as an instrument for shaping the future family structure and family life.

As a result, the true core of family law is increasingly seen as supporting and helping the parties to use the freedom of action they enjoy responsibly and creatively. The way in which this support is structured and the nature of the dispute resolution process take many different forms. Even the *sharia* councils in England can provide assistance in these negotiations. What all the various available forms of advice, support and procedures have in common is that they leave the decisions relating to concrete questions and issues with the parties concerned.

To sum up, the primary tasks of the law of the state should be those of defining areas of autonomy, promulgating compulsory law and putting in place procedures, all of which serve to allow creative and fair consensus to be found. Procedure-based reference to family law aims to bring individual decision processes as close as possible to the ideal discourse situation, in which law evolves within the decision-making process and is the outcome of a procedure of free and reasoned deliberation among equal individuals. Legal procedures should be directed only marginally and subjected to minimal controls, but they should be organised, accompanied and safeguarded.

Issues and Projects

Numerous projects being carried out in various countries are testimony to the growing use of procedural and deliberative approaches in family law as a means of resolving conflicts resulting from references to culturally inspired norms.

Admittedly, these initiatives have not delivered concepts which are generally applicable, since the issues and dynamics involved, the historical ramifications and the cultural and legal circumstances are all too diverse. Perceptions and understandings of the boundaries between state control, individual autonomy and group authority also vary according to circumstance, location and culture. The following sections discuss both efforts made in Europe *de lege lata* (that means within the framework of the family-law institutions currently in place) as well as a number of *de lege ferenda* ideas with the potential to contribute towards achieving a system of family law which is attuned to the needs of a plural society.

Arbitration

An initiative of extensive procedural incorporation of alien, religious law has taken place in Canada, where, based on the Ontario *Arbitration Act*,[38] efforts have been made in that province to institutionalise arbitration courts which draw on the *sharia* as a transnational legal source and method of legal decision making in family-law matters. The idea is that the parties should be allowed to resolve family-law disputes outside the traditional court system. The initiative has been the object of exhaustive scientific and legal-policy discussion. A comprehensive review was positive in its assessment of family arbitration procedures also applying religious law, remarking that, 'The Review did not find any evidence to suggest that women are being systematically discriminated against as a result of arbitration of family-law issues. Therefore the Review supports the continued use of arbitration to resolve family-law matters.'[39] The review does, however, propose a number of protective measures. Specifically, these recommend granting authority to a court to overturn arbitration agreements in cases where these are not in the best interests of the child or where one of the parties had not received independent legal advice. The review also recommended that – in order to ensure that any choice to apply religious law is made with the full knowledge of all parties as to the consequences of that choice – the arbitrators should be appropriately qualified, the parties should receive independent legal advice, the processes employed should be transparent and the arbitrators should be granted certain powers. A final recommendation was that only arbitration agreements which are reached after the specific dispute they aim to resolve has arisen should be binding.[40] The authorisation of arbitration courts to issue judgments according to Islamic law principles did, however, attract vehement criticism.[41] One of the objections voiced was:

---

38 This also provided for family-law issues to be submitted to arbitration; regarding this, see Bader 2009, 59.

39 Cf. Boyd 2004, 133.

40 Cf. Boyd 2004, 109.

41 For a rejection of the Boyd report and arbitration in family-law matters applying religious law, see Bakht 2005, 56.

> While it is possible that a feminist interpretation of sharia law or an interpretation of Islam that incorporates international human-rights standards may result in arbitral awards that deal fairly with women, it is also feasible that under the current *Arbitration Act* a regressive interpretation of sharia will be used to seriously undermine the rights of women.[42]

A further objection was that private agreements, in which the state would not intervene, would tend to replicate both inequalities between the sexes and pre-existing distributions of authority and resources in the private sphere, thus potentially consolidating current power structures within individual communities and families. The critics thus argued that, while arbitration may be suitable in a commercial-law context, it was entirely inappropriate in family law, where gender dynamics, unequal power relations and discrimination are always a factor.[43]

The Canadian debate ultimately resulted in arbitration decisions based on the application of religious law being declared non-binding, and, as a result, Ontario's *Arbitration Act* was modified by the *Family Statute Law Amendment Act* of 2005. The potential which arrangements of this kind would have to ensure cultural autonomy in European countries, however, has yet to be fully investigated, since the assessment of the feasibility of arbitration in family-law matters has so far been quite limited. It is worth considering the extent to which limited, procedurally and substantively regulated recognition of arbitration in family-law disputes would make it possible to accommodate cultural and religious diversity within the framework of a uniform system of family law.

In 2007, a Muslim Arbitration Tribunal was established under the UK's *Arbitration Act 1996*. This institution's website describes its scope as follows:

> The Muslim Arbitration Tribunal (MAT) was established in 2007 to provide a viable alternative for the Muslim community seeking to resolve disputes in accordance with Islamic Sacred Law and without having to resort to costly and time consuming litigation. The establishment of MAT is an important and significant step towards providing the Muslim community with a real opportunity to self determine disputes in accordance with Islamic Sacred Law.[44]

This development can be linked to the much-debated speech by the Archbishop of Canterbury in 2008, in which he stated that the accommodation of some aspects of *sharia* law practices would be inevitable, and called for discussion of the current condition of cultural, social and conceptual plurality and its implications for the law.[45] The *Arbitration Act 1996* provides a clearly defined legal framework for

---

42 Bakht 2005, 27.

43 Bakht 2005, 31.

44 [Online] Available at: http://www.matribunal.com/ [accessed: 9 November 2010].

45 Brown, Russell 2008; for extensive discussion of the speech, its significance and the ensuing debate, see Shah 2009, 77.

the activities of the Muslim Arbitration Tribunal. The tribunal cannot grant a civil divorce or make a binding determination with respect to the custody of children. However, the parties can ask an arbitrator to decide on the distribution of assets upon divorce according to religious law. The result would be treated in the same way as would an agreement between the parties, that means it would be binding, but the court could override or modify it.[46] The *Arbitration Act 1996* contains a number of safeguards, and courts may refuse to enforce an arbitration award if, for example, a party was in some way incapacitated or if an award related to a matter which is not capable of being settled by arbitration, or if it would be contrary to the public order to enforce an award.[47]

Arbitration in family-law matters requires that the legal system of the jurisdiction concerned recognises arbitrability, that choice of applicable law and arbitration agreements are both effective and that the principles of due process under the rule of law are respected. An important consideration in the context of Islamic law is that while non-state law cannot be chosen on conflict-of-laws grounds,[48] this restriction does not apply if both parties have agreed on arbitration. Clearly, the scope of the decisions the arbitrator would be permitted to make would have to be precisely defined and due heed would have to be paid to the duty of protection placed on family law.

The difference between recognising arbitration decisions in family-law matters and recognising parallel family-law canons is that the latter effectively delegates legislation and jurisdiction in family-law matters. Arbitration, on the other hand, requires the state to define a legal framework within which arbitration is authorised and plurality of applicable law is recognised. Under arbitration, the parties agree to have their dispute settled by an arbitrator upon whom they have jointly agreed and who will apply the law the parties have chosen. The arbitrator's decision is then binding on the parties, and it is legally enforceable by the state. It is a private system which is entered into by agreement. Arbitration does not, therefore, give rise to autonomous systems of family law for individual communities. However, since arbitration allows the parties to choose the law applicable to their case, it does, of course, also lead to pluralistic legal structures. Nevertheless, the design of the institution of arbitration – as well its regulation and procedural and substantive safeguards – can ensure that minimum standards are upheld and common ground continues to be shared.

---

46 Lowe, Douglas 2007, 1006, see also Matrimonial Causes Act 1973 (c. 18), sections 34 and 35.

47 Arbitration Act 1996 (c. 23), sections 68 and 103.

48 Although the *sharia* is religious law and transcends specific legal orders, its various manifestations today nevertheless have clear national characteristics. Because it is not a self-contained, complete system of law, it is primarily a method for reaching decisions on legal matters. *Sharia* is religious in its legitimation and claims applicability in all areas of life.

Culturally Open Procedures

A less far-reaching approach can be seen in efforts aimed at incorporating various notions of family and family law and interacting with different actors, as well as in initiatives to fashion open procedures with the objective of accommodating the cultural dimensions of family law. Such efforts avoid relinquishing the state's prerogatives for legislation and application of the law, attempting instead to make family-law institutions more inclusive in their effect. Cultural and religious practices can be drawn into the law in a variety of ways here.

Marriage ceremony

There are, for example, some areas where cultural inclusion would already be guaranteed by the requirement that religious and cultural acts, such as the celebration of marriage, must be subject to state registration in order for legal effect to devolve from them. Spain, for example, recognises registered religious marriage ceremonies and in England organisational and statutory measures have been taken so that civil and religious marriages can take place at the same time and in the same place.[49] In some instances, imams can also assume the role of the marriage registrar.[50]

The continuing popularity of Islamic marriages in migrant communities is well documented.[51] It is hard to cite any current public interests which would justify making civil marriage ceremonies compulsory. Civil weddings first became possible towards the end of the sixteenth century, and were introduced in countries with a denominational minority, so as to allow members of that minority a religiously neutral means of marrying. The French Revolution then began the trend towards obligatory civil marriages, in order to limit the power of the church, though democratised marriage kept its Christian engravings. Europe now has religious minorities again, but at a time when the conflict between state and church has already been decided. The principal tasks of marriage ceremony legislation today are to ensure that the prerequisites for marriage are met, that the spouses are entering into marriage of their own free will and that they are aware of the legal consequences of the marriage ceremony, or of the lack of such consequences where the marriage ceremony is a purely religious one. Also, as long as civil law and other legal consequences devolve from marriage, it is in the public interest for it to be known who is married and who is not. The law's

---

49 With the enactment of the Marriage (Registration and Buildings) Act 1990, the previous requirement that marriages had to take place in separate buildings was dropped. Marriages can now take place in buildings which themselves form part of another building.

50 Cf. Yilmaz 2005, 71.

51 For England, see Yilmaz 2005, 74, or Pearl, Menski 1998, 52. For France, cf. Fulchiron 1999, note 110, notes 111 *et seq.* and notes 588 *et seq.* The key issue for Muslims is to ensure that a child is 'legitimate', particularly since an illegitimate child is placed in a weak and ambivalent position in the Muslim context, cf. Foblets 2003, 244.

duty of protection will have been adequately discharged in this regard if, prior to marriage, the spouses are required to obtain a marriage licence certifying that they meet such requirements as minimum age, soundness of mind and free will and if the person performing the marriage ceremony then reports the marriage officially or, alternatively, if the spouses are required to register their marriage immediately after the marriage ceremony itself, in order for the marriage to take legal effect. This last procedure is not, however, sufficient to ensure that couples who have opted for a religious marriage ceremony are necessarily aware that no legal effect devolves from the religious ceremony itself. Failure to have their marriage registered in those circumstances can have far-reaching consequences.

In any case, truly enlightened thinking, thinking which sees marriage without any mystery or magic, without ultimate justifications on philosophical or theological grounds, would logically conclude that couples should be free to choose the form of their marriage ceremony. This would apply particularly if the essential family-law consequences of a relationship were in any case not dependent on whether marriage had occurred but related rather, in line with the duty of protection which falls on family law, to benefits and costs resulting from the relationship, to the sharing of various tasks, or to the partners' relationship to their children. It is interesting to note that, in order to establish certain claims and in the context of common law, English courts have sometimes been prepared to presume a marriage to exist on the basis of long cohabitation, even though no civil marriage ceremony has occurred and no marriage has been registered. This has enabled minority legal acts to be accommodated within the English legal structure.

Following Shachar's approach of distinguishing between a 'demarcating' and a 'distributive' function for family law, and attributing the governance of status to the first of these functions and property rights to the second, produces similar results.[52] According to Shachar, group authority may prevail over the demarcating aspects, whereas the state should exercise authority over distribution matters.[53] On the basis of these different functions, one can argue that while marriage may be sanctioned by religious ritual, it remains the duty of the state to guarantee protection to each partner and to ensure equitable compensation for contributions to family life, and equitable sharing of its burdens, irrespective of marriage.

Divorce

In the case of divorce, it is necessary to co-ordinate the state's control requirements on the one hand with culturally determined decision processes on the other hand. A *talaq* could, for example, also be pronounced and acknowledged within the framework of proceedings under the laws of European countries. Such a course of action is being considered in Germany in the context of applying foreign law according to conflict-of-laws rules. While divorce by repudiation is undoubtedly at odds with the principles of gender equality and human dignity, in effect this

52 Cf. Shachar 2001, 120.

53 Cf. Shachar 2001, 131.

objection would not, however, apply in cases where the wife is given the right to be heard and agrees to a divorce by mutual consent, or in cases where even the prerequisites for unilateral divorce under the law of the European country concerned are met. In some cases the right to pronounce a *talaq* is contractually delegated to the wife. Under this procedure (called *tafwid al-talaq*), a wife may represent her husband when pronouncing the *talaq*. Applying the family law of European countries, where the *talaq* is an alien concept, it would be possible, should the party concerned need this, to grant the husband or the wife the right to pronounce the *talaq* according to their own rules and rituals and also to have this documented in their application for divorce. If a verbal divorce procedure is conducted, the pronouncement of the *talaq* could also be included in the divorce declaration without thereby according it any effective legal consequence in and of itself. This may be appropriate in cases where the ritual of *talaq* is so deeply rooted in the parties' moral and religious beliefs that not to be able to express it would be perceived as surrendering cultural identity and therefore be unacceptable. It is worth noting in this context that European family-law reform in recent decades has constantly reduced the period of time which must elapse before a unilateral divorce can be carried out. Divorce-law reform in Spain in 2005, for example, made unilateral divorce possible without any prior period of separation, provided that the marriage had lasted for at least three months.[54]

Islamic law prescribes a process of reconciliation and mediation as a preliminary step in the divorce process, with the family playing a vital role in the attempts to reconcile the parties. Relatives are frequently also involved in negotiations on the consequences of a divorce.[55] Permitting the parties' families to participate in divorce processes conducted in Europe is in tune with the idea of making the most of the resources available to the couple and providing them with scope to contribute. A couple's relatives could, for example, be entrusted with reconciliation and mediation tasks, or the expertise of people with specific religious and cultural authority could be sought. Involving the community in this way also helps to ensure that the decisions reached carry the authority vested in older family members, thus making such agreements more binding. Contrary to an arbitration process, which involves a choice of applicable law in certain matters, the general objective of these alternative dispute resolution methods is to ensure that – within dispositive provisions of law as provided for by every family-law system – cultural and religious considerations and surroundings are accorded appropriate respect. Alternative dispute resolution does not, however, involve an arbitration court making a binding judgment.

Whether a court of law's decision should necessarily continue to adhere to a pre-defined list of possible grounds for divorce, or whether the court may simply

---

54 Article 81 of the Código Civil, Ley 15/2005, de 8 de julio, por la que se modifican el Código Civil y la Ley de Enjuiciamiento Civil en materia de separación y divorcio. Martín-Casals, Ribot 2008, 428.

55 Cf. Bano 2007, 54.

offer a set of rules, which either spouse may opt in to in the event of the couple disagreeing among themselves, depends on the importance attached to certainty of expectations of the law. In any event, defined lists of acceptable grounds for divorce afford little practical protection of the marriage or the parties. A contractualised family-law system must permit a marital union to be dissolved at any time if this is the wish of both spouses and it should also permit such dissolution in cases where this is the wish of one spouse only – though in this case it may be appropriate to require a specific period of time to elapse before dissolution. It may be sufficient if the pronouncements relating to the dissolution of the marriage are procedurally taken into account and registered.

A further relevant consideration here is whether *de lege ferenda* divorces in Europe should necessarily maintain the requirement that marriage dissolution be pronounced by a court. If marriage ceases to be the basis on which legal effects rest, it follows that the institution of divorce becomes redundant. The dissolution of a marriage need not necessarily be pronounced by a court, as comparative law shows,[56] and the role of the courts in this area has recently also been somewhat reduced in Europe, as administrative divorces have become possible.[57] In many countries, as the principle of fault in divorce-law matters has been abandoned, there has been a concomitant move away from divorces pronounced by the courts. It is certainly true that as family law has become contractualised – and the courts' monopoly in divorce matters is largely explained by the state's traditional claim to uphold social order and its protection of marriage as an institution – the role of the courts in divorce matters has tended to diminish, and the state's monopoly in the divorce arena, which has proved to be at the very least problematical in the light of the plurality of living arrangements and of cultural understandings of the family prevalent today, is attracting criticism.

A family-law system whose purpose is reduced to that of affording protection will concern itself principally with ensuring equitable distribution of assets, compensation for contributions to family life and the sharing of its burdens and thus the consequences of the dissolution of the relationship. Many jurisdictions now allow the consequences of divorce to be agreed by mediation or alternative dispute resolution – England being a noteworthy example[58] – though given the protective role assigned to family law, there are areas where compulsory rules – especially concerning children – and some control by the court or another state institution over the financial aspects of divorce remains necessary as a mechanism for ensuring that the material outcome is reasonably fair.[59] In contrast to solutions based on arbitration or parallel, community-based family-law systems, alternative dispute resolution merely defines the scope within which autonomy is granted to the parties. Regulatory and judiciary functions, on the other hand, remain the

56 Cf. Gärtner 2008, 3.

57 Cf. Gärtner 2008, 7, concerning Scandinavia.

58 Lowe, Douglas 2007, 10, 282, 988; Poulter 1998, 234.

59 Cf. Büchler 2004, 23.

sole preserve of the state. Conversely, as far as the informal settlement of disputes through processes of counselling and mediation is concerned, there is certainly scope for *sharia* councils to make a significant contribution.[60]

Contracts

Given the nature of marriage, contractual agreements are of particular importance in Islamic law contexts, and they are often an important means of protecting the position of the wife.[61] In addition to defining the *mahr*, such contractual agreements sometimes also define other financial matters, possible reasons for divorce and the exercise of parental care of the children. Stipulations in the marriage contract often seek to clarify or modify the duties and obligations of husband and wife, as well as other parameters of conjugal life, in an approach which is known to be rooted in classical Islamic law and practice.[62]

The *nikah* contract – the Islamic marriage contract – is probably most akin to a regular contractual arrangement, and the intent of 'marriage contracts' of this kind should be realised and enforced within the bounds of what is legally permissible. Of course, a marriage contract cannot be permitted to circumvent compulsory family-law provisions, particularly in the area of child law. Nevertheless, contractual autonomy should also allow reference to understandings of the law based on religious belief. It is also possible that the parties may agree in their marriage contract to remove religious barriers after a civil divorce, by, for example, agreeing to carry out a religious divorce ritual so that they can be allowed to remarry according to their own religion. In cases where the parties have completed civil divorce proceedings and the husband then refuses to pronounce the *talaq*, this then raises the question of the relevance of the couple's contractual agreement. The religious divorce ritual agreed to in the contract cannot, of course, be carried out by force, as this would impinge on the husband's personal and religious freedom. In such a case it would, however, be conceivable for damages to be awarded to the wife on the grounds of breach of contract.[63]

60 Cf. Poulter 1998, 234.

61 Regarding the legal tradition of the Islamic marriage contract, cf. Tucker 2008, 41. Regarding the significance – especially also for women – and the possible content of marriage contracts in the context of Islamic family law, cf. Pearl, Menski 1998, 176; Büchler 2003, 63; Carroll 1982.

62 Concerning developments in various countries and the struggles undertaken to have certain stipulations included in a standard marriage contract, see Welchman 2007, 99.

63 The decision of the Supreme Court of Canada in *Bruker v. Markovitz*, [2007] 3 S.C.R. 607 is remarkable in this respect, in that it condemned the husband to pay damages because of breach of contract. The husband refused to provide his wife with Jewish religious divorce after civil divorce despite an agreement to do so. The court argued that any impairment to the husband's religious freedom was significantly outweighed by the harm to his wife personally and to the public's interest in protecting fundamental values such as

Within Europe's various family-law systems there are, however, considerable variations in the scope of contractual freedom and in the permissibility, prerequisites, content and form of marriage contracts. It is certainly true that the trend towards contractualisation warrants a re-examination and possible extension of contractual freedom in family-law matters.

Fosterage and child protection

Finally, diversified law in the area of fosterage will allow the inclusion of arrangements whose function is to protect children, such as *kafala*.

Procedural mediation and models which employ inter-cultural mediation and ethno-psychiatric expertise can be effective even in, or indeed particularly in, areas related to children.[64] Besides expertise in dealing with cases involving children, procedural competence is one important requirement for the ability to practise in a culturally aware manner. Key ingredients are participative processes which involve not only the parents but also the children, the use of community resources, awareness among decision-makers that their own standards are conditioned by society and the ability to respect cultural differences without culturalising – since the use of cultural defence arguments can promote stereotypes – and without permitting 'culture' to be used as a strategic resource. Success can be said to have been achieved when the parents' co-operative attitude leads to a solution which is favourable to the child. It is for this reason that French law expressly requires the *juge de l'enfant* to make all efforts to secure parental agreement.[65]

Participation by minors in decision-making processes is worthy of special mention here. The UN Convention on the Rights of the Child expressly emphasises that children and young people should have the right to participate in all areas of life affecting them. Participation in this context means taking part in decision-making processes. The process by which decisions are reached is as important here as the results of the decisions themselves. Including children and young people in the actual design and implementation of child-protection measures certainly helps to increase their acceptance of such interventions considerably. Participation in decision making requires the children and young people to have a certain level of awareness, to be able to express their views and to exert some influence on the decision. Clearly, the extent to which the child is capable of assessing the matters affected by a particular decision, his or her power of judgment, will be a decisive factor in determining the extent of his or her involvement in it. Involving the child by hearing his or her views, should, however, happen as a matter of course.

Involving children and young people in decision making in culturally diverse contexts is of particular importance. Indeed, it is precisely in situations where children and young people have multiple and ambivalent points of cultural

---

equality rights and autonomous choice in marriage and divorce as well as the public benefit in enforcing valid and binding contractual obligations.

64 Cf. Cottier 2005, 703.

65 See article 375–1, para. 2 of the Code Civil.

reference that participative processes enable the differing points of view of parents and their children to be expressed and understood. Participative processes also have a creative and formative potential which can assist mediation.

Theoretical Concepts, Scope and Limits of Discursive and Proceduralised Incorporation of Different Understandings of Family Law

Reducing the scope of family law to its core functions and placing greater emphasis on discourse and procedure is very much in keeping with the processes of de-institutionalisation and contractualisation currently affecting family law in Europe. In particular, it opens up the prospect of a family-law system which is better equipped to meet the demands placed on it by the plurality of society today.

Dynamic Interactions

Family-law thinking based on discourse and procedure does not accept an existentialised concept of culture or the manipulative abuse of contextual specificity or cultural relativity and avoids clothing social conflicts in primordial arguments. By co-ordinating discourse and moderating conflicts, it is thus better placed to grasp and understand differentiations, dynamic interactions and diversity of perspectives within a society.[66]

Also, and in contrast to the dogma of applying law on the basis of an individual's nationality, such thinking recognises that the law is not an idiopathic manifestation, but instead is able to develop its content, its meaning and its effect only in a given cultural context, and that these are therefore susceptible of transformation. Within the social and economic conditions prevailing in Europe, Islamic law codifications have specific connotations and functions. Transplanted legal institutions are subject to a translation and reframing in their new cultural context given its specific requirements and expectations.[67]

However, the environment in the adopted society itself is also subject to change once it integrates alien elements. A normative syncretisation is being set in motion, as can be seen in processes of trans-culturalisation, where self-referencing cultures, once viewed as mutually distinct, begin to impinge upon each other. Elements of one legal order may change under the influence of another such order, thus resulting in new legal forms emerging. Interlegality is the term which has been coined to describe this phenomenon, 'a process of adoption of elements of a dominant legal order, both national and international, and of the frames of meaning that constitute these orders, into the practices of a local legal order and/

66 Cf. Deveaux 2005, 340.

67 Cf. also Rude-Antoine 1991, 95.

or the other way round'.[68] Shifts in the dominant interpretation of concepts such as marriage or divorce, or the best interests of the child, can result from incorporating various culturally informed notions and values. Incorporation is not the same as recognition, however, since the latter implies the legalisation of a whole set of foreign norms, thereby officialising their parallel existence. Moreover, it is also the case that the legal perceptions and values which are incorporated – and are initially viewed as alien – themselves undergo transformation as a result of being included in a shared framework.

This does, however, also require two things: first, a willingness somewhat to relinquish consistency and coherence of terminology and dogma, to let go of uniform systems of meaning, and to give up the ideal theory of law with its privileged meta-narratives and norm hierarchies; second, in the space thus created, where discourse and procedure hold their rightful places, to embrace a heterarchical family-law system, characterised by open texts and by the unpredictability and puzzle-solving tasks which the meeting of cultures brings with it.

Individual Rights

The incorporation of some awareness of Islamic family-law tradition into family-law procedures in Europe is very much of a piece with the evolution towards a more contractual and less institutional approach to family law seen in recent decades in Europe. The increasing plurality of modes of living people are now choosing means that narrowly prescriptive family-law models require particular justification. The approach to family-law conflicts based primarily on discourse ethics and procedural arrangements aims to ensure that cultural plurality can be accommodated within the framework of the rights of the individual. Only individuals hold civil rights and liberties. Culture has no intrinsic value of its own, and cultural identity is accorded legal guarantees only indirectly: that is, through the person claiming it. Cultural traditions do, however, have value, because they provide people with a variety of options for how they live their lives. Certainly, culture is not a category to which one is faithfully committed and bound for life. Rather, it is the result of a flexible, contradictory and dualistic dovetailing of interpretation and symbolisation. Appreciations of culture are also relational, in the sense that they are different only in relation to other cultural appreciations and that they permanently interact with them. Culture is therefore not static and insular, but is something which is constantly created through relationships. Therefore, the law should keep taking its cue not from the interests of the group, but rather from those of the individual. In this way, the law and legal practice will uphold diversity of family arrangements whether or not they are reflective of differences in culture or religion.

---

68 Hoekema 2005, 11. Hoekema explains the concept by reference to several exemplary cases.

An approach based on individual positions rather than on group interests focuses, on the one hand, on shared meanings while on the other hand being able to grasp differences in positions and interests within groups, different self-conceptions, self-images and legal understandings. It follows from this that a search for the true interpretation of Islamic legal institutions is not necessary. The question of what Islamic law allows and what it forbids is irrelevant. This does not mean, however, that representatives of religious and ethnic minorities, their institutions and understanding of family law and its practice are irrelevant, since in closed social settings these will be influential or even dominant. In family-law procedure, however, it is only the individual who matters. Institutional, dominant or traditional perceptions of religious family law are part of the discourse only in as far as they are argued for in the area left available for autonomous decisions by the parties.

Autonomy and Procedural Guarantees

Based on the recognition that cultural and collective autonomy on the one hand, and individual autonomy on the other hand both originate from the same source – since it is only through socialisation that persons acquire individuality – the discursive, procedure-based approach to questions of family law not only recognises the articulated collective identities and life contexts which secure identity, it primarily also protects the self-interpretation of cultural imperatives and the individual's autonomy in setting his or her own life agenda. For autonomy to be substantive, however, it must enable the individual to choose between various options without coercion. There are a number of prerequisites for this, not the least of which being institutional and procedural guarantees. The institutional prerequisite is that there should be independent decision-making bodies, sanctioned by law. The procedural requirement is that the individual should have access to such bodies, that the proceedings be fair, and, in particular, that legal arguments be heard.[69]

Gender Equality

There remains the problem of inequality between the sexes in terms of their structural, familial and cultural circumstances. The discourse of accommodation of cultural and religious identity in family law notably focuses on the question of violation of gender equality by means of religious law, often suggesting a binary opposition between culture and religion on the one hand and human rights and gender equality on the other, and therefore positing culture and women's rights in competing terms and viewing human rights values and gender equality as external to culture.[70]

---

69 These are the guarantees set out in article 6, para. 1 of the Convention for the Protection of Human Rights and Fundamental Freedoms; cf. Grabenwarter 2009, 343.

70 Cf. Mehra 2007, *passim*.

The problems of the binary structure of the discourse of gender equality and culture are manifold.

First, the focus on cultural practices affecting migrant women implies a 'gendered dimension of the culture clash hypothesis',[71] while at the same time diverting attention away from gender discrimination closer to home. Susanne Baer calls it 'othering of sex inequality, which uses religion or culture as a stigma to shield a majority from critique and change'.[72] The rhetoric is all too often one which suggests that non-Western family law and practices are culturally inspired, whereas European ones are rational. Culture tends to be invoked selectively and only in relation to the characteristics and behaviour of minorities,[73] European behaviour and values being perceived to be acultural in character. The result is that actions are perceived to be culturally driven if they are carried out by members of a minority group. This view overlooks the specific manner in which gender structures social relationships. Arguments about the roles of the sexes and gender equality do not take place between closed cultural groups. Rather, these are societal conflicts which also take place within specific single cultural contexts. Moreover, it is not culture itself which dictates that women should be discriminated against, but rather particular interpretations of cultural traditions, sometimes quite deliberately invoked. Nonetheless, as Anne Phillips points out, one should not simply understand culture and gender as generating competing claims to equality, since gender exists within culture, and is never separate from it.[74]

Second, this discursive strategy and its concomitant suggestion of a binary opposition between culture or religion and gender equality essentialises the notions of culture and gender and constructs an unassailable link between gender roles and specific cultural contexts while at the same time assuming that gender inequality is integral only to certain cultures. Yet cultural understandings within communities are vibrant, fluid, contradictory and constantly changing, rather than fixed or homogeneous, as the discourse of culture opposing women's rights has suggested.[75] Linking specific, unequal gender roles to specific cultural or religious entities, such as Islam, effectively limits women's possible courses of action to a choice between constantly distancing themselves from their religion or committing themselves to Islam and thus being symbolically coralled into supporting the continuation of an oppressive code of honour and being perceived as complicit in its authoritarian family practices. Women are therefore left with the choice between cultural or religious affiliation on the one hand, or gender equality

71 Powell 2005/2006, 334. Powell, conversely, focuses in her paper on how cultural claims were advanced to limit women's human rights in the United States during the process of rejecting the ratification of CEDAW and how the cultural assumptions behind this were obscured by framing the debate in terms of constitutionalism.

72 Baer 2010, 58, 61.

73 Cf. Volpp 2001, 1185.

74 Cf. Phillips 2005, 122.

75 Cf. Mehra 2007, 18.

rights on the other, and those who challenge cultural interpretations from within are labelled as traitors to their cultural traditions. Women, however, encouraged by the discourse of cultural identity, are also able to stand up for close links between gender codes and cultural authenticity and, in so doing, respond to processes of alienation and discrimination within the ranks of the social majority, which are themselves a reaction to the rapid social changes which migration has brought in its wake.

Third, assumptions of women's vulnerability are often rooted in paternalism. The discourse very much tends to victimise women belonging to a foreign culture, 'it denies their potential to be understood as emancipatory subjects'.[76] It assumes that 'other' women are victims of their culture and are passively waiting to be rescued from cultural dictates, it denies them agency and autonomy and it does not recognise their potential to negotiate their own position within the family and the community. This perspective thus objectifies women and obscures the complexities of women's lives, leaving unconsidered the interplay of gender and culture with other factors like social status and economic resources.[77] Muslim women in Europe are adamant in explaining that they are not subjugated by their faith, and that following Islamic practices is not an imposition but a rational source of personal morality which they want to be free to follow, while at the same time rejecting the imposition of unnecessarily strict norms of conduct by religious leaders and the judgmental mentality of closely-knit minority communities. They feel discriminated against when they are prevented from practising their faith as they would like and also feel that representations of them as being passively subjugated to Islam are unfounded.[78]

Finally, it also undermines the work of women in the Islamic context and misrepresents many members of the community who do not share and would never support certain practices and their cultural justification. Women can challenge the validity of cultural claims and also provide alternative interpretations to the mainstream, male-dominated reading of religious texts. Moreover, the solutions argued for need not leave the Islamic context behind, since the potential for change also exists within the Islamic frame of reference. A similar struggle took place in Europe, too, during which it should be remembered that the culturally decisive forces within European modernism took a long time to come to terms with the idea of gender equality, leaving women to fight an interpretation of equality in which they themselves were not included.[79]

---

76 Volpp 2001, 1205. See also Mehra 2007, 31.

77 Cf. also Bano 2007, 41.

78 Cf. Silvestri 2008, 6.

79 Basically, the claim of the Enlightenment for equal rights referred only to men; the French Revolution and the Declaration of the Rights of Man and of the Citizen of 1789 for example did not extend equal rights to women. In response to the exclusion of women, Olympe de Gouges published the Declaration of Rights of Woman and the Female Citizen. See Mousset 2003, 17 and 84.

Nevertheless, since Foucault,[80] no discourse can elude the power structure on which it is built. Procedural justice can, however, be achieved only if the positions from which each party is negotiating are fundamentally equally strong, each party's arguments are accorded equal respect, and each party's interests can be formulated freely.

Empirical social studies show that while women living in Islamic communities in Europe do not wish to relinquish their ultimate right of resorting to state law, individual and collective identities are, however, closely interwoven and individual identity can be stabilised only in the context of the social network. Many women originating from countries with a Muslim population and living in Europe acknowledge and stress the heterogeneity of law in their everyday lives. They recognise, negotiate and contest different cultural identities and legal practices. They do not wish to lose the privileges they have acquired through European law, nor have they any desire to alienate themselves from their Islamic community. Sometimes they empower religious authorities to regulate their lives according to specific religious and cultural values. On occasion, they may leverage their position by playing legal systems off against one another.[81]

Women are certainly free to follow the prescriptions of their religion, by, for example, asking for their marriages to be dissolved according to religious law, even if such dissolution is less favourable to them and runs counter to the principle of gender equality. However, as Phillips points out, such legitimate behaviour by individual women seeking redress is problematic on a different level, since

> the fact that some individuals choose to regulate their lives according to alternative legal principles will sometimes have the effect of putting pressure on others to take the same route. Where this happens, something that looks like a benign way of helping women reach a religiously sanctioned solution to their difficulties could have the effect of enhancing authoritarian powers.[82]

Recognising the rights and needs of an individual can therefore result in lending authority to a group with the potential to exercise coercion on its other members. A better assessment of the needs of women and their empowerment within the procedure and discourse of state family law provides a solution to this dilemma.

Where women avail themselves of the law of the state, by filing a legal case aimed at improving their position vis-à-vis their family, this amounts to a shift of power away from the family and the community and towards the state. This can sometimes give rise to problems of its own, however, since state law and its application are by no means neutral, but are mediated through a prism of cultural and social understanding which is clearly gendered. Moreover, in such cases, the loyalties of women from migrant communities often tend to be ambivalent.

80 Foucault 1971.

81 See Shah-Kazemi 2001, *passim*; Phillips 2007, 172.

82 Phillips 2007, 175.

A familiar discursive environment, encompassing people living in the same cultural and social context, favours the disclosure of interests involved, thus making it harder to retreat to purely culturalised attitudes. Such an approach fosters a sense of cultural security, which in turn strengthens individual autonomy. Accordingly, family-law interventions should focus on identifying the potential for change in the relationship between the sexes within cultural and religious communities, and on appreciating and supporting discourses which contest fundamentalist versions and representations of the community's culture. Rather than assuming that practices which are discriminatory towards women are preordained by a community's culture, the strategy should be to question cultural assertions, to unravel cultural constructs and to deconstruct culture. In this regard, Islam can also be seen as a flexible resource which is adaptable to different circumstances.

Admittedly, there are limits to what the law can achieve in a single case. Rather, financial, human and social resources are needed for members of closed communities to succeed in freeing themselves from the constraints placed on them and securing their individual rights to freedom.

Ayelet Shachar advocates a joint governance and transformational accommodation approach to resolve the conflict between commitments to cultural diversity and gender equality. She favours legal structures which encourage increasing co-operation and co-ordination between religious groups and national authorities, and is convinced that this can help to decrease gender inequalities within different communities. The goal of restricting state intervention to the protection of the interests of individuals put at risk by their group, while still allowing their group maximum jurisdictional autonomy, is at the core of Shachar's model of transformative accommodation. According to Shachar, family law has a demarcating function, delineating who is inside the collective and who is outside, and this function is mainly carried out by religious and cultural groups. Distributive functions, on the other hand, would be primarily the task of the state. In a joint governance system, authority would be divided and shared, so that a fluid and dynamic conception of power and jurisdiction would prevail.[83] The idea of inter-cultural and inter-institutional co-operation and dialogue underlying Shachar's

---

83 Shachar 2001, *passim*, especially 117. Shachar defines the process of transformative accommodation as follows: 'This is a variant that takes the two different locuses of authority – the *nomoi* group and the state – and, instead of viewing their conflict of interests as a problem, considers it as an occasion for encouraging each entity to become more responsive to *all* its constituents. Through an arrangement of *non-exclusive* competition for the loyalties of those citizens who overlap both jurisdictions, transformative accommodation seeks to adapt the power structures of both *nomoi* group and state in order to accommodate their most vulnerable constituents. Each intersection of jurisdictions provides each authority with an opportunity to increase its accountability and sensitivity to otherwise marginalized group members, since each entity must now "bid" for these individuals' continued adherence to its sphere of authority rather than take it for granted' (117).

proposal is certainly to be welcomed. Legal certainty and equality before the law can, however, be jeopardised by these proposals and there is at least a suggestion of legal eclecticism. What is lacking is a concept of where the lines between non-negotiable constitutional essentials on the one hand, and practices and rights governed by cultural and religious groups on the other, should be drawn. It thus remains uncertain whether Schachar's idea will enable greater gender equality to supersede the paradox of multicultural vulnerability.[84] The model is also highly unsuitable for a civil law culture.

Not Necessarily beyond Nations but beyond Culture

We are confronted with the elusive nation. The processes of globalisation, with their twin dimensions of transnationalisation and fragmentation, have shaken the model of the nation-state with a culturally homogeneous population to its foundations. The characteristics of 'we' or 'us' are becoming increasingly amorphous. The demand for respect and the pursuit of difference, and the pressure for normative diversity which they bring in their wake, all challenge the notion of the nation-state. The nation-state is faced with the task of integrating a society which is becoming increasingly diversified, and the two main instruments it has deployed to that end are its constitution and human rights.[85]

The discourse on legal pluralism, for its part, challenges the notion of state law as the only source of law – and one enjoying special privileges – and offers conceptions of law which go beyond the state. Mostly, however, the debate on legal and normative pluralism has focused on where to draw the definitional boundaries of the law.

Nevertheless, the nation-state still has a function to perform, particularly so in the realm of the law, where its foremost task is to secure democratic legitimacy and an adjudicative structure. Yet even if concepts of legal order must necessarily be subject to geographical boundaries, the law is nevertheless becoming more global and transversal in other ways. Family law beyond nations is now beginning to take shape – this is certainly true for Europe – partly as a result of being reduced to its essential core functions, but not least because of the harmonisation and convergence in family law which international law has fostered.

However, to the extent that the nation-state maintains its status as the frame of reference for legal considerations, we can think of a family law beyond culture and beyond religion, provided it focuses on its core tasks and provided it is devoid of religiously informed content. This would mean that family law no longer affords exclusive protection to any single morality, but rather that it dissolves those moralities, thus reconciling nation-state and social plurality or, to put it another way, integrating diversity into the nation-state. After all, it is not only the hegemonic culture within a society – the culture which often is not marked and

---

84 Cf. Benhabib 2002, 128.

85 Cf. Habermas 1996, 144.

which is experienced as being invisible – which is hybrid, fluid and constantly transforming itself, and which is contradictory and subject to contestation from within its ranks. The same also applies to the minorities which deviate from the hegemonic norm. Thinking of a system of family law beyond culture means dismissing the need, or indeed even the potential, to preserve cultural identities as established and delineable entities. It also means accepting the internal complexity and essential contestability of cultures. Seyla Benhabib puts this quite explicitly when she writes:

> But movements for maintaining the purity or distinctiveness of cultures seem to me irreconcilable with both democratic and more basic epistemological considerations. Philosophically, I do not believe in the purity of cultures, or even in the possibility of identifying them as meaningfully discrete wholes. I think of cultures as complex human practices of signification and representation, of organization and attribution, which are internally driven by conflicting narratives. Cultures are formed through complex dialogues with other cultures.[86]

Thus, family law beyond culture is most likely to succeed in accommodating the general hybridisation of cultural legacies, the blurring and shifting of unboundaried cultural beliefs, and the sense of multiple belongings many experience today, thus overcoming the tendency for people and their actions to be mapped onto opposing sides of an us/them divide. Family law itself would then lose its so intensely debated cultural and moral imprint and would, in its restatement, focus on the primary general tasks of private law, thereby reducing the complexity of legal pretensions, while at the same time recognising the complexity in family lives, and allowing for 'multiculturalism without culture'.[87]

Transformations of the Islamic Law Context

Although a theory and practice of family law which concentrates on its protective role – but otherwise allows for areas of autonomy and supports self-interpretations – does not therefore need to concern itself with Islamic law institutions and their interpretation, a description of congruent developments which amounts to a harmonisation of the principles of family law and identifies common values may nevertheless be of considerable help in furthering the general acceptance of limits to autonomy.

An important initial point to note is that Islamic family law has a number of characteristics which in fact facilitate its integration into the European legal context. First, as far as substantive law is concerned, Islamic marriage is regarded as a contract between a bride and a groom and not as an institution, and its effects and dissolution are thus both largely subject to negotiated agreements. Second,

86 Benhabib 2002, ix.

87 This is the title of the particularly relevant work on this subject by Phillips (2007).

Islamic law provides a graduated approach to resolving marital differences, in which arbitrators, preferably drawn from both families, play a part. This is significant, since family-law systems in Europe are now increasingly providing for contractual elements in marriage and accord considerable weight to out-of-court agreements. As a result, all legal systems have similar scope for areas of autonomy and the contractual viewpoint is becoming increasingly prevalent among them all.

Generally speaking, Islamic family-law structures are largely self-regulating, informal in nature, situation-specific and essentially flexible.

More importantly, Islamic law is inherently suited to reform. Many efforts are being undertaken to reread classical Islamic law and to liberate it from rigidities. There is a growing global movement of scholars who are rereading the foundational and canonical Islamic texts for a perspective which does not essentialise or engage in a generalising construction of Islamic law. This is an engagement which is redynamising Islamic thought.

While independent interpretation of religious sources was something early Islamic scholars took for granted, over time the practice became increasingly restricted. No later than the tenth century, a broad consensus had become established to the effect that the 'gate to independent interpretation (*ijtihad*)' had closed, that Islamic law had been comprehensively structured and interpreted and that its formulation had reached such a stage of completeness and finality that all future generations were bound by the views of their antecessors, who were alone in being authorised to engage in *ijtihad*. The creative legal enthusiasm of Islamic scholars of jurisprudence gradually dried up along with their hermeneutic freedom, with the result that Islamic law became a rigid, ossified and systematically self-contained set of norms on which external influences exerted little sway.[88]

Major changes in Islamic societies, partly due to the fact that Western ways of life and Western science were beginning to infiltrate the Islamic world, prompted new, reform-oriented hermeneutic interpretation of religious source texts. Efforts by Muslim intellectuals to bring about social, political and legal reform were particularly prevalent in the nineteenth century. Today's modern Islamic legal scholars are adopting a variety of methodological approaches in order to circumvent the narrow restrictions placed on their work by classical Islamic scholarly tradition and the literal adherence to source texts which its exegesis demands. Reference to the history of Islam and the historicisation of certain *sharia* legal concepts is being used for interpretative initiatives, not in the sense that Islam should be abandoned as a point of reference, but rather that inspiration should again be drawn from its core and that the law should be moved closer to its original intent of achieving justice.[89] One view put forward in this context is that the density of family-law texts in the Qur'an demonstrates the efforts to grant women a stronger position

88 Cf. Saeed 2006, 145; Büchler 2009, 197.

89 For a groundbreaking contribution to this debate see, for example, An-Na'im 1992; Abu Zayd 2006; Wadud 1999. Regarding various modern hermeneutic interpretations, cf. Büchler 2009, 200.

than that which they had in pre-Islamic times: 'The principal sources of the Sharia and Islamic family laws, the Quran and Sunna, represent progressive values – the legal regulations that are extrapolated from both these sources advocate, in particular, welfare of women and children.'[90] It is indeed paradoxical that, at the time of Islamic revelation, the very verses and regulations which are currently at the centre of criticism and contestation in fact heralded a revolution. From a historical perspective, religious Islamic sources should be viewed against the background of pre-Islamic times, which Muslims call the *jahiliya* or 'time of ignorance'. One of the essential objectives of Islam's message was to bring about a significant improvement in the status of women and to establish the family as the core constituent unit in society. It was this which ushered in the transformation from a tribal culture to a family-based structure, in the course of which protecting the members of a family became the paramount imperative. For the first time, women were accorded legal personality and legal rights, and ceased to be treated as chattels. Specific rights granted to them included that of owning and having charge over property. Women were also granted inheritance rights. The bride's consent became a prerequisite for marriage. Islam forbad the killing of newborn baby girls, a practice which had been widespread in pre-Islamic times. Polygamy was restricted. Some restrictions were also placed on the divorce rights which husbands had enjoyed in pre-Islamic times and wives were also granted certain separation rights of their own. Dowers were to be paid to the wife and no longer to her tribe. Finally, women were granted the same status as religious believers as men.[91] Admittedly, the reforms ushered in by Islam served less to turn existing social order on its head than to place as many restrictions on the customary laws which had prevailed in pre-Islamic times as the society of the day was prepared to accept and understand. The degree of detail in which certain verses of Islamic family law are formulated is largely a reflection of the efforts being made at that time to provide women with effective protection. However, it is precisely this density of regulation which is proving a constant hindrance to the ongoing development of family law towards greater gender equality – unless, of course, the Qur'an is read in its historic context, based on its spirit of introducing a gradual and progressive change of the status of women in the context of the transition from a tribal to an Islamic society, as its ideals anticipated. Many Islamic legal scholars emphasise that the basic ethical norm of the Qur'an is equality between the sexes.[92]

In family law, the process of codification, as an arena for the contestation of different positions, is the main force driving reform. The first national family-law codes were promulgated in the 1950s and the process of reform with its patterns of consultation, reciprocal borrowings of jurisprudential arguments and advocacy

90 Rehman 2007, 113. Cf. also Coulson 1964, 14.

91 Qur'an, *sura* 33, verse 35.

92 Cf. the numerous detailed references in Ali 2000, 50.

for progress continue to this day.[93] Although no two codes are the same, since legislation is subject to political contingency reflecting national and international dynamics, the family-law reforms undertaken in many Islamic Arab countries are nevertheless testimony to processes of modernisation. Polygamy, for example, has been made contingent on certain conditions being met, divorce by repudiation has been made harder, women's rights to petition for divorce have been strengthened, registration requirements for marriage and divorce have been introduced, post-divorce maintenance under certain circumstances has been introduced, the parental custody rights of the mother have been extended and the marriageable age has been raised.[94] Pleas for systematic further progress along this route are occasionally heard:

> the Sharia and Islamic family laws that eventually emerged during the second and third centuries of the Muslim calendar were heavily influenced by the socio-economic, political and indigenous tribal values of the prevailing times. In the development of the classical legal schools, the Islamic jurists frequently adopted male-centric approaches towards women's rights and family laws. A cardinal mistake in the subsequent history of Islam was an insistence upon Taqlid or imitation. Although not without its controversies, for centuries the dominant voices within Muslim societies continued to argue that the doors to Ijtihad had been closed. Such an argument undermined the essence of Islam, which is based on change, reform and re-interpretation ... The Quran as well as Sunna provide excellent examples of dealing with situations in a humanitarian and pragmatic manner, with reform and creativity as vital elements of the process. The generations subsequent to the Prophet appear not to have carried this message forward.[95]

Rehman addresses the significance of this view for Europe, when he writes:

> Finally, it is submitted that a deeper, more profound meaning of religious as well as social values can be established through a proper understanding of the Quran and Sunna; these principal sources of the Sharia emphasize pragmatism and reform in accordance with demands of the society. The law-makers and judiciary in the UK may find the pragmatic message of the Sharia useful since

93 The process of codification of Islamic family law began in the Middle East with the Ottoman Law of Family Rights of 1917. In the 1920s and 1940s Egypt enacted some laws concerning family-law matters without issuing an overall code.

94 See Rohe 2009b, 209, 214 and 226; for a comparative analysis encompassing several countries, see Welchman 2007, *passim*; Esposito, Delong-Bas 2001, 47. Important material on this can also be found in An-Na'im 2002, 26, 40, 67, 93, 153, 191, 204, 247, 284.

95 Rehman 2007, 124.

> there is a need for re-evaluation of established English family laws including a re-interpretation of such traditional concepts as family, marriage and divorce.[96]

The understanding and substantiation of Islamic law is very contextual and it can present a content and form very similar to those found in European law. This means that while reformers must also ensure that their ideas and proposals remain clothed in Islamic raiment, and while the theoretical rationale for reform proposals must, in order to gain approval, create the impression that the proposed changes are undoubtedly commensurate with Islam, the emphasis of their approach can and must also be broadly parallel to that of current European family law. Debate must thus be conducted in a less ideological and abstract manner, and be as detailed, concrete and relevant to its context as possible.

The Prism of Postmodernity

Finally, a discursive and procedural conception of family-law conflicts which have cultural connotations can be seen in the conceptual changes which recent works in the field of legal theory have examined in such great detail. These changes are sometimes seen as a linguistic turn, as a move towards a normative pluralism viewed through the prism of postmodernity. They do not deal primarily with the conflict between social and state norms within the same social plane, but recognise instead a network of communicative processes, of equal-ranking discourses on the codes of right and wrong, which in turn generate normative expectations and are thus part of the legislative process.[97] Family law is an area in which the communicative process has a special effect. Admittedly, and contrary to the scepticism towards common normative projects which postmodern theories of law generally espouse, it should not be possible to subject human rights in family-law matters to individual interpretation or to generative and relational communication, and to the random outcomes which these can produce. Rather, human rights should create the framework within which diversity can bring the full force of its creative and productive potential to bear.

96 Rehman 2007, 124.

97 For a fundamental discussion, see Teubner 1995, especially 200: 'Also folgen wir der linguistischen Wende! Der entscheidende konzeptuelle Wandel, so scheint mir, ist der von Struktur zu Prozess, von Norm zu Aktion, von Einheit zu Differenz, und, am wichtigsten für das rechtliche Proprium, von Funktion zu Code. Dies rückt den dynamischen prozessualen Charakter des Rechtspluralismus in den Vordergrund, und hebt gleichzeitig das "Rechtliche" deutlich von anderen Typen des sozialen Handelns ab.'

Chapter 6
Seven Theses to Sum Up and Conclude

New Cartographies: within Society rather than between Societies

The Semantics of Identity in Postmodern Thought

What we are witnessing today is 'a contemporaneity of the non-contemporaneous'.[1] On the one hand, the values, forms and codes governing family life are multiplying and a new dimension of discursive heterogeneity is emerging. Plurality is the defining epistemological attribute of the postmodern.[2] On the other hand, holistic understanding of culture is enjoying a renaissance, there is an insistence – be it as an *apologia* or with critical intent – on ascribed attributes of the self and of that which is other, on characteristics being not only assigned to people but incorporated into them. This is no paradox, however. In a globalised context all these phenomena can be conceived of without contradiction.

Admittedly, the cultural identity of families is determined by a plethora of social processes. Constructivist analysis makes these imagined evidences visible. The result of these processes by which family cultural identity is forged is not an illusion, a fiction or a deception, however, but a reality which has the potential of changing. To understand religion, family and nation as cultural constructs and products of social imagination does not detract from their practical relevance to, and potency in shaping, everyday life. It is for this reason that cultural identity deserves the attention of family law.

Within European societies today, diverging legal concepts, understandings and notions of family often collide, so that family-law theory and practice may encounter conflicts of cultures and norms. A positive approach to diversity which simultaneously heeds integration policy objectives is the key challenge which modern societies have to meet today.

---

1 Rothenbacher 1998, 4.

2 Cf. Töpperwien 2001, 1: 'Modernity aimed at integration. Postmodernity embraces diversity.'

Inclusion or Exclusion of Alien Family Law?

Europe's Search for the Self and that which is Other, for Balance and for Permissible Diversity

Islamic law has a part to play in the application of law in European countries, because private international law refers to it and accords it applicability. From a comparative law standpoint, I observe that all the countries examined here are engaged in seeking assurance in their quest for balance in the degree of plurality in family law which commands sufficiently wide acceptance. While commonalities and convergences dominate, presumably because the countries concerned are addressing comparable problems, differences in emphasis are also apparent. It is in France that *ordre public* considerations under private international law most evidently serve to protect self-affirmation. Switzerland pursues a policy of integration, as is evident from its tendency to recognise domicile as the connecting factor in private international law: that is, to apply Swiss family law to foreign nationals living in Switzerland. Germany, by contrast, identifies strongly with its own cultural codes. Its frequent recourse to the law of Islamic countries and its noteworthy reticence in giving precedence to German law on *ordre public* grounds can be seen as both a defence mechanism and a demarcation line within its borders as well as evidence of its respect for differences. Spain takes account of its Islamic past, thereby opening up new fields of cultural autonomy. Finally, England's social structures display signs of communitarianism. Despite applying law based on an individual's domicile, the state shows willingness to allow different culture-based canons of family law to co-exist with a very considerable degree of legal autonomy. The Muslim community in England has thus largely maintained its legal traditions, albeit in a modified form.

The observation is, therefore, that the degree of permissible diversity in the context of family law can be seen as an epiphenomenon of different variants of political modernity and national self-definitions in Europe – neither more, nor less.

The (De-)construction of Binary Oppositions

Inadequacies in Private International Law Discourse in Post-National and Post-Secular Societies

In the 'post-national' and 'post-secular' society which Habermas postulates,[3] attempting to use national borders to decide the relevant context for the determination of identity ultimately amounts to legal reductionism. Serious misgivings also apply to determining the family law applicable to an individual on the basis of their nationality, particularly since this is an approach based on exclusion. Nationality is not the appropriate connecting factor in international family law. It is an approach which anticipates a difference, which it then re-emphasises with every decision. It is thus a performative act, engaging in the binary logic of the self and that which is other. That said, determination of applicable law based on nationality is in decline, ceding ground to a determination of the applicable law based on shared living space and choice of laws, the objective being to find common ground.

The Deconstruction of European Family-Law Codes

The Dissolution of the Meaning of Marriage and other Seismic Shifts

The ethical imperative of respect for cultural and religious identities, coupled with the axiom of their equivalence, poses a challenge to the integration of differing systems of family law. In Europe, increasing convergence in substantive family law has been accompanied by a gradual erosion of the importance accorded to marital status. In particular, traditional interpretations of marriage as an institution have proved to be historically obsolete, and the economic and social need to structure society by means of family-law policy has become atavistic. A system of family law free of metaphysical and political constraints, which has returned to its basic protective tasks, has considerable integrative potential.

3 Regarding post-secular society, see Habermas 2001, *passim*, in particular 12.

Incorporating Diversity through the Application of Substantive Family Law; an Eclectic Process

Concretising Norms on Hermeneutic Principles, Autonomous Determination of Law and Culturally Diversified Sets of Laws

An approach to recognising cultural identity and diverging understandings of family law within the scope of substantive law aims to find common ground. Such common ground can be found in many areas, and the encounters are of differing intensity. While it is rare that the law applicable to a given situation can be chosen from a broad range of family-law institutions drawing on different cultures, accommodation of alien legal concepts in the process of interpretation of a uniform substantive law is nevertheless more frequent. In order to incorporate culturally or religiously alien legal formulations, the process of norm concretisation needs to be sufficiently open to cultural and normative diversity. Such a process is, however, essentially an eclectic one, rather than one determined by theory.

Normative Pluralism in Family Law: Empirical Findings from Anthropological Investigations

Pluralism of Legal Cultures and Equality of Normative Obligation

Legal or normative pluralism, conversely, is a field of anthropological investigation. Legal anthropology teaches us that social space is not a normative vacuum. Pluralistic normative structures derived from a postmodern perception of the law, unconstrained by the dictates of legal positivism, challenge the modern idea that legislative monopoly rests with the state, thus – according to von Benda-Beckmann[4] – releasing the law from the panoptic of reifications in which many have imprisoned it. Such pluralism highlights the limits to the extent to which state law can direct society, and brings into sharp focus the enormous interdependence and complexity which exists in the relationship between law and society – as separate social entities – and between legal systems and social practices. It is thanks to the anthropological theory of legal or normative pluralism that jurisprudence has turned its attention to this complexity, to the empirically observable law as it is actually lived.

Nevertheless, parallel systems of family law based around religious communities are not a realistic and desirable prospect for Europe, especially since they must necessarily pose a challenge which the theory of law tailored to the individual cannot possibly meet. The right to cultural identity in the context of family law does not rule out every equality of normative obligation, precisely because this right also needs a foundation, a basis, in order for its own validity to be guaranteed. Moreover, in a democratic and secular state, the culturally inclusive effects exerted

4 von Benda-Beckmann 1991, 116.

by family-law institutions and procedures are indispensable. Finally, religious, community-based, normative orders in family matters pose a threat both to the cohesion of society as a whole and to the weaker members of the group.

Beyond Cultural and Religious Identity in Family Law: Discursive Practice and 'Legitimisation by Proceedings'[5]

Challenges to Diversity in Family-Law Contexts: Protecting Choice – Promoting Inclusion

Nevertheless, there is considerable scope for accommodating a plurality of views about the family. We need a plurality-conscious methodology which matches pluralist realities and goes at least some way towards accommodating cultural and religious minorities. Furthermore, we cannot ignore the normative reality which the autonomous structures in place in certain Muslim communities create. I believe that empirical and normative perspectives can ultimately best be combined in a family-law context based on discourse and procedure and that this will displace and overcome interpretations narrowly focused on norms and institutions and the boundaries between nation-states. The genesis of legal values from dialogue and the clarification of the core tasks of family law should have as their starting point the notion of autonomy of the individual. Depending on the area it is regulating, family law in Europe can limit itself to recognising self-determined proceedings, to integrating culture-based institutions, rules and values – despite the legislative prerogative which the state obviously holds – or, finally, to finding procedures within its state monopoly for reconciling differing positions. Autonomy ensures recourse to familiar discourse and to interpretative sovereignty. The limits to autonomy are set by human rights law and the constitution of the country concerned. Nevertheless, the heterarchical encounters which will necessarily occur will give rise to cultural and normative syncretisation extending way beyond the positions held by the various parties involved. The increasingly multicultural fabric of societies can result in individual objectives becoming more closely aligned with each other. This process, however, need not require that cultural considerations and the identity which they confer be abandoned. To address plurality, to be aware of one's own history, to refrain from the application of stigmatising stereotypes, to be aware of the contingent nature of cultural constructions and of the inherent potential for change: these are the essential elements of integrative family-law order and practice.

The converging development of family law provides additional impetus to this integrative approach, and Islamic countries are very much involved in this process. An irreducible core of family-law values which is sufficiently abstract and to which everyone could subscribe can integrate both cultural plurality and

5 Cf. Luhmann 1983.

other growing differentiations within society. The task now is to protect choice and promote inclusion, by means of a family law which accommodates cultural identity without sacrificing justice. That task involves nothing less than reshaping family law in order to reconcile a diversity of cultures and beliefs within the unitary family-law institutions of modern states. In everyday practice, debate in this area needs to be less abstract and ideological, and more detailed, concrete and context-related. It is an ambitious objective, but a worthwhile one.

Conclusion

Boundaries are Common Ground

Traces of Otherness on the Way to the Self

We are back where we started: with Levinas. Alterity is innate to the construction of identity as the experience of being identical with oneself. Boundaries between identity and otherness are common ground wherever and however they occur. While there is no ontological approach or Espistemological gateway to the idea of alterity, exploring its boundaries and venturing over them from time to time does bring us closer to ourselves.

If family law follows the path of otherness, there will be consequences. Discourse on the legal recognition of cultural identity and diversity points way beyond its subject. If we expose the law to alterity, then we inevitably abandon the path of legal positivism. And if we do so, what remains? A suggestion of agony. Agony in the face of the puzzle which the encounter and engagement with the other poses. And yet, in Levinas's words, it is in this encounter, in this engagement, that language and responsibility have their origins. In fact, that encounter and engagement form the essence of mutual cultural understanding in family law.

Bibliography

Abu Zayd, N. 2006. *Reformation of Islamic Thought. A Critical Historical Analysis*. Amsterdam: Amsterdam University Press.

Ali, S.S. 2000. *Gender and Human Rights in Islam and International Law. Equal before Allah, Unequal before Man?* The Hague: Kluwer Law International.

Anderson, B. 1983. *Imagined Communities*. London: Verso.

Andrae, M. 2007. Anwendung des islamischen Rechts im Scheidungsverfahren vor deutschen Gerichten. *Neue Juristische Wochenschrift*, 24, 1730–1733.

An-Na'im, A. 1992. *Toward Islamic Reformation. Civil Liberties, Human Rights, and International Law*. Cairo: American University in Cairo.

An-Na'im, A. 1994. Cultural Transformation and Normative Consensus on the Best Interests of the Child. *International Journal of Law and the Family*, 8(1), 62–81.

An-Na'im, A. 2002. *Islamic Family Law in a Changing World. A Global Resource Book*. London: Zed Books.

Antokolskaia, M. 2004. Human Rights as a Basis for the Harmonisation of Family Law?, in *Family Life and Human Rights*, edited by P. Lødrup, E. Modvar. Oslo: Gyldendal Akademisk, 29–47.

Antokolskaia, M. 2006. *Harmonisation of Family Law in Europe. A Historical Perspective. A Tale of Two Millennia*. Antwerp: Intersentia.

Bade, K.J., Oltmer, J. 2007. Deutschland, in *Enzyklopädie. Migration in Europa. Vom 17. Jahrhundert bis zur Gegenwart*, edited by K.J. Bade, P.C. Emmer, L. Lucassen, J. Oltmer. Paderborn: Ferdinand Schöningh, 141–170.

Bader, V. 2009. Legal Pluralism and Differentiated Morality: Shari'a in Ontario?, in *Legal Practice and Cultural Diversity*, edited by R. Grillo, R. Ballard, A. Ferrari, A.J. Hoekema, M. Maussen, P. Shah. Farnham: Ashgate, 48–72.

Baderin, M.A. 2005 (originally published 2003). *International Human Rights and Islamic Law*. Oxford: Oxford University Press.

Badry, R. 1999. Zur 'Mädchenbeschneidung' in islamischen Ländern: religiös-rechtliche Aspekte und feministische Kritik. *Freiburger FrauenStudien*, 2, 211–232.

Baer, S. 2010. A Closer Look at Law: Human Rights as Multi-Level Sites of Struggles over Multi-Dimensional Equality. *Utrecht Law Review*, 6(2), 56–76.

Bainham, A. 1995. Family Law in a Pluralistic Society. *Journal of Law and Society*. 22(2), 234–247.

Bakht, N. 2005. *Arbitration, Religion and Family Law. Private Justice on the Backs of Women*. Ottawa: National Association of Women and the Law.

Ballard, R. 2006. Ethnic Diversity and the Delivery of Justice: The Challenge of Plurality, in *Migration, Diasporas and Legal Systems in Europe*, edited by P. Shah, W. Menski. Abingdon, New York: Routledge Cavendish, 29–56.

Ballard, R. 2008. Inside and Outside: Contrasting Perspectives on the Dynamics of Kinship and Marriage in Contemporary South Asian Transnational Networks, in *The Family in Question. Immigrant and Ethnic Minorities in Multicultural Europe*, edited by R. Grillo. Amsterdam: Amsterdam University Press, 37–70.

Ballard, R. 2009. Human Rights in Contexts of Ethnic Plurality: Always a Vehicle for Liberation?, in *Legal Practice and Cultural Diversity*, edited by R. Grillo, R. Ballard, A. Ferrari, A. Hoekema, M. Maussen, P. Shah. Farnham: Ashgate, 299–329.

Bano, S. 2007. Muslim Family Justice and Human Rights: The Experience of British Muslim Women. *The Journal of Comparative Law*, 2(2), 38–66.

Basedow, J. 2001. Das Internationale Privatrecht in den Zeiten der Globalisierung, in *Festschrift für Hans Stoll zum 75. Geburtstag*, edited by G. Hohloch, R. Frank, P. Schlechtriem. Tübingen: Mohr Siebeck, 405–416.

Beck-Gernsheim, E. 2000. *Was kommt nach der Familie? Einblicke in neue Lebensformen*. 2nd Edition. München: Beck.

Beck-Gernsheim, E. 2007. Transnational lives, transnational marriages: a review of the evidence from migrant communities in Europe. *Global Networks*, 7(3), 271–288.

Belhoul, S.M. 2005. Religionspluralismus: Europäischer 'Normal-' oder 'Notfall'?, in *Religiöser Pluralismus. Empirische Studien und analytische Perspektiven*, edited by M. Baumann, S.M. Belhoul. Bielefeld: transcript, 145–169.

Benhabib, S. 2002. *The Claims of Culture. Equality and Diversity in the Global Era*. Princeton: Princeton University Press. Bernecker, W.L. 1995. *Religion in Spanien, Darstellung und Daten zu Geschichte und Gegenwart*. Gütersloh: Gütersloher Verlagshaus.

Bielefeldt, H. 2007. *Menschenrechte in der Einwanderungsgesellschaft. Plädoyer für einen aufgeklärten Multikulturalismus*. Bielefeld: transcript,.

Bielefeldt, H. 2010. Das Islambild in Deutschland. Zum öffentlichen Umgang mit der Angst vor dem Islam, in *Islamfeindlichkeit: Wenn die Grenzen der Kritik verschwimmen*, edited by T.G. Schneiders. 2nd Edition. Wiesbaden: VS Verlag für Sozialwissenschaften, 173–206.

Bistolfi, R. 1995. Approches de l'islam dans l'Union Européenne, in *Islams d'Europe. Intégration ou insertion communautaire?*, edited by R. Bistolfi, F. Zabbal. La Tour d'Aigues: Editions de l'Aube, 13–63.

Boele-Woelki, K. 2003. *Perspectives for the Unification and Harmonisation of Family Law in Europe*. Antwerp: Intersentia.

Boele-Woelki, K., Braat, B., Sumner, I. 2003. *European Family Law in Action, Volume 1. Grounds for Divorce*. Antwerp: Intersentia.

Bosse-Platière, H. 2010a. Chapitre 150. Nature juridique et evolution du PACS, in *Droit de la Famille*, edited by P. Murat. 5th Edition. Paris: Dalloz, 477–478.

Bosse-Platière, H. 2010b. Chapitre 151. Formation du PACS, in *Droit de la Famille*, edited by P. Murat. 5th Edition. Paris: Dalloz, 489–497.
Boyd, M. 2004. *Dispute Resolution in Family Law. Protecting Choice, Promoting Inclusion.* [Online, 20 December]. Available at: http://www.attorneygeneral.jus.gov.on.ca/english/about/pubs/boyd/fullreport.pdf [accessed: 9 November 2010].
Briggs, A. 2008. *The Conflicts of Law*. 2nd Edition, Oxford: Oxford University Press.
Brophy, J., Jhutti-Johal, J., Owen, C. 2003. *Significant Harm. Child Protection Litigation in a Multi-Cultural Setting*. London: Lord Chancellor's Department.
Brown, C., Russell, B. 2008. Archbishop of Canterbury warns sharia law in Britain is inevitable. *The Independent*, 8 February.
Bucher, A. 2008. Internationales Scheidungsrecht in der Praxis, in *Vierte Schweizer Familienrecht§Tage*, edited by I. Schwenzer, A. Büchler. Bern: Stämpfli, 33–76.
Büchler, A. 2003. *Das islamische Familienrecht. Eine Annäherung unter Berücksichtigung des Verhältnisses des klassischen islamischen Rechts zum geltenden ägyptischen Familienrecht*. Bern: Stämpfli.
Büchler, A. 2004. Das Scheidungsverfahren in rechtsvergleichender Sicht, in *Auf dem Weg zum Familiengericht*, edited by R. Vetterli. Bern: Stämpfli, 19–43.
Büchler, A. 2007. Zwangsehen in zivilrechtlicher und internationalprivatrechtlicher Sicht. Rechtstatsachen – Rechtsvergleich – Rechtsanalyse. *Die Praxis des Familienrechts*, 4, 725–751.
Büchler, A. 2009. Hermeneutik und Recht in der Tradition des Islam, in *Rechtswissenschaft und Hermeneutik. Kongress der Schweizerischen Vereinigung für Rechts- und Sozialphilosophie*, 16 and 17 May 2008, University of Zurich, edited by M. Senn, B. Fritschi, Stuttgart: Franz Steiner-Verlag, 185–206.
Büchler, A., Fink, S. 2008. Eheschliessungen im Ausland. Die Grenzen ihrer Anerkennung in der Schweiz am Beispiel von Ehen islamischer Prägung. *Die Praxis des Familienrechts*, 1, 48–68.
Cadet, F. 2005. *L'ordre public en droit international de la famille. Etude comparée France/Espagne*. Paris: L'Harmattan.
Carroll, L. 1982. Talaqi-Tafwid and Stipulations in a Muslim Marriage Contract: Important Means of Protecting the Position of the South Asian Muslim Wife. *Modern Asian Studies*, 16(2), 277–309.
Cesari, J. 2003. Muslim Minorities in Europe: The Silent Revolution, in *Modernizing Islam. Religion in the Public Sphere in the Middle East and Europe*, edited by J.L. Esposito, F. Burgat. London: Hurst & Company, 251–269.
Cesari, J., Caerio, A., Hussain, D. 2004. *Islam and Fundamental Rights in Europe*, Final Report of October 2004, [Online, 25 October]. Available at:http://ec.europa.eu/justice_home/doc_centre/rights/studies/docs/islam_fundamental_rights_final_25_10_2004_en.pdf [accessed: 9 November 2010].

Chaïbou, A. 1998. La jurisprudence nigérienne en droit de la famille à l'émergence de la notion 'coutume urbaine'. *Journal of Legal Pluralism*, 42, 157–170.

Cherribi, O. 2003. The Growing Islamization of Europe, in *Modernizing Islam. Religion in the Public Sphere in the Middle East and Europe*, edited by J.L. Esposito, F. Burgat. London: Hurst & Company, 193–213.

Chiba, M. 1986. Introduction, in *Asian Indigenous Law in Interaction with Received Law*, edited by M. Chiba. London, New York: Kegan Paul International, 1–12.

Chiba, M. 1998. Other Phases of Legal Pluralism in the Contemporary World. *Ratio Juris*, 11(3), 228–245.

Clifford, J. 1986. Introduction: Partial Truths, in *Writing Culture. The Poetics and Politics of Ethnography*, edited by J. Clifford, G.E. Marcus. Berkeley: University of California Press, 1–26.

Coester-Waltjen, D. 2006. Anerkennung im Internationalen Personen-, Familien- und Erbrecht. *Praxis des Internationalen Privat- und Verfahrensrechts*, 4, 392–400.

Coester-Waltjen, D., Kronke, H., Kokott, J. 1998. *Die Wirkungskraft der Grundrechte bei Fällen mit Auslandsbezug*. Heidelberg: C.F. Müller.

Collier, J.G. 2001. *Conflict of Laws*. Cambridge: Cambridge University Press.

Collins, L. 2006. *Dicey, Morris & Collins on The Conflict of Laws*, 1, 2. 14th Edition. London: Sweet & Maxwell.

Cottier, M. 2005. Weibliche Genitalverstümmelung, zivilrechtlicher Kindesschutz und interkulturelle Verständigung. *Die Praxis des Familienrechts*, 4, 698–717.

Coulson, N.J. 1964. *A History of Islamic Law*. Edinburgh: Edinburgh University Press.

Crossette, B. 1999. Testing the Limits of Tolerance as Cultures Mix; Does Freedom Mean Accepting Rituals That Repel the West? *The New York Times*, 6 March.

Dannemann, G. 2004. *Die ungewollte Diskriminierung in der internationalen Rechtsanwendung. Zur Anwendung, Berücksichtigung und Anpassung von Normen aus unterschiedlichen Rechtsordnungen*. Tübingen: Mohr Siebeck.

Deveaux, M. 2005. A deliberative approach to conflicts of culture, in *Minorities within Minorities. Equality, Rights and Diversity*, edited by A. Eisenberg, J. Spinner-Halev. Cambridge: Cambridge University Press, 340–362.

Devers, A. 2010. Chapitre 421. Formation du mariage, in *Droit de la famille*, edited by P. Murat. 5th Edition. Paris: Dalloz, 1202–1216.

Donders, Y.M. 2002. *Towards a Right to Cultural Identity?* Antwerp: Intersentia.

Eekelaar, J. 2003. The End of an Era? *Journal of Family History*, 28(1), 108–122.

Ehringfeld, K. 1997. *Eltern-Kind-Konflikte in Ausländerfamilien*. Berlin: Duncker & Humblot.

Ehrlich, E. 1989. Grundlegung der Soziologie des Rechts, in *Schriftenreihe zur Rechtssoziologie und Rechtstatsachenforschung*, edited by M. Rehbinder. 4th Edition. Berlin: Duncker & Humblot, 69.

Esposito, J.L., DeLong-Bas, N.J. 2001. *Women in Muslim Family Law.* 2nd Edition, Syracuse, New York: Syracuse University Press.

Feinberg, J. 2007. The Child's Right to an Open Future, in *Philosophy of Education. An Anthology*, edited by R. Curren. Oxford: Blackwell Publishing, 112–123.

Ferrand, F. 2006. Aktuelle Entwicklungen im französischen Familienrecht. *Zeitschrift für das gesamte Familienrecht mit Betreuungsrecht, Erbrecht, Verfahrensrecht, Öffentlichem Recht*, 18, 1316–9.

Fischer-Lescano, A., Teubner, G. 2007. Fragmentierung des Weltrechts: Vernetzung globaler Regimes statt etatistischer Rechtseinheit, in *Weltstaat – Weltstaatlichkeit: Beobachtungen globaler politischer Strukturbildung*, edited by M. Albert, R. Stichweh. Wiesbaden: VS Verlag für Sozialwissenschaften, 37–61.

Foblets, M.C. 1999. Conflicts of Law in Cross-Cultural Family Disputes in Europe Today. Who will Reorient Conflicts Law?, in *Relations familiales interculturelles / Cross cultural family relations, Oñati Papers*, edited by M.C. Foblets, F. Strijbosch, 8, 27–45.

Foblets, M.C. 2000. Migrant Women Caught between Islamic Family Law and Women´s Rights. The Search for the Appropriate 'Connecting Factor' in International Family Law. *Maastricht Journal of European and Comparative Law*, 7(1), 11–34.

Foblets, M.C. 2001. Conflits conjugaux en immigration. Libérer malgré elle, la femme musulmane immigrée marocaine?, in *Die Bedeutung der Lehre vom Rechtskreis und der Rechtskultur*, edited by H. Scholler, S. Tellenbach. Berlin: Duncker & Humblot, 33–54.

Foblets, M.C. 2003. L'enfant d'une famille musulmane. Questions particulières relatives à la gestion par le droit de l'appartenance, in *L'enfant et les relations familiales internationales*, edited by J.L. Renchon. Bruxelles: Bruylant, 235–263.

Foblets, M.C., Reyntjens, F. 1998. Urban Normative Fields in Africa Today. *Journal of Legal Pluralism*, 42, 1–8.

Fondation Surgir 2006. *La prévalence du mariage forcé en Suisse: Rapport de l'enquête exploratoire*. Lausanne.

Foucault, M. 1971. *L'Ordre du discourse.* Paris: Gallimard.

Fournier, P. 2009. Transit and Translation: Islamic Legal Transplants in North America and Europe. *Journal of Comparative Law*, 4(1), 1–38.

Fulchiron, H. 1999. *L'étranger en France, face et au regard du droit. Rapport, Centre de droit de famille Université Jean Moulin Lyon 3*. Lyon.

Fulchiron, H. 2007. Adoption sur *kafala* ne vaut (à propos des arrêts Civ. 1re, 10 octobre 2006). *Recueil Dalloz*, 183(12), 816–821.

Fux, B. 2002. Which Models of the Family are Encouraged or Discouraged by Different Family Policies?, in *Family Life and Family Policies in Europe. Vol. 2: Problems and Issues in Comparative Perspective*, edited by F.-X. Kaufmann, A. Kuijsten, H.-J. Schulze, K.P. Strohmeier. Oxford: Clarendon Press, 363–418.

Gannagé, P. 1998. Cour de cassation, 1ère chambre civile, décision du 2ème décembre 1997. *Revue critique de droit international privé, 87*. Paris: Dalloz, 632–7.

Gärtner, V. 2008. *Die Privatscheidung im deutschen und gemeinschaftsrechtlichen Internationalen Privat- und Verfahrensrecht: aussergerichtliche Ehescheidung im Spannungsfeld von kultureller Diversität und Integration*. Tübingen: Mohr Siebeck.

Geuss, R. 2002. *Privatheit: eine Genealogie*. Frankfurt am Main: Suhrkamp.

Giménez Costa, A. 2004. El matrimonio musulman: problemas de adaptación al derecho español, in *Perspectivas del derecho de familia en el siglo XXI: XIII Congreso Internacional de Derecho de Familia*, Instituto de Desarrollo y Análisis del Derecho de Familia en España. Sevilla.

Glenn, H.P. 1991. Reception and Reconciliation of Laws, in *Monismus oder Pluralismus der Rechtskulturen? Anthropologische und ethnologische Grundlagen traditioneller und moderner Rechtssysteme, Rechtstheorie. Zeitschrift für Logik, Methodenlehre, Kybernetik und Soziologie des Rechts*, edited by P. Sack, C. Wellmann, M. Yasaki. Berlin: Duncker & Humblot, Beiheft 12, 209–214.

Gräb, W. 2007. Säkularisierung – das Ende der Religion oder der Verfall der Kirchen?, in *Säkularisierung. Bilanz und Perspektiven einer umstrittenen These*, edited by C. von Braun, W. Gräb, J. Zachhuber. Berlin: LIT-Verlag, 75–95.

Grabenwarter, C. 2009. *Europäische Menschenrechtskonvention*. 4th Edition. München: Beck.

Griffiths, J. 1986. What is Legal Pluralism? *Journal of Legal Pluralism*, 24, 1–55.

Grillo, R. 2008. The Family in Dispute: Insiders and Outsiders, in *The Family in Question. Immigrant and Ethnic Minorities in Multicultural Europe*, edited by R. Grillo. Amsterdam: Amsterdam University Press, 15–35.

Grimm, D. 2001. *Die Verfassung und die Politik: Einsprüche in Störfällen*. München: Beck.

Gutmann, D. 2009. *Droit International Privé*. 6th Edition. Paris: Dalloz.

Habermas, J. 1983. *Moralbewußtsein und kommunikatives Handeln*. Frankfurt am Main: Suhrkamp.

Habermas, J. 1985. *Theorie des kommunikativen Handelns*. Band I, Handlungsrationalität und gesellschaftliche Rationalisierung. 3rd Edition. Frankfurt am Main: Suhrkamp.

Habermas, J. 1991. *Erläuterungen zur Diskursethik*. Frankfurt am Main: Suhrkamp.

Habermas, J. 1993. Anerkennungskämpfe im demokratischen Rechtsstaat, in *Multikulturalismus und die Politik der Anerkennung*, edited by C. Taylor. 2nd Edition. Frankfurt am Main: Fischer, 147–196.

Habermas, J. 1996. *Die Einbeziehung des Anderen. Studien zur politischen Theorie*. Frankfurt am Main: Suhrkamp.

Habermas, J. 2001. *Glauben und Wissen*. Frankfurt am Main: Suhrkamp.

Haeri, S. 1989. *Law of Desire. Temporary Marriage in Shi'i Iran*. New York: Syracuse University Press.

Hallaq, W.B. 2005. *The Origins and Evolution of Islamic Law*. Cambridge: Cambridge University Press.

Harris, D.J., Boyle, M.O., Bates, E.P., Buckley, C.M. 2009. *Harris, O'Boyle & Warbrick Law of the European Convention on Human Rights*. 2nd Edition. Oxford: Oxford University Press.

Henrich, D. 2001. Abschied vom Staatsangehörigkeitsprinzip?, in *Festschrift für Hans Stoll zum 75. Geburtstag*, edited by G. Hohloch, R. Frank, P. Schlechtriem. Tübingen: Mohr Siebeck, 437–449.

Henrich, D. 2004a. Die Morgengabe und das Internationale Privatrecht, in *Privatrecht in Europa: Vielfalt, Kollision, Kooperation, Festschrift für Hans Jürgen Sonnenberger zum 70. Geburtstag*, edited by M. Coester, D. Martiny, K.A. Prinz von Sachsen Gessaphe. München: Beck, 389–400.

Henrich, D. 2004b, Parteiautonomie, Privatautonomie und kulturelle Identität, in *Festschrift für Erik Jayme*, Band I, edited by H.P. Mansel, T. Pfeiffer, H. Kronke, C. Kohler, R. Hausmann. München: Sellier, 321–9.

Herfarth, C. 2000. *Die Scheidung nach jüdischem Recht im internationalen Zivilverfahrensrecht*. Heidelberg: Universitätsverlag Winter.

Hicks, S. 1991. A Model of Society for the Comparative Study of Law, in *Monismus oder Pluralismus der Rechtskulturen? Anthropologische und ethnologische Grundlagen traditioneller und moderner Rechtssysteme, Rechtstheorie. Zeitschrift für Logik, Methodenlehre, Kybernetik und Soziologie des Rechts*, edited by P. Sack, C. Wellmann, M. Yasaki. Berlin: Duncker & Humblot, Beiheft 12, 215–222.

Hinz, M.O. 1990. 'Folk Law': Recht von unten – Zur Theorie des 'Legal Pluralism', in *Kritik und Vertrauen, Festschrift für Peter Schneider zum 70. Geburtstag*, edited by E. Denninger, M.O. Hinz, P.C. Mayer-Tasch, G. Roellecke. Frankfurt am Main: Hain, 122–142.

Hinz, M.O. 1995. Das Recht auf das eigene Recht. Rechtspluralismus und Rechtsgleichheit in Kanada, in *Rechtsgleichheit und Rechtspluralismus*, edited by E.-J. Lampe. Baden-Baden: Nomos, 75–88.

Hoekema, A.J. 2005. European Legal Encounters between Minority and Majority Culture: Cases of Interlegality. *Journal of Legal Pluralism*, 51, 1–28.

Hussain, D. 2003. The Holy Grail of Muslims in Western Europe: Representation and their Relationship with the State, in *Modernizing Islam. Religion in the Public Sphere in the Middle East and Europe*, edited by J.L. Esposito, F. Burgat. London: Hurst & Company, 215–250.

Huzel, P. 2006. Eherecht in Spanien, in *Eherecht in Europa*, edited by R. Süss, G. Ring. Angelbachtal: Zerb Verlag, 1195–1249.

The Islamic Shari'a Council of Great Britain and Northern Ireland, *An Introduction*, Leyton.

Jayawickrama, N. 2002. *The Judicial Application of Human Rights Law. National, Regional and International Jurisprudence*. Cambridge: Cambridge University Press.

Jayme, E. 1993. *Narrative Normen im Internationalen Privat- und Verfahrensrecht*. Tübingen: Mohr Siebeck.

Jayme, E. 2003a. Die kulturelle Dimension der Rechts – ihre Bedeutung für das Internationale Privatrecht und die Rechtsvergleichung. *Rabels Zeitschrift für ausländisches und internationales Privatrecht*, 67, 211–230.

Jayme, E. 2003b. *Internationales Privatrecht und Völkerrecht, Studien – Vorträge – Berichte*. Heidelberg: C.F. Müller, Heidelberg.

Jivraj, S., Herman, D. 2009. 'It is difficult for a white judge to understand': Orientalism, Racialisation, and Christianity in English Child Welfare Cases. *Child and Family Law Quarterly*, 21(3), 283–308.

Kälin, W. 2000. *Grundrechte im Kulturkonflikt. Freiheit und Gleichheit in der Einwanderungsgesellschaft*. Zürich: NZZ Verlag.

Kamali, M.H. 2003. *Principles of Islamic Jurisprudence*. 3rd Edition. Cambridge: The Islamic Text Society.

Kaufmann, F.-X. 2002. Politics and Policies towards the Family in Europe. A Framework and an Inquiry into their Differences and Convergences, in *Family Life and Family Policies in Europe. Vol. 2: Problems and Issues in Comparative Perspective*, edited by F.-X. Kaufmann, A. Kuijsten, H.-J. Schulze, K.P. Strohmeier. Oxford: Oxford University Press, 419–490.

Kegel, G., Schurig, K. 2004. *Internationales Privatrecht*. 9th Edition. München: Beck.

Kepel, G. 2006. Der Islam Europas zwischen Integration und Kommunitarismus, in *Der Islam in Europa. Zwischen Weltpolitik und Alltag*, edited by U. Altermatt, M. Delgado, G. Vergauwen. Stuttgart: Kohlhammer, 23–39.

Keshavjee, M. 2007. Alternative Dispute Resolution in a Diasporic Muslim Community in Britain, in *Law and Ethnic Plurality. Socio-Legal Perspectives*, edited by P. Shah. Leiden: Martinus Nijhof, 145–175.

Kohler, C. 2006. Einfluss der Globalisierung auf die Wahl der Anknüpfungsmomente, in *Internationales Familienrecht für das 21. Jahrhundert. Symposium zum 65. Geburtstag von Ulrich Spellenberg*, edited by R. Freitag, S. Leible, H. Sippel, U. Wanitzek. München: Sellier, 9–27.

Kohler, C. 2008. Zur Gestaltung des europäischen Kollisionsrechts für Ehesachen: Der steinige Weg zu einheitlichen Vorschriften über das anwendbare Recht für Scheidung und Trennung. *Zeitschrift für das gesamte Familienrecht mit Betreuungsrecht, Erbrecht, Verfahrensrecht, Öffentlichem Recht*, 18, 1673–1681.

Korbin, J.E. 1981. Introduction, in *Child Abuse and Neglect. Cross-Cultural Perspectives*, edited by J.E. Korbin. Berkeley, Los Angeles, University of California Press, 1–12.

Krause, H.D. 2006. Comparative Family Law, Past Traditions Battle Future Trends – and vice versa, in *The Oxford Handbook of Comparative Law*, edited by M. Reimann, R. Zimmermann. Oxford: Oxford University Press, 1099–1129.

Krawietz, B. 2002. Cut and Paste in Legal Rules: Designing Islamic Norms with Tafliq. *Die Welt des Islams. International Journal for the Study of Modern Islam*, 42, 3–40.

Kropholler, J. 2004. *Internationales Privatrecht*. 5th Edition. Tübingen: Mohr Siebeck.

Kymlicka, W. 1995. *Multicultural Citizenship. A Liberal Theory of Minority Rights*. Oxford: Clarendon Press.

Lauser, A., Weissköppel, C. 2008. Einleitung: Die neue Aufmerksamkeit für Religion in der Migrations- und Transnationalismusforschung. Ein Plädoyer für die ethnografische Mikro- und Kontextanalyse, in *Migration und religiöse Dynamik. Ethnologische Religionsforschung im transnationalen Kontext*, edited by A. Lauser, C. Weissköppel. Bielefeld: transcript, 7–32.

Lemouland, J.-J. 2010. Chapitre 111: Exigences de fond du mariage, in *Droit de la famille*, edited by P. Murat. 5th Edition. Paris: Dalloz, 38–76.

Levinas, E. 1967. *En découvrant l'existence avec Husserl et Heidegger*, Réimpression conforme à la 1ère édition suivie d'Essais nouveaux. Paris: Librairie philosophique J. Vrin.

Levinas, E. 1991. *Entre nous. Essais sur le penser-à-l'autre*. Paris: Grasset.

Looschelders, D. 2001. Die Ausstrahlung der Grund- und Menschenrechte auf das Internationale Privatrecht. *Rabels Zeitschrift für ausländisches und internationales Privatrecht*, 65, 463–491.

Lösch, K. 2005. Begriff und Phänomen der Transdifferenz: Zur Infragestellung binärer Differenzkonstrukte, in *Differenzen anders denken. Bausteine zu einer Kulturtheorie der Transdifferenz*, edited by L. Allolio-Näcke, B. Kalscheuer, A. Manzeschke. Frankfurt am Main: Campus, 26–49.

Loussouarn, Y., Bourel., P., de Vareilles-Sommières, P. 2007. *Droit international privé*. 9th Edition. Paris: Dalloz.

Lowe, N.V., Douglas, G. 2007. *Bromley's Family Law*. 10th Edition. Oxford: Oxford University Press.

Luhmann, N. 1983. *Legitimation durch Verfahren*. Frankfurt am Main: Suhrkamp.

Mahajan, G. 2005. Can intra-group equality co-exist with cultural diversity? Re-examining multicultural frameworks of accommodation, in *Minorities within Minorities. Equality, Rights and Diversity*, edited by A. Eisenberg, J. Spinner-Halev. Cambridge: Cambridge University Press, 90–112.

Mahlmann, M. 2006. Ethische Duldsamkeit und Glauben – (Rechts-)Philosophische Grundlagen religiöser Toleranz, in *Ein neuer Kampf der Religionen? Staat Recht und religiöse Toleranz*, edited by M. Mahlmann, H. Rottleuthner. Berlin: Duncker & Humblot, 75–98.

Mankowski, P. 2004. Kulturelle Identität und Internationales Privatrecht. *Praxis des Internationalen Privat- und Verfahrensrechts*, 4, 282–290.

Mansel, H.P. 2008. Die kulturelle Identität im Internationalen Privatrecht, in *Pluralistische Gesellschaften und Internationales Recht: Referate und Thesen*, edited by G. Nolte, H. Keller, A. von Bogdandy, H.P. Mansel, A. Büchler, C. Walter. Heidelberg: C.F. Müller, 43, 137–214.

Martín-Casals, M., Ribot, J. 2008. Spain. The Postmodern Family and the Agenda for Radical Legal Change, in *The International Survey of Family Law, 2008 Edition*. Bristol: Jordan Publishing, 411–436.

Martinez-Torrón, J. 2000. The Legal Status of Islam in Spain, in *Islam and European Legal Systems*, edited by S. Ferrari, A. Bradney. Aldershot: Ashgate, 47–71.

Mayss, A. 2000. Recognition of Foreign Divorces: Unwarrantable Ethnocentrism, in *Ethnic Minorities, their Families and the Law*, edited by J. Murphy. Oxford: Hart Publishing, 51–68.

Mehra, M. 2007. Women's Equality and Culture in the Context of Identity Politics. *The Journal of Comparative Law*, 2, 6–37.

Menski, W. 2006. Rethinking Legal Theory in the Light of South–North Migration, in *Migration, Diasporas and Legal Systems in Europe*, edited by P. Shah, W. Menski. Abingdon, New York: Routledge Cavendish, 13–28.

Menski, W. 2009. Indian Secular Pluralism and its Relevance for Europe, in *Legal Practice and Cultural Diversity*, edited by R. Grillo, R. Ballard, A. Ferrari, A.J. Hoekema, M. Maussen, P. Shah. Farnham: Ashgate, 31–47.

Meulders-Klein, M.-T. 2004. Family Law, Human Rights and Judicial Review in Europa. Heterogeneity and Complexity, in *Family Life and Human Rights*, edited by P. Lødrup, E. Modvar. Oslo: Gyldendal Akademisk, 477–493.

Mills, C. 2003. The Child´s Right to an Open Future? *Journal of Social Philosophy*, 34, 499–509.

Mirza, M., Senthilkumaran, A., Ja'far, Z. 2007 (reprint 2009). *Living Apart Together. British Muslims and the Paradox of Multiculturalism*. London: Policy Exchange.

Mitchell, R. 2001. Family Law in Algeria before and after the 1404/1984 Family Code, in *Islamic Law. Theory and Pracice*, edited by R. Gleave, E. Kermeli. London: I.B. Tauris Publishers, 194–204.

Moch, L.P. 2007. Frankreich, in: *Enzyklopädie Migration in Europa. Vom 17. Jahrhundert bis zur Gegenwart*, edited by K.J. Bade, P.C. Emmer, L. Lucacssen, J. Oltmer. Paderborn: Ferdinand Schöningh, 122–140.

Mousset, S. 2003. *Olympe de Gouges et les droits de la femme*. Paris: Editions du Félin.

Murphy, J. 2000a. The Discretionary Refusal of Recognition of Foreign Marriages, in *Ethnic Minorities, their Families and the Law*, edited by J. Murphy. Oxford: Hart Publishing, 71–86.

Murphy, J. 2000b. Child Welfare in Transracial Adoptions: Colour-blind Children and Colour-blind Law, in *Ethnic Minorities, their Families and the Law*, edited by J. Murphy. Oxford: Hart Publishing, 33–48.

Nasir, J.J.A. 2009. *The Islamic Law of Personal Status*, 3rd Edition. Leiden: Brill.

One Law For All campaign, *Sharia Law in Britain. A Threat to one Law for All & Equal Rights*, June 2010.

Owen Hood, P., Jackson, P., Leopold, P. 2001. *O. Hood Phillips and Jackson. Constitutional and Administrative Law*. 8th Edition. London: Sweet & Maxwell.

Pearl, D. 1999. Islamic Family Law and its Reception by the Courts in the West: the English Experience, in *Islamic Law and its Reception by the Courts in the West. Congress from 23 to 24 October 1998 in Osnabrück*, edited by C. von BaR. Cologne: C. Heymanns Verlag, 111–115.

Pearl, D., Menski, W. 1998. *Islamic Family Law*. 3rd Edition. London: Sweet & Maxwell.

Phillips, A. 2005. Dilemmas of Gender and Culture. The Judge, the Democrat and the Political Activist, in *Minorities within Minorities. Equality, Rights and Diversity*, edited by A. Eisenberg, J. Spinner-Halev. Cambridge: Cambridge University Press, 113–134.

Phillips, A. 2007. *Multiculturalism without Culture*. Princeton: Princeton University Press.

Pintens, W. 2006. Materielles Familienrecht in Europa – Rechtseinheit oder -vielfalt?, in *Internationales Familienrecht für das 21. Jahrhundert*, edited by R. Freitag, S. Leible, H. Sippel, U. Wanitzek. München: Sellier, 137–153.

Poulter, S. 1987. Ethnic Minority Customs, English Law and Human Rights. *International and Comparative Law Quarterly*, 36(3), 589–615.

Poulter, S. 1990. The Claim to a Separate Islamic System of Personal Law for British Muslims, in *Islamic Family Law*, edited by C. Mallat, J. Connors. London: Graham & Trotman, 147–166.

Poulter, S. 1998. *Ethnicity, Law and Human Rights. The English Experience*. Oxford: Clarendon Press.

Powell, C. 2005/2006. Lifting Our Veil of Ignorance. *Hastings Law Journal*, 57, 331–383.

Randeria, S. 2002. Entangled Histories of Uneven Modernities: Civil Society, Caste Solidarities and Legal Pluralism in India, in *Unraveling Ties*, edited by Y. Elkana, I. Krastev, E. Macamo, S. Randeria. Frankfurt am Main: Campus, 284–311.

Randeria, S. 2003. Transnationalisierung des Rechts. Zur Rolle zivilgesellschaftlicher Akteure. *WZB-Mitteilungen*, 101, 19–22.

Rauscher, T. 2004. Heimatlos in Europa? – Gedanken gegen die Aufgabe des Staatsangehörigkeitsprinzips im IPR, in *Festschrift für Erik Jayme*, Band I, edited by H.-P. Mansel, T. Pfeiffer, H. Kronke, C. Kohler, R. Hausmann. München: Sellier, 719–745.

Rehman, J. 2007. The Sharia, Islamic Family Laws and International Human Rights Law: Examining the Theory and Practice of Polygamy and Talaq. *International Journal of Law, Policy and the Family*, 21, 108–127.

Reitman, O. 2005. On Exit, in *Minorities within Minorities. Equality, Rights and Diversity*, edited by A. Eisenberg, J. Spinner-Halev, J. Cambridge: Cambridge University Press, 189–208.

Renteln, A.D. 2004. *The Cultural Defense*. New York: Oxford University Press.

Reuter, L.R. 2002. Zuwanderung nach Deutschland: Rechtliche, politische und gesellschaftliche Aspekte, in *Demokratie in Staat und Wirtschaft, Festschrift für Ekkehart Stein zum 70. Geburtstag*, edited by H. Faber, G. Frank. Tübingen: Mohr Siebeck, 387–409.

Revillard, M. 2006. *Droit international privé et communautaire: pratique notariale*. 6th Edition. Paris: Defrénois.

Rohe, M. 2003. Religiös gespaltenes Zivilrecht in Deutschland und Europa?, in *Festschrift für Christoph Link zum 70. Geburtstag*, edited by H. De Wall, M. Germann. Tübingen: Mohr Siebeck, 409–429.

Rohe, M. 2004. The Application of Islamic Family law in German Courts and its Compatibility with German Public Policy, in *Iranian Family and Succession Laws and their Application in German Courts*, edited by J. Basedow, N. Yassari. Tübingen: Mohr Siebeck, 19–32.

Rohe, M. 2006. Eheschliessung in islamischen Staaten – Prüfung der Wirksamkeit durch deutsche Behörden. *Das Standesamt. Zeitschrift für Standesamtswesen, Familienrecht, Staatsangehörigkeitsrecht, Personenstandsrecht, internationales Privatrecht des In- und Auslands*, 4, 93–102.

Rohe, M. 2009a. Shari'a in a European Context, in *Legal Practice and Cultural Diversity*, edited by R. Grillo, R. Ballard, A. Ferrari, A.J. Hoekema, M. Maussen, P. Shah. Farnham: Ashgate, 93–114.

Rohe, M. 2009b, *Das Islamische Recht. Geschichte und Gegenwart*. München: Beck.

Romano, G. 2005. Religion und soziale Ordnung – Wie viel Multikulturalität braucht die Gesellschaft?, in *Religiöser Pluralismus Empirische Studien und analytische Perspektiven*, edited by M. Baumann, S. M. Behloul. Bielefeld: transcript, 223–240.

Rosman, D. 2003. *The Evolution of the English Churches 1500–2000*. Cambridge: Cambridge University Press.

Rothenbacher, F. 1998. Social Change in Europe and its Impact on Family Structures, in *The Changing Family. International Perspectives on the Family and Family Law*, edited by J. Eekelaar, T. Nhlapo, T. Oxford: Hart Publishing, 3–31.

Rottleuthner, H. 2006. Wie säkular ist die Bundesrepublik?, in *Ein neuer Kampf der Religionen? Staat, Recht und religiöse Toleranz*, edited by M. Mahlmann, H. Rottleuthner. Berlin: Duncker & Humblot, 13–42.

Rude-Antoine, E. 1991. Muslim Maghrebian Marriage in France: A Problem for Legal Pluralism. *International Journal of Law and the Family*, 5, 93–103.

Saeed, A. 2006. *Interpreting the Qur'ān. Towards a Contemporary Approach*. London: Routledge.

Schiffauer, W. 2008. *Parallelgesellschaften. Wie viel Wertekonsens braucht unsere Gesellschaft? Für eine kluge Politik der Differenz*. Bielefeld: transcript.

Schnyder, A. K. 2006. *Internationales Privat- und Zivilverfahrensrecht*. 2nd Edition. Zürich: Schulthess.

Scholz, P. 2002. Islam-rechtliche Eheschließung und deutscher ordre public. *Das Standesamt. Zeitschrift für Standesamtswesen, Familienrecht, Staatsangehörigkeitsrecht, Personenstandsrecht, internationales Privatrecht des In- und Auslands*, 11, 321–334.

Schulze, G. 2003. Datum-Theorie und narrative Norm – Zu einem Privatrecht für die multikulturelle Gesellschaft, in *Kulturelle Identität und Internationales Privatrecht*, edited by E. Jayme. Heidelberg: C.F. Müller, 155–177.

Schwenzer, I. 2003. Methodological Aspects of the Harmonisation of Family Law. *Die Praxis des Familienrechts*, 3, 318–332.

Schwenzer, I., Dimsey, M. 2006. *Model Family Code. From a Global Perspective*. Antwerp: Intersentia.

Scolnicov, A. 2007. The Child's Right to Religious Freedom and Formation of Identity. *International Journal of Children's Rights*, 15, 251–267.

Sellmann, M. 2007. *Religion und soziale Ordnung. Gesellschaftstheoretische Analysen*. Frankfurt am Main: Campus.

Shachar, A. 2001, *Multicultural Jurisdictions. Cultural Differences and Women's Rights*. Cambridge: Cambridge University Press.

Shachar, A. 2007. Feminism and Multiculturalism: Mapping the Terrain, in *Multiculturalism and Political Theory*, edited by A.S. Laden, D. Owen, D. Cambridge: Cambridge University Press, 115–147.

Shah, P. 2003. Attitudes to Polygamy in English Law. *International and Comparative Law Quarterly*, 52(2), 369–400.

Shah, P. 2005. *Legal Pluralism in Conflict. Coping with Cultural Diversity in Law*. London: Glass House.

Shah, P. 2007. Rituals of Recognition: Ethnic Minority Marriages in British Legal Systems, in *Law and Ethnic Plurality. Socio-Legal Perspectives*, edited by P. Shah. Leiden: Martinus Nijhof, 177–202.

Shah, P. 2009. Transforming to Accommodate? Reflections on the Shari'a Debate in Britain, in *Legal Practice and Cultural Diversity*, edited by R. Grillo, R. Ballard, A.Ferrari, A.J. Hoekema, M. Maussen, P. Shah. Farnham: Ashgate, 73–91.

Shah-Kazemi, S.N. 2001. *Untying the Knot. Muslim Women, Divorce and the Shariah*. London: The Nuffield Foundation.

Siehr, K. 2007. Inländische Adoption von Kindern aus islamischen Staaten, in *Grundfragen der juristischen Person, Festschrift für Hans Michael Riemer zum 65. Geburtstag*, edited by P. Breitschmid, W. Portmann, H. Rey, D. Zobl. Bern: Stämpfli, 371–391.

Silvestri, S. 2008. *Europe's Muslim Women. Potential, Aspirations and Challenges*. Research Report, Brussels: King Baudouin Foundation.

Speelman, G. 1995. Muslim Minorities and the Shari'ah in Europe, in *Religion, Law and Society. A Christian–Muslim Discussion*, edited by T. Mitri. Geneva: WWC Publications, 70–77.

Staudinger, J., Mankowski, P. 2003. *Art 13-17b EGBGB; Anhang zu Art 13 EGBGB: Verlöbnis und nichteheliche Lebensgemeinschaft (Internationales*

Eherecht), J. von Staudingers Kommentar zum Bürgerlichen Gesetzbuch, Einführungsgesetz zum Bürgerlichen Gesetzbuche/IPR, Neubearb. 2003. Berlin: Sellier-de Gruyter.

Tamanaha, B. 2001. A Non-Essentialist Legal Pluralism, in *A General Jurisprudence of Law and Society*. Oxford: Oxford University Press, 171–205.

Tamanaha, B. 2008. Understanding Legal Pluralism: Past to Present, Local to Global. *Sydney Law Review*, 30, 375–411.

Taylor, C. 1992. *Multiculturalism and 'The Politics of Recognition'*. Princeton: Princeton University Press.

Taylor, C. 1994. *Quellen des Selbst: die Entstehung der neuzeitlichen Identität*, translated by J. Schulte. Frankfurt am Main: Suhrkamp.

Teubner, G. 1995. Die zwei Gesichter des Janus: Rechtspluralismus in der Spätmoderne, in *Liber Amicorum Josef Esser. Zum 85. Geburtstag am 12. März 1995*, edited by E. Schmidt, H.-L. Weyers. Heidelberg: C.F. Müller, 191–214.

Teubner, G. 1996. Globale Bukowina. Zur Emergenz eines transnationalen Rechtspluralismus. *Rechtshistorisches Journal*, 15, 255–290.

Thomson, A. 2004. Incorporating Muslim Personal Law into UK Domestic Law, *AMSS (UK) 5th Annual Conference – Fiqh Today, Sunday 22nd February 2004*. [Online: 22 February] Available at: http://www.wynnechambers.co.uk/pdf/AMSS-ATNotes220204.pdf [accessed: 9 November 2010].

Tiesler, N.C. 2007. Europäisierung des Islam und Islamisierung der Debatten. *Aus Politik und Zeitgeschichte* (APuZ), 26–27, 24–32.

Töpperwien, N. 2001. *Nation-State and Normative Diversity*. Basel: Helbing & Lichtenhahn.

Tschentscher, A. 2000. *Prozedurale Theorien der Gerechtigkeit. Rationales Entscheiden, Diskursethik und prozedurales Recht*. Baden-Baden: Nomos.

Tucker, J.E. 2008. *Women, Family, and Gender in Islamic Law*. Cambridge: Cambridge University Press.

van der Veer, P. 1994. *Religious Nationalism. Hindus and Muslims in India*. Berkeley: University of California Press.

Vikør, K.S. 2005. *Between God and the Sultan. A History of Islamic Law*. London: Hurst & Company.

Vlaardingerbroek, P. 2002. Trends in the Development of Family Law in Europe – Comparative Perspectives, in *Family Life and Family Policies in Europe. Vol. 2: Problems and Issues in Comparative Perspective*, edited by F.X. Kaufmann, A. Kuijsten, H.J. Schulze, K.P. Strohmeier. Oxford: Clarendon Press, 120–148.

Volpp, L. 2001. Feminism versus Multiculturalism. *Columbia Law Review*, 101(5), 1181–1218.

von Benda-Beckmann, F. 1991. Unterwerfung oder Distanz: Rechtssoziologie, Rechtsanthropologie und Rechtspluralismus aus rechtsanthropologischer Sicht. *Zeitschrift für Rechtssoziologie*, 12, 97–119.

Von Hoffmann, B., Thorn, K. 2007. *Internationales Privatrecht*. 9th Edition. München: Beck.

von Krosigk, C. 2000. *Der Islam in Frankreich: Laizistische Religionspolitik von 1974 bis 1999*. Hamburg: Kovač 2000.

Vuilleumier, M. 2007. Schweiz, in *Enzyklopädie. Migration in Europa. Vom 17. Jahrhundert bis zur Gegenwart*, edited by K.J. Bade, P.C. Emmer, L. Lucassen, J. Oltmer. Paderborn: Ferdinand Schöningh, 189–204.

Wadud, A. 1999. *Qur'an and Woman. Rereading the Sacred Text from a Woman's Perspective*. Oxford: Oxford University Press.

Wasserstein Fassberg, C. 2005. Religious Diversity and Law, in *Human Diversity and the Law*, edited by M. Bussani, M. Graziadei. Bern: Stämpfli, 25–41.

Weber, M. 1968. *Economy and Society. An Outline of Interpretive Sociology*. New York: Bedminster Press.

Welchman, L. 2007. *Women and Muslim Family Laws in Arab States. A Comparative Overview of Textual Development and Advocacy*. Amsterdam: Amsterdam University Press.

Welstead, M. 2008. Judicial Reform or an Increase in Discretion – The Decision in Miller v Miller; McFarlane v McFarlane (2008), in *The International Survey of Family Law, 2008 Edition*. Bristol: Jordan Publishing, 61–75.

Welstead, M., Edwards, S. 2008. *Family Law*. 2nd Edition. Oxford: Oxford University Press.

Wicker, H.R. 1998. Zu Rasse, Kultur, Nation und ethnischer Identität. Oder zur Frage: Wer gehört dazu und wer nicht?, in *Blickwechsel. Die multikulturelle Schweiz an der Schwelle zum 21. Jahrhundert*, edited by S. Prodolliet. Luzern: Caritas-Verlag, 21–36.

Wurmnest, W. 2005. Die Brautgabe im Bürgerlichen Recht. *Zeitschrift für das gesamte Familienrecht mit Betreuungsrecht, Erbrecht, Verfahrensrecht, Öffentlichem Recht*, 22, 1878–1885.

Wurmnest, W. 2007. Die Mär von der *mahr* – Zur Qualifikation von Ansprüchen aus Brautgabevereinbarungen. *Rabels Zeitschrift für ausländisches und internationales Privatrecht*, 71, 527–558.

Yahyaoui Krivenko, E. 2009. *Women, Islam and International Law. Within the Context of the Convention on the Elimination of All Forms of Discrimination Against Women*, Graduate Institute of International and Development Studies, 8. Leiden and Boston: Nijhoff.

Yassari, N. 2006. Die Anwendung islamisch geprägter Sorgerechtsnormen vor deutschen Gerichten. *Recht der Jugend und des Bildungswesens. Zeitschrift für Schule, Berufsbildung und Jugenderziehung*, 2, 197–206.

Yilmaz, I. 2003. Muslim Alternative Dispute Resolution and Neo-Ijtihad in England. *Alternatives: Turkish Journal of International Relations*, 2(1), 117–139.

Yilmaz, I. 2005. *Muslim Laws, Politics and Society in Modern Nation States. Dynamic Legal Pluralism in England, Turkey and Pakistan*. Aldershot: Ashgate.

Yusuf 'Ali, A. 1999 (reprint 2004), *The Meaning of The Holy Qur'an*. 10th Edition. Beltsville, Maryland: Amana Publications.

Zachuber, J. 2007. Die Diskussion über Säkularisierung am Beginn des 21. Jahrhunderts, in *Säkularisierung. Bilanz und Perspektiven einer umstrittenen These*, edited by C. von Brau, W. Gräb, J. Zachhuber. Berlin: Lit, 11–42.

Zentrum für Islamische Frauenforschung und Frauenförderung 2005. *Ein einziges Wort und seine grosse Wirkung. Eine hermeneutische Betrachtungsweise zum Qur'an, Sure 4 Vers 43, mit Blick auf das Geschlechterverhältnis im Islam.* Köln: Zentrum für Islamische Frauenforschung und Frauenförderung.

Index